BANKING SECTOR AND HUMAN RESOURCES

CHANGING SCENARIO

BANKING SECTOR AND HUMAN RESOURCES

CHANGING SCENARIO

Edited by

Talluru Sreenivas

MBA, M Com, M Phil, Ph D.
Reader, Department of Management Sciences
RVR & JC College of Engineering
Guntur 522 019
(Andhra Pradesh)

Foreword by

Prof. L. Venugopal Reddy

Vice-Chancellor, Andhra University
Visakhapatnam 530 003
(Andhra Pradesh)

DISCOVERY PUBLISHING HOUSE
NEW DELHI-110002

Edition - 2009

Reprinted: 2013

ISBN 81-8356-048-2

Published by

DISCOVERY PUBLISHING HOUSE

4831/24, Ansari Road, Prahlad Street,
Darya Ganj, New Delhi-110002 (India)
Phone: 23279245 • Fax: 91-11-23253475
E-mail:dphtemp@indiatimes.com

Printed at

Dynamic Printer Delhi

Dedicated to my teachers

Sri Nandipati Sivarama Krishnayya
Head Master
Sri Patibandla Sitharamaiah High School
Guntur (Andhra Pradesh)

and

Sri Yadla Muralidhara Rao
Teacher (Retd.)
Sri Patibandla Sitharamaiah High School
Guntur (Andhra Pradesh)

Where the mind is without fear and the head is held high,
Where knowledge is free,
Where the world has not been broken up into fragments
by narrow domestic walls,
Where words come out from the depth of truth,
Where tireless strying stretches its arms towards perfection,
Where the clear stream of reason has not lost its way
into the dreary desert sand of dead habit,
Where the mind is led forward by thee
into ever-widening thought and action
into that heaven of freedom, my father, *let my country awake.*

–Rabindranath Tagore

FOREWORD

Finance and growth are intimately interlinked. As the economy grows and becomes more sophisticated, the banking sector has to develop *pari passu* in a manner that it supports and stimulates such growth. With increasing global integration, the Indian banking system and financial system as a whole have to be strengthened so as to be able to compete. India has had more than a decade of financial sector reforms during which period there has been substantial transformation and liberalisation of the whole financial system. It is, therefore, an appropriate time to take stock, and assess the efficacy of our approach. It is useful to evaluate in an objective manner how the financial system has performed in the recent years. This is important because India's path of reforms has been different from most other emerging market economies : it has been a measured, gradual, cautious and steady process, devoid of many flourishes that could be observed in other countries.

The initiation of financial sector reforms in the country during the early 1990s was to a large extent conditioned by the analysis and recommendations of various committees / working groups set up to address specific issues. The process has been marked by gradualism with measures being undertaken after extensive consultations with experts and market participants. From the beginning of financial sector reforms, India has resolved to attain standards of international best practices by fine tuning of the process through extensive consultations keeping in view the underlying institutional and operational considerations. Reform measures introduced across sectors as well as within each sector were planned in such a way as to reinforce each other. Attempts were made to simultaneously strengthen the institutional framework while enhancing the scope for commercial decision making, and market forces in an increasingly competitive framework. At the same time, the process did not lose sight of the social responsibilities of the financial sector. Attempts were made to provide operational flexibility and incentives so that the desired ends are attended through broad interplay of market forces. M. Narasimham Committee Report, one on Financial System (1991), and two on Banking Sector Reforms (1998) constituted the main committee reports which laid the road map for the reform process in the financial sector.

Financial sector reforms can be broadly grouped into five parts, *viz.*, (a) banking sector reforms, (b) debt markets reforms, (c) forex markets reforms, (d) reforms in other segments of the financial sector, and (e) monetary and credit policy changes.

The major aim in the early phase of reforms, known as first generation of reforms, was to create an efficient, productive and profitable financial service industry operating within the environment of operating flexibility and functional autonomy. While these reforms were being implemented, the world economy also witnessed significant changes, 'coinciding with the movement towards global integration of financial services'. The focus of the second phase of financial sector reforms starting from the second half of the 1990s, therefore, has been the strengthening of the financial system, and introduction of structural improvements. Despite several changes in the government at the Centre and in the states, there has not been any reversal of the direction in the financial sector reform process, over the last decade and a half. The same is true of the totality of economic reform process, though there are areas where decision-making and pace of reform implementation has slackened in certain periods.

All along, the direction has been to move towards international best practices and standards in several crucial areas of importance such as monetary policy, banking supervision, data dissemination, corporate governance, and the like. A Standing Committee on International Financial Standards and codes was constituted under the chairmanship of the present Governor of Reserve Bank of India, Y. Venugopal Reddy, and recommendations made by the Committee have either been implemented or are in the process of being implemented.

I am delighted to learn of the importance given to financial and banking sector reforms in the themes included for the National Seminar on *Emerging India : Challenges and Opportunities* organised by RVR & JC College of Engineering, Guntur during March 2004. This publication covers two key areas of implementation in reform policies, *viz.*, Banking and Finance, and Human Resource Management. In all these themes, the changing scenario was highlighted by the contributors, and perspectives for implementation in future have been pinpointed. I had the unique opportunity of inaugurating the Seminar, and observe the meticulous care taken by the organisers in planning and execution, and the effort put in by the delegates through their contributions. Enthusiastic response to the Seminar from the academic and professional circles is praiseworthy. I would like to congratulate the management of the college, and in particular Dr. Talluru Sreenivas, Reader in the Department of Management Sciences who undertook the responsibility for organising the National Seminar, and bringing out the papers and proceedings of the Seminar in the form of four publications covering various facets on which the discussions took place.

I have great pleasure in commending this publication to policy makers, administrators and implementers associated with the themes covered here. Academics and researchers would find it very absorbing to note the trends of analysis, and pointers for the future. I am sure the ideas and suggestions contained in the publication can stimulate further research, and more effective implementation of action-oriented policies.

Guntur
Nov.1, 2004

Professor L Venugopal Reddy
Vice-Chancellor
Acharya Nagarjuna University
Guntur, Andhra Pradesh

PREFACE

The significant transformation of the banking industry in India is clearly evident from the changes that have occurred in the financial markets, institutions and products. While deregulation has opened up new vistas for banks to augment revenues, it has entailed greater competition, and consequently greater risks. Cross-border flows and entry of new products, particularly derivative instruments, have impacted significantly on the domestic banking sector, forcing banks to adjust to the product mix, as also to effect rapid changes in their processes and operations in order to remain competitive to the globalised environment. These developments have facilitated greater chance for consumers, who have become more discerning and demanding. These have compelled banks to offer a broader range of products through diverse distribution channels. The traditional face of banks as mere financial intermediaries has since altered, and risk management has emerged as their defining attribute.

There is a growing realisation that the ability of countries to conduct business across national borders, and the ability to cope with the possible downside risks would depend, *inter alia*, on soundness of the financial system. This has consequently meant the adoption of a strong and transparent, prudential, regulatory, supervisory, technological, and institutional framework in the financial sector on par with international best practices. All this necessitates a transformation: a transformation in the mindset, a transformation in the business processes, and finally, a transformation in knowledge management. This is a continuous process; and key strategies need to be initiated at certain periods.

Financial services are at the centre of the present trend in globalisation. On the other hand, increasing integration of economies and markets is making global banking a reality while, on the other, global banks are drivers behind global trade and corporate globalisation. Deregulation of capital markets in both the developed and developing countries in the 1990s has resulted in larger and freer flow of capital. With capital flows across continents becoming significant, the provision of financial services on a global scale is gaining in importance. In fact, international banking is a key component of the global economy. It is central to the flow of capital around the world through provision of loans, supply of financial advice, and involvement in securities markets.

Global banking, of course, extends beyond international banking which in its narrower sense relates to delivery of trade products and services to business and trade customers. The surge in globalisation of finance has gained momentum with technological advancements, particularly in information and communication technology. Technological advances, while reducing costs and speeding up financial transactions, have also effectively overcome national burden in the financial services business. It is now possible to market financial products and services on a global basis. Widespread use of internet banking has widened the frontiers of global banking.

In the coming years, globalisation will spread further with the likely opening up of financial services under the World Trade Organisation (WTO). India is one of the 104 signatory countries of the Financial Services Agreement (FSA) of 1997. This gives the country's financial sector including banks an opportunity to expand their business on *quid pro quo* basis. Accordingly, the role of Indian banks will be shaped, among other factors, by increasing globalisation of financial markets. According to the Indian Banks Association Report, *Banking Industry Vision 2010*, there will be greater presence of international players in the Indian financial system, and some of the Indian banks will become global players in the coming years. Thus, the new mantra for Indian banks is to go global in search of new markets, customers and profits. They will now have to cope with a rapidly changing competitive situation as a result of further globalisation. The competition is not only on foreign front but also in the domestic field as well from foreign banks operating in India. The complexity of operations and sophistication of financial products call for new skills and expertise. However, a combination of factors including regulatory support and technological upgradation will enable Indian banks to achieve their global aspirations. Appropriate sequencing and repacking of financial sector reform measures with changed emphasis, and relative speed of reforms at various sectoral levels would ultimately determine whether India would be able to leapfrog into the new growth trajectory.

The emerging landscape of competitive banking calls for organisation-wide human resource reforms in public sector banks to begin with. Human resource (HR) management covers all sectors, particularly manufacturing and service sectors. Developing human resource as a strategic strength in the competitive environment warrants a number of new initiatives. The purpose is to bring about improvements in employee productivity, implementation of performance measurement and management system, development of leaders for critical roles, compensation, motivation and reward mechanism, development of competency-based strategic HR systems, implementation of HR management system, knowledge management initiatives for learning and growth, skill development, attitude reorientation and managing diversities, training and development agenda, career management systems, and organisational renewal.

The papers presented at the National Seminar on Emerging India : Challenges and Opportunities, organised during March 2004 by RVR & JC College of Engineering, Guntur, incorporated in this publication refer to two areas: (a) Banking and Finance, and (b) Human Resource Management. In addition to select papers received for the seminar, efforts have been made to include a few more special contributions from prominent professionals and researchers on themes relevant for the publication. A wide variety of topics have been covered in each section. Special care has been taken in these papers to examine the recent trends, and bring out suggestions for effective implementation of programmes in future. Conclusions and suggestions brought out by the contributors deserve special consideration of the policy making and implementing organisations. Researchers, academics and professional bodies will benefit from the methodologies followed, and conclusions drawn in the papers. The editor acknowledges the valuable contribution of the authors, and commends them for adoption extensively in the concerned sectors.

Guntur **Talluru Sreenivas**

June 1, 2005

ACKNOWLEDGEMENT

Inspired by the article which I co-authored recently with my Research Director, Professor G Prasad, Department of Commerce and Business Administration, Acharya Nagarjuna University, entitled, Health Care in India – Strategies for Globalisation, I embarked on the humble venture of organising a National Seminar on the very fascinating topic, dearest to our young minded, dynamic first citizen of our country, his Excellency Bharat Ratna Dr. A.P.J. Abdul Kalam, Emerging India – Challenges and Opportunities. The present publication is the outcome of the proceedings of the seminar held under the editor's secretaryship during March 2004 at RVR & JC College of Engineering, Guntur (Andhra Pradesh).

Sizeable number of papers on different functional areas and in different sectors were received from academics, research scholars, and practitioners. These papers deal with various topics which were taken up for discussion in different technical sessions. The sessions were captioned as : (i) Is India Emerging?, (ii) Industry, Infrastructure and Agriculture, (iii) Service Sector and Developed India, and (iv) Human Resources as a strategic strength. In addition to select papers received for the seminar, efforts have been made to include a few more special contributions from prominent professionals and researchers on themes relevant for the publication. The Seminar organisers are highly indebted to all the contributors for their painstaking efforts to make the presentation highly thought-provoking and instructive. We would like to convey our gratefulness to all of them, and look forward to their bringing out greater insight on these themes in future. These papers are distributed over four publications : (i) Service Sector in Indian Economy, (ii) Perspectives of Indian Agriculture, Industry and Infrastructure, (iii) Banking Sector and Human Resources – Changing Scenario, and (iv) Globalisation and Emerging India.

I acknowledge with gratitude the help I received from Professor D Dakshina Murthy, Former Dean, Faculty of Commerce and Business Administration, Acharya Nagarjuna University, who currently heads the Department of Management Sciences of our College, and all other colleagues in our Department for their constant guidance, encouragement and support.

It gives me great pleasure to place on record my indebtedness to Professor G Prasad, whose guidance gave me the strength and courage to bring out this publication. His scholarly guidance and encouragement are responsible for my success in this venture. He has been a continuous source of inspiration to me.

I would like to convey my gratefulness to a number of elders and well wishers for the substantial encouragement and support given to me on various occasions. These include Dr KRR Mohan Rao, former Vice-Chancellor, Acharya Nagarjuna University, Guntur; Professor P Murali, former Vice-Chancellor, Sri Venkateswara University, Tirupati; Professor V Balamohan Das, Vice-Chancellor, Acharya Nagarjuna University, Guntur; Professor GN Brahmanandam, Dean, Faculty of Commerce & Management Studies, Acharya Nagarjuna University, Guntur; Professor DAR Subrahmanyam, Principal, Mahatma Gandhi College, Guntur; Dr K Chandrasekhara Rao, Head, Department of Commerce, Pondicherry University, Pondicherry; Professor PS Sankara Rao, Andhra University, Visakhapatnam; Dr R Murali Babu Rao, Professor of Cardiology on special duty, Guntur General Hospital, and Guntur Medical College, Guntur; and Professor NV Narasimham, School of Management Studies, IGNOU, New Delhi.

I am grateful to Professor L Venugopal Reddy, the then Vice-Chancellor, Acharya Nagarjuna University, Guntur; presently Vice-Chancellor, Andhra University, Visakhapatnam, for writing the foreword to this work in spite of his busy schedule. I am highly obliged to Professor DL Narayana, Chairman, Third Finance Commission of Andhra Pradesh for delivering the keynote address at the Seminar, and enlightening all the delegates with his extensive research highlights.

It is my privilege to express deep sense of gratitude to the Management of RVR & JC College of Engineering, particularly to our beloved President, Dr K Basavapunnaiah, and our dynamic Secretary & Correspondent, Dr M Gopalkrishna, Sri R Gopala Krishna,

Treasurer, and Professor K Pameswara Rao, Principal, Professor B Ravindra Babu, Vice-Principal, PS Somayajulu, Registrar, NV Srinivasa Rao, Administrative Officer, G Anantha Narayana, Office Manager, and other senior faculty in the College for providing me conducive work environment to organise this mega event. I specially acknowledge the support of Sri DSR Anjaneyulu, and Sri SV Rattaiah who helped me in the completion of this gigantic task.

I am greatly indebted to Dr C Ramachandra Prabhu, faculty of Department of Physics, RVR & JC College of Engineering, Dr D Nagayya, former Director, National Institute of Small Industry Extension Training (NISIET), Hyderabad, and Professor S Krishna Sharma, formerly of the Dept. of English, Acharya Nagarjuna University, Guntur for the encouragement, help and support extended to me while working on this publication.

My special thanks are due to the Management of Discovery Publishing House, New Delhi for bringing out this publication in an elegant manner in record time.

I also want to thank a number of personal friends for their solid support and involvement in a variety of ways in my academic ventures. These include : Smt & Sri GS Ram Prasad, Smt & Sri K Shyam Babu, Smt & Sri G Subrahmanyam, Smt & Sri M Subba Rao, Smt & Sri Y Durga Prasada Rao, Smt & Sri PN Uday Kumar, Smt & Sri R Vasu, Smt & Sri V Srinivasa Rao and Smt & Sri M Venkateswara Rao.

All my family members have patiently borne the inconvenience due to my involvement in a number of academic activities including the release of this publication, and encouraged me a great deal. I acknowledge their silent and valued contributions.

Talluru Sreenivas

LIST OF CONTRIBUTORS

Smt. Anitha G
Lecturer, Dept. of Business Admn.
NNS Vidya College of PG Studies
Chirala, Prakasam Dist., AP

Smt. Aruna Kumari AV
Lecturer, Dept. of Bank Management
Theivanai Ammal College for Women
Villipuram, Tamil Nadu

Dr. Bhaskara Rao VK
Reader, PG Dept. of Commerce & Management Studies
VRS & YRN College
Chirala, Prakasam Dist., AP

Professor Brahmanandam GN
Dean, Faculty of Commerce and Management Studies
Dept. of Commerce & Business Administration
Acharya Nagarjuna University
Nagarjuna Nagar - 522 510 (Andhra Pradesh)

Dr. Chalam GV
Associate Professor & Head
Dept. of Commerce & Business Administration
Acharya Nagarjuna University
Nagarjuna Nagar - 522 510

Dr. Chandrasekhara Rao K
Head, Department of Commerce
Pondicherry University
Pondicherry - 605 014

Smt. Esther Sujana L
Lecturer, JB Institute of PGCourses
Tirupathi, AP

Dr. Jayachandra K
Reader, Dept. of Commerce
Sri Venkateswara University
Tirupathi, AP

Professor Kamaraju Panthulu N
Dean, School of Social & Behavioral Sciences (Rtd.)
Sri Venkateswara University
Tirupathi

Sri Khamruddin Sk
Lecturer in Management
Vignan School of PG Studies
Guntur - 522 006

Sri Kiran Kumar N
Lecturer, Dept. of Management Studies
JB Institute of PG Courses
Tirupathi, AP

Professor Krishnamacharyulu CSG
Chairman, Board of Studies
School of Business Management
Sri Venkateswara University
Tirupathi, AP

Sri Kumar Ch HKS
Lecturer in Management
Alhabeeb College of Engineering
Hyderabad

Ms. Lakshmi Soujanya N
Lecturer, PGDept. of Management Studies
KBN College
Vijayawada, AP

Dr. Nagaraju T
Sr Lecturer, Dept. of Management Sciences
RVR & JC College of Engineering
Guntur - 522 019

Dr. Nagayya D
Former Director
National Institute of Small Industry Extension Training (NISIET)
Hyderabad

Dr. Narasimha Rao V
Reader & Head
PG Dept. of Business Administration
Akkineni Nageswara Rao College
Gudivada, Krishna Dist., AP

Dr. Narayana MS
Reader & Principal
DonBosco PG College
Guntur - 522 017

Dr. Niranjan Reddy P
Associate Professor
Rayalseema Institute of Information and Management Sciences
Tirupathi, AP

Professor Prasad G
Dept. of Commerce & Business Administration
Acharya Nagarjuna University
Nagarjuna Nagar – 522 510

Smt. Poornima Y
Sr Lecturer
Dept. of Commerce & Business Administration
PB Siddartha College of Arts & Sciences
VIjayawada - 520 010

Sri Prasada Rao YVS
Lecturer, PG Dept. of Management Studies
TJPS College
Guntur - 522 006

Sri Purnachandra Rao P
Faculty Member
Dept. of Commerce & Business Administration
Acharya Nagarjuna University PG Centre
Ongole, Prakasam Dist., AP

Sri Raghava Satya Murthy B
Lecturer, Dept. of Commerce
KBN College
Vijayawada - 520 001

Dr. Rajasekhar M
Dept. of Commerce
Sri Venkateswara University
Tirupathi, AP

Dr. Ramachandra Prabhu C
Dept. of Physics
RVR & JC College of Engineering
Guntur - 522 019

Dr. Ramachandra Reddy B
Reader, Dept. of Commerce
Sri Venkateswara University
Tirupathi, AP

Dr. Ravi Dasari
Associate Professor
Dhruva College of Management
Kacheguda, Hyderabad - 500 027

Dr. Sreenivas Talluru
Reader, Dept. of Management Sciences
RVR & JC College of Engineering
Guntur - 522 019

Sri Sreekrishna T
Sr Lecturer, Dept. of Management Sciences
RVR & JC College of Engineering
Guntur - 522 019

Sri Srinivas L
Research Scholar
Dept. of Commerce & Business Administration
Acharya Nagarjuna University
Nagarjuna Nagar
Guntur - 522 510

Sri Sriram P
Lecturer, PG Dept. of Business Administration
PB Siddhartha College of Arts & Science
Vijayawada - 520 010

Professor Subrahmanyam DAR
Principal, Mahatma Gandhi College
Guntur - 522 006

Dr. Sudhakar Reddy K
PG Dept. of Business Administration
Akkineni Nageswara Rao College
Gudivada, Krishna Dist., AP

Smt. Suguna K
Lecturer
JB Institute of PG Courses
Tirupathi, AP

Mrs. Suja S Nair
Lecturer, Dept. of Management Studies
JB Institute of PG Courses
Tirupathi, AP

Dr. Surya Prakasha Rao BK
Reader, Dept. of Management Sciences
RVR & JC College of Engineering
Guntur - 522 019

Sri. Syed Ahmad S
Research Scholar, Dept. of Commerce
Pondicherry University
Pondicherry - 605 014

Dr. Tessy Kurian
Asst. Prof. in Development
Debub University
Awassa, Ethiopia

Dr. Venkateswara Rao Malapati
Professor and Head
Dept. of Chemical Engineering
RVR & JC College of Engineering
Guntur - 522 019

Dr. Venkateswarlu M
Lecturer, Dept.of Commerce
Sri Venkateswara University
Tirupathi, AP

Sri Venu Gopal Rao KS
Associate Professor
Dhruva College of Management
Kacheguda, Hyderabad - 500 027

Sri Yuvaraja Reddy B
Research Scholar
Dept. of Commerce
Sri Venkateswara University
Tirupathi, AP

CONTENTS

SECTION–I
BANKING AND FINANCE

1

VENTURE CAPITAL
RECENT TRENDS IN THE LIBERALISATION CONTEXT

Dr. Talluru Sreenivas* and **Dr. D. Nagayya****

The paper reviews development of Venture Capital Funds (VCFs) and Venture Capital Investment (VCI) in the country. Concept, evolution, characteristics and scope of venture capital as an equity mechanism are discussed. This is also referred to as private equity (PE) - an investment in a company with equity securities that are generally not publicly traded. Private Equity focuses on active private equity investments that enable them to acquire a large or controlling interest in a firm with solid growth potential. As a result, PE firms can oversee, assist, and if necessary, redirect the company's activities or its management.

Indian environment of venture capital funds, particularly through institutional sources like Industrial Development Bank of India (IDBI) and Small Industries Development Bank of India (SIDBI) is presented in detail. To make the programme dynamic to meet the needs of entrepreneurial interests in the small and medium enterprises sector, changes taking place are covered in some depth. Role of the nodal agency, Securities and Exchange Board of India (SEBI) in supervising and monitoring the functioning of venture capital funds is highlighted. Involvement of the Indian Venture Capital Association

* Reader, Department of Management Sciences, RVR & JC College of Engineering, Chowdavaram, Guntur - 522 019.

** Consultant on Small Enterprises at Guntur; and former Director(Industrial Development), National Institute of Small Industry Extension Training (NISIET), Hyderabad.

(IVCA) in pursuing with the Government of India for revision of guidelines for Venture Capital Funds at different periods is recapitulated.

Introduction

Venture Capital is defined as "an equity by which an investor supports an entrepreneur with finance and business skills to exploit market opportunities; thus obtain long-term market gains." Venture capital is primarily for new entrepreneurial ventures, which involve high risk, but at the same time promise high reward. Commercialisation of new technologies developed indigenously is one of the directions supported by venture capital. Venture capital is made available in the form of equity and equity-related instruments. The institutions / investors providing venture capital assistance get themselves deeply involved in the venture by providing necessary managerial and marketing support, and networking opportunities till the venture reaches the take off stage of becoming successful.

Venture capitalist combines risk capital with entrepreneurial management and advance technology to create new products, new companies and new wealth. Risk finance and venture capital environment can bring about innovation, promote technology, and harness knowledge-based ventures. In this sense, venture capital is different from other types of financing such as (a) development finance, (b) seed capital, (c) term loan/conventional financing, (d) passive equity investment support, and (e) R&D funding sources. Venture capital is a source of investment in the form of seed capital in unproven areas, products or start-up situations. The concept of venture capital is relatively new to the Indian economy, and is gaining prominence in the recent years.

In developed countries such as U.S.A. and U.K., venture capital financing, entirely through private initiative, with hardly any involvement of the government institutions, has achieved miracles in stimulating entrepreneurial growth in unproven and risky ventures which offered high potential for growth. In developing countries like Taiwan, Singapore, South Korea, and Israel, the scheme has contributed phenomenally to economic growth. Indian approach is modelled on the U.S.A. and U.K. patterns, with pro-active role of the Government and a regulatory environment to secure benefits to the small and medium enterprises (SMEs) in particular.

Concept of Venture Capital

Venture capitalists in India follow a flexible and broad approach to venture capital. They supply funds to new, high risk, not necessarily high tech ventures, and also extend management, marketing and financial skills to assisted ventures. Initially the emphasis was on supporting high tech unproven technologies. It has been broadbased in the light of the experience of the first few years. Venture capitalists (a) expect the assisted enterprise to have a very high growth rate, (b) provide management and business skills, (c) expect medium to long-term gains, and (d) do not expect any collateral to cover the capital provided. Venture capitalist cannot afford to invest in start-ups unless there is a rare combination of product opportunity, market opportunity, and proven management. The fundamental principle underlying the operations of a venture capital fund is "No return without risk; and greater the risk, greater will be the returns."

In developed countries, where venture capital funds have developed well, angel investors are the initial funding sources for a new venture. Angel investors provide funding by 'first round' financing for risky investment. Angels are persons with less profit orientation, but who play an active role in making an early - stage company work. They are persons with enough hands-on experience in industry, and are experts in their own fields. They take it as a challenge to support start-ups in activities in which they have the specialization. In other words, they consider adopting a new born enterprise, to enable it to become successful. Angels bring both technical expertise and finances to the doorsteps of an entrepreneur. While choosing and angel, it is important to consider his experience in the relevant industry, reputation, qualifications and track record. In the Indian context, where it may not be easy to find 'angel investors' in large numbers, the venture capitalists play that role.

Venture capitalists finance innovation and ideas, which have potential for high growth but with inherent uncertainties. This makes it high risk and high return investment. Apart from finance, venture capitalists provide networking, management and marketing support as well. In a broad sense, therefore, venture capital refers to risk finance as well as managerial support. This blend of risk financing and handholding of entrepreneurs by venture capitalists creates an environment particularly suitable for knowledge and technology-based enterprises.

The ultimate aim of the venture capitalist is the same as that of the promoters, i.e., the long-term profitability and viability of the invested company. Venture capitalists function in a dual capacity, i.e., as a financial partner, and as a strategic advisor. They monitor and evaluate the projects regularly. They keep a hand on the pulse of the project. They are actually involved in the management of the invested unit. They promote expert business counsel, to ensure the survival and growth of the enterprise. As professionals in this unique method of financing, they may have innovative solutions to maximize the chances of success of the project.

Historically, private equity/venture capital funds have significantly out- performed public equities and mutual funds over the long term. This is because an active PE investor can improve returns by among other things, developing corporate strategies with management, implementing incentive programmes for management and employees, and identifying appropriate add on acquisitions. PE funds do not generally make passive investments involving limited participation in the company's operation. In such cases, the investor has little or no influence on the management's direction of the company. Naturally, the investment increases in value if the company prospers. However, the passive investor has no ability to exert influence if the company loses direction, and may watch helplessly if the value of the investment declines. Hence, PE funds negotiate either a Board seat or super majority rights, which ensure that they have a significant say in the company.

Investments in PE and VC funds are characterised by long-term perspective, relatively high risk, lack of liquidity (as typically there are no secondary markets where these investments can be traded), and difficulty in determining their valuations on a mark to market basis, as the underlying investments are not usually traded except on the category of private investment in public enterprises.

Method of Venture Financing

The venture capitalist makes an investment through equity, quasi-equity, conditional loans, and income notes.

Equity: Investment in the form of equity is the most desirable form of venture financing, as it reflects an approach of sharing risks and rewards; and does not put any pressure on the cash flow of the company in the initial teething period. Equity contribution from the venture capitalist should be slightly lower than that of the promoters' equity.

Quasi-equity: The quasi-equity instruments are instruments that are converted into equity at a later date. The convertible instruments include convertible debentures and convertible preference shares.

Conditional Loan: The conditional loan is not really a loan because there is no repayment of principal; and there is no interest on such loans. In this instrument, the company pays royalty to the venture capital undertaking that is linked to the turnover, after the unit goes into regular production. This is based on the true concept of sharing risk and reward.

Income Notes: It is a hybrid of simple loan and conditional loan. The outstanding debt carries concessional rate of interest and royalty attached to the turnover.

Divestment Mechanism

The most crucial stage in any venture capital investment is the exit. The goal of the venture capitalist is to sell the investment in a period ranging from three to seven years at a considerable gain. The different possible routes for exit from venture investment or disinvestments or divestment are: (i) Initial Public Offer (IPO), (ii) trade sale, (iii) promoters buy back, (iv) company buy back, (v) management buy out, (vi) sale to another venture capitalist, (vii) employee stock option, (viii) sweat equity and recognition of intellectual capital.

Initial Public Offer (IPO): The most preferred exit route for a venture capitalist is the IPO. The company can go to the public through stock exchanges.

Trade Sale: In a trade sale, the venture capitalist sells his stake to a strategic buyer, which already owns a business similar/ complementary or plans to enter into the target industry. This helps the strategic buyer to produce a synergistic increase in its value. The promoter may or may not sell this stake to the strategic buyer.

Promoter Buy Back: In this pattern, the promoter buys back the venture capitalist's stake at a pre-determined price. This is not very popular since the promoter as a first generation entrepreneur is hard pressed for money.

Company Buy Back: In this, the company buys back the venture capitalist's stake at a pre-determined price. The company buy back has been recently announced.

Management Buy Out: In this, the operating management group acquires the business by buying the equity held by the promoters. It usually involves revitalizing an operation with entrepreneurial management acquiring a significant equity interest.

Report of the R.H. Patil Committee (2000) appointed by SIDBI to look into various issues relating to opening up of capital markets to small scale industries as a viable means for tapping capital and debt in various forms as also for providing a safe exit route for equity provider to the sector is under the consideration of the Government. Action needs to be initiated on the recommendations of the Committee to enable SSI units to raise funds from the capital markets with minimum efforts, and also to provide safe exit for the investors in SSI units. At present, there is no market for trading in unlisted securities, and also due to the unsatisfactory performance of OTCEI (Over The Counter Exchange of India). The threshold limit placed by various stock exchanges generally of Rs.5 crore equity acts as a deterrent for listing companies of SSI units with smaller equity base. SEBI can facilitate the process by lowering of the threshold limit for public issue / listing for companies backed by venture capital funds.

Structure of Venture Capital Funds in India

The structure of VCFs can be classified into domestic funds and offshore funds.

Domestic Funds: Most of the domestic venture capital funds created their funds under the Indian Trust Act, 1882. There is either a two-tier structure or three-tier structure. In the two-tier structure, an Asset Management Company (AMC) is formed which also acts as a trustee to the funds. The funds are settled as close-ended funds. In the three-tier structure, an asset management company and a separate Trustee Company are formed. The Board of Trustees gives the policy guidelines to the AMC for making investments and disinvestments. This facilitates launching of more funds, each with a different objective or focus by the VC companies which normally act as the AMC.

These two structures are very similar to the Limited Partnership Act which is the structure through which VC funds are operated in U.S.A. and U.K. IDBI operates its venture capital activities through a separate division. SIDBI, which also operated VC earlier through a separate division, has formed an asset management company and a Trustee Company in 1999 - 2000 to operate venture capital activities.

Offshore Funds: With the liberalisation trends in the country from 1991, mobility of international funds in India has steadily increased. The funds are set up outside India in U.S.A., Singapore, Hong Kong, etc. These are very large funds, and make large investments. Their investments are generally in existing big companies. The fund is set up usually either with the sole contribution from one company or with contributions channelled through the foreign investors. Most of the funds that make investment exclusively in India create the fund in Mauritius. AMC is also based in Mauritius. These offshore funds create an advisory board that makes investment and divestment decisions. The funds are routed through Mauritius for investment in Indian companies. This is primarily done to save taxes under a double tax treaty between India and Mauritius. The Mauritius - based companies are totally exempted from paying capital gains tax. Such investments are also subject to Foreign Investment Promotion Board (FIPB) approval.

Comparison of the domestic funds and offshore private equity funds is given here

	Feature	*Domestic Funds*	*Offshore Funds*
1.	Base	Based in India	Based usually in Mauritius
2.	Guidelines	Follow SEBI guidelines and need to get registered with SEBI	Follow SEBI guidelines, and need to get registered with SEBI
3.	Corpus size	Smaller in size, up to Rs. 30 crore	Larger in size up to US $30 million
4.	Invested companies	Investment primarily in start-up small and medium enterprises	Investment primarily in existing large companies
5.	Investment size	Average of Rs.50 lakh to Rs.2.5 crore per enterprise	Average of Rs.8 crore Rs.10 crore per enterprise
6.	Structure	Registered as a Trust under Indian Trust Act, 1882	——

The venture capital industry has grown manifold over the last decade and a half. The number of venture capital funds increased from 12 in 1990 to 31 in 1997, and 45 in 2000. The total corpus increased from Rs.200 crore in 1990 to Rs.4,000 crore in 1997, and Rs.5,000 crore in 2000. However, there has been almost stagnant growth in the domestic funds, whereas 19 offshore private equity funds have started making investment in Indian companies. From 2001, inflow of venture capital from offshore funds has been quite substantial, after the implementation of the recommendations of the *Report of the Working Group on Structure of Venture Capital Funds*, chaired by K.B. Chandrasekhar, a NRI (Non-Resident Indian) from Silicon Valley, U.S.A.

The domestic venture funds created in India are all based largely on public sector institutional initiatives. These include IDBI, IFCI, ICICI, SIDBI, SBI and a number of other public sector banks. In U.S.A., venture funds are largely or wholly out of private sector initiative. There is no regulatory mechanism in U.S.A. In the Indian context, regulatory mechanism is considered necessary. In U.S.A., pension funds, insurance companies and corporate bodies provide resources for venture capital funds. It is suggested that this practice may be followed in the Indian context. If mutual funds are allowed to invest up to 5 per cent of their corpus in VCFs by SEBI, it may lead to increased availability of resources for VCFs.

Guidelines on Venture Capital Funds and Incentives announced by Government of India

Government of India issued guidelines on venture capital in November 1988, giving capital gains tax concessions to technology ventures which met the stipulated criteria. These were modified in 1996, when revised guidelines were issued under the supervision of SEBI. In September 1995, Government of India issued guidelines for overseas investment in venture capital in India. These guidelines restricted the setting up of VCFs only to banks or financial institutions.

The venture capital guidelines of SEBI were announced with the primary objective of protecting the interest of investors, and providing enough flexibility to fund managers to make suitable investment decisions. Participation by very small investors has been restricted, and only high net worth individuals and institutions, both domestic and foreign, are allowed to participate with a minimum investment of Rs.5 lakh.

As per the guidelines issued by Central Board of Direct Taxes (CBDT) and other guidelines of Government of India of September 1995, a venture capital fund can invest up to 40 per cent of the paid up capital of the invested company or up to 20 per cent of the corpus of the fund in one undertaking. SEBI regulations and the guidelines of CBDT require that at least 80 per cent of the corpus of the venture fund should be invested in unlisted equity shares of the VC undertakings. The regulations permit investment by VCFs in listed companies of sick industrial undertakings.

Later during 1999 - 2000, *SEBI has been made the nodal agency for all VCFs.* Domestic and foreign VCFs have to get registered with SEBI. That will entitle them to avail of the facilities made available by different institutions. Guidelines issued by different agencies were harmonised through SEBI, as per the recommendation of the Chandrasekhar Working Group. A number of concessions were announced by Government of India thereafter. In the 1998 - 99 Union Budget, in the Income Tax Act 1961, a new section 10 (23FA) was introduced in respect of investments made by VCFs. VCFs are exempted from dividends and long-term capital gains on unlisted equity shares, and would cover investments in a number of product lines / services. These included software development, IT, basic drugs in the pharmaceutical sector, biotechnology, agriculture and allied sectors, and other areas as notified by the Government from time to time. Union Budget 2000 - 01 provided a big boost to the VC industry. Any income of such VCFs or VC company is exempted from tax under section 10 (23FB). Section 115U was introduced with effect from the assessment year 2001 - 02 to establish pass-through.

- To simplify the procedures, SEBI has been designated as the nodal agency for registration and regulation of both domestic and overseas VCFs.
- No approval of VCFs by tax authorities would be required.
- The Principle of 'pass-through' would be applied in tax treatment of VCFs, whose income would be free of tax, except when not distributed within the period that may be prescribed in the SEBI guidelines. Income in the hands of its investors, which would otherwise be taxable, would also be kept tax free; and there would only be a one-time

payment of tax by the VCF at the rate of 20 per cent, when the fund distributes its income to the investors. The same rate would apply to the undistributed income also.

Earlier in the Monetary and Credit Policy announced by the Reserve Bank of India (RBI) in April 1999, to encourage the finance for venture capital, the overall ceiling of investment by banks in ordinary shares, convertible debentures of corporates, and units of mutual funds, etc., which was earlier at 5 per cent of their incremental deposits, was increased to the extent of bank's investment in venture capital. It was also decided to include investments in venture capital as part of priority sector lending.

The VC industry is governed by the SEBI through the VCF Regulations. The regulations define a VCF to mean a fund established in the form of a trust or company, and registered under these regulations which has a dedicated pool of capital raised, and which invests in VC Undertakings (VCUs). The term VCU has been defined to mean a domestic company where shares are not listed in India, and which is engaged in a business which does not fall within the negative list which mainly includes gold financing, and such other activities that may be notified by SEBI or the Government.

In addition, VCF regulations lay down several investment restrictions on VCFs. These restrictions are as follows:

1. VCFs shall not invest more than 25 per cent of the fund in one VCU;
2. VCFs shall not invest in the associated companies;
3. VCFs shall make investments as enumerated below:
   (a) at least two-thirds of the investible funds should be invested in unlisted equity shares or equity-linked instruments of VCUs
   (b) not more than one-third of the investible funds may be invested by way of :
      (i) subscription to initial public offer of a VCU whose shares are proposed to be listed,
      (ii) debt or debt instrument of a VCU in which VCF has already made an investment by way of equity,

(iii) preferential allotment of equity shares of a listed company subject to lock in period of one year,

(iv) the equity shares or equity-linked instruments of a financially weak company or a sick industrial company whose shares are listed,

(v) special purpose vehicles which are created by a VCF for the purpose of facilitating or promoting investment in accordance with these regulations.

Growth of Venture Capital Funds (VCFs) in India

Evolution: Venture capital financing as a source of providing funds to new, high risk, not necessarily high-tech ventures is of recent origin in the Indian context. As conventional financing schemes are generally security oriented, and are meant for projects based on established / proven technology, the need for venture capital finance was keenly felt by small and medium enterprises (SMEs) in particular. For meeting the risks of projects promoted by entrepreneurs who take to unproven innovative projects, and those with professional background and experience, venture capital finance is of utmost necessity. As commercialisation of Research and Development (R & D) work involves definite risk; more so, when the processes have not been commercialised, specific incentives are provided by a number of institutions for entrepreneurs opting for these technologies. Venture capital finance is also to be dovetailed with these incentives.

The concept of venture capital as a new financial service was introduced in India in the fiscal budget for the year 1986-87, followed by promulgation of Research and Development Cess Act, 1986. The Act imposed 5 per cent cess on all know-how import payments to create a pool of funds for, *inter alia*, venture capital activities initiated by Industrial Development Bank of India (IDBI). Consequently in March 1987, IDBI introduced Venture Capital Fund (VCF) scheme for financing ventures seeking development of indigenous technologies / adaptation of foreign technology to wider domestic applications. Similarly, Industrial Credit and Investment Corporation of India (ICICI) started financing technology-oriented innovative companies. ICICI in association with Unit Trust of India (UTI) formed a venture capital subsidiary called TDICI - Technology Development and Information

Company of India - with headquarters at Bangalore, for taking up venture capital activity. Industrial Finance Corporation of India (IFCI) formed Risk Capital and Technology Finance Corporation (RCTC), with headquarters at New Delhi. TDICI is now known as ICICI Venture Funds Management Company Ltd. or ICICI Venture; and RCTC is now known as IFCI Venture Capital Funds Ltd. (IVCF). Their main focus is on development and commercialisation of viable indigenous, often, untried technologies. Almost at the same time, Credit Capital Venture Finance Limited was started in the private sector. This has mobilised funding from global funding agencies, with the joint sponsorship of Commonwealth Development Corporation, London (U.K.), Credit Capital Finance Corporation, Asian Development Bank (ADB), and Bank of India, a public sector bank in India.

In November 1988, Government of India announced the first venture capital guidelines in the Parliament. The guidelines were aimed at providing Venture finance to technology start-ups, promoted primarily by first generation entrepreneurs. In 1989, the World Bank selected four institutions to start venture capital activities in different parts of the country under its Industrial Technology Development Project. These included ICICI at Mumbai, Gujarat Industrial Investment Corporation (GIIC) in Ahmedabad, Andhra Pradesh Industrial Development Corporation (APIDC) in Hyderabad, and Canara Bank in Bangalore. Later on, two more institutions were added. These are IFCI at New Delhi, and Infrastructure Leasing and Financial Services Ltd. (IL & FS) at Mumbai. All these institutions formed separate companies for handling venture capital activity; and have been following Government of India guidelines. Names of the parent companies, and the nomenclature of the Venture Capital Funds promoted by them are given here.

Parent Institution	*Venture Fund Promoted*
ICICI	TDICI, renamed as ICICI Venture Funds Management Company or ICICI Venture
IFCI	RCTC, renamed as IFCI Venture Capital Funds Ltd. (IVCF)
IL & FS	Pathfinder
GIIC	Gujarat Venture Capital Finance Ltd. (GVCFL), with all India coverage
APIDC	APIDC Venture Capital Ltd., with coverage as Andhra Pradesh
Canara Bank	Canfina - VCF, with focus on southern states

Among the public sector banks, State Bank of India (SBI) and Canara Bank took the lead. SBI Capital Markets, promoted by SBI is operating VCF. A few other public sector banks followed the direction later. Punjab National Bank is one among them, which started PNB Financial Services. From 1996, there has been an increased level of activity in the venture capital industry. More funds have been set up both by existing companies and by new ones in the public and private sectors. There has also been an increased availability of foreign funds for Indian venture capital investments.

The World Bank made a significant contribution towards the development of Venture Capital industry in the country, through its support in the early stages in particular. It developed manpower resources, created international exposure, encouraged networking, and interactions among venture capital companies in India to foster cohesiveness, and contributed to professionalisation of venture capital companies.

The Indian Venture Capital Association (IVCA) which was formed in 1992 by 12 domestic VCFs, took vigorous follow-up with the Government of India to streamline the guidelines for venture capital in the country. Securities and Exchange Board of India (SEBI) was granted statutory powers in 1992 with the main objective to regulate and develop the Indian securities market. The SEBI Act empowered SEBI to *inter alia* regulate the venture capital funds, as these funds are part of the overall securities market; and is a source of capital. All the VCFs including the new ones are to be registered with SEBI. With economic liberalisation and reforms, several Mauritius - based offshore private equity funds started investing in India, from 1996; and more so from 2001.

IDBI Venture Capital Fund (IDBI VCF)

IDBI has been operating the Venture Capital Scheme since 1987 for providing assistance for ventures involving commercialisation of indigenously developed technology, adaptation of imported technology to wider domestic applications, as also for all software / Information Technology (IT) ventures.

The scheme is applicable to existing and new enterprises concerned with proposals relating to development of technology from the level of the laboratory or bench scale onwards till the stage where it is mature for commercial application. Assistance under the scheme covers capital expenditure as well as operating expenditure (including market development expenses) during the agreed development period. The amount of assistance will be decided on a case-to-case basis after allowing for an appropriate involvement / stake of the promoter. It is proposed to have a flexible approach in this regard but typically, a minimum promoter's contribution of 10 per cent in case of schemes costing up to Rs.50 lakh, and 15 per cent for projects above Rs.50 lakh cost is envisaged. The focus of IDBI was on small and medium projects. After SIDBI started the Venture Capital scheme for small enterprises in 1992, IDBI's coverage has been limited to medium enterprises.

IDBI would provide assistance in the form of both equity as well as loan. The assistance to equity may be in the form of equity capital and / or interest free soft loan carrying a service charge of one per cent per annum. In case, it is in the form of interest free soft loan, IDBI would be free to raise the interest to normal applicable rate after a maximum period of three years. The loan assistance would be at the rate of 6 per cent per annum; but IDBI would be free to review and raise it to the normal applicable rate, once the commercial size of the unit starts making profits. The composition of assistance in various forms will be structured to suit the nature of the proposal.

A normal repayment period up to 10 years including an initial moratorium of three years is envisaged. In order to enable a faster recycling of funds under the scheme, IDBI would negotiate with the assisted concern for accelerated repayment of loan instalments and for buy back of its equity holdings. Besides, there would be provision for sharing of royalties, profits, etc. IDBI may explore possibilities of exit from these projects through take over, merger, etc., where necessary. In the event of development projects becoming unsuccessful, assistance given under the scheme along with the promoter's stake may be written off.

SIDBI - Promoted Venture Capital Funds

SIDBI constituted Venture Capital Fund in October 1992 to increase the flow of venture funds to the SSI sector. As most of the venture funds are increasingly funding larger companies, SIDBI stepped in to fill the gap, as a long felt need of SSI units. The corpus of SIDBI Venture Capital Fund started with an initial contribution of Rs.10 crore. It has progressively increased it to Rs.125 crore by March 2003. The fund is being utilised for venture capital assistance to SSI units directly, and for subscribing to the corpus of the existing/ prospective venture capital funds, including industry - specific funds, with the objective of enlarging SIDBI's outreach to small scale units. As per the policy initiatives spelt out in the Union Budget 1996 - 97, SIDBI can participate in VCFs set up by public sector institutions, as well as private companies set up at state / regional level, and sector - specific funds, up to 50 per cent of the total corpus of the funds, provided such a fund is dedicated to the financing of small scale enterprises. SIDBI's entire contribution is to be utilised for SSI units. The first dedicated SSI Venture Fund was set up in Gujarat by GIIC as Gujarat Venture Finance Ltd. (GVFL) with all India coverage. Its corpus is Rs.40 crore, out of which SIDBI's contribution is Rs.20 crore. APIDC in Andhra Pradesh started a Venture Fund about the same time with 50 per cent contribution from SIDBI.

SIDBI Venture Capital Scheme

The focus of the VC scheme has been to assist innovative small size projects which have features of high risk, high growth, and higher than normal returns. In view of the risk associated with the VC assistance, it is sanctioned on a highly selective basis. The technology evaluation done by SIDBI consists of in-house evaluation, feedback from outside experts, and appraisal by the screening Committee of Experts. Assistance has been extended under the scheme to a wide range of industries including software and Information Technology, biotechnology, food processing, electronics, chemicals, etc. The projects involved either of the features like manufacture of the products for the first time in the country, new untried indigenous technologies, and import substitute projects. Instruments of finance used are equity, equity - related instruments, and conditional loan. Besides interest, conditional loan requires payment of royalty on sales. In the initial years, assistance was made by way of conditional loan only, but gradually the equity component is being increased. Entire assistance by way of equity only is not possible because of the small equity base of SSI units, and reluctance of SSI units to part with equity. Conditional loan has its limitations as there is an outflow of funds which limits the availability of funds for the assisted unit's growth, particularly where there is delay in project implementation. It is expected that with more favourable conditions being created for equity participation by investors in 'small cap' companies, there would be greater momentum to VC financing.

SIDBI's Creation of An Integrated Venture Fund Structure

In order to facilitate the availability of VC assistance to SMEs, SIDBI has promoted a three-tier integrated VC system for development of SSIs in software / IT-related sectors in all its comprehensiveness, at regional, national and international level so as to effectively integrate and enhance the opportunities for the industry, both in domestic and international markets.

Regional strategy

As a first - tier programme, SIDBI has taken steps for setting up state / regional level VC funds dedicated to SSIs in software / IT industry with participation from state level institutions/banks/private sector. Up to March 2003, SIDBI has contributed to the corpus of 15 state/ regional level funds. Out of them, 10 are at state / regional level, and 5 at all India level. Ten states covered are: Andhra Pradesh, Gujarat, Karnataka, Kerala, Maharashtra, Orissa, Punjab, Rajasthan, Tamil Nadu and Uttar Pradesh. SIDBI is setting up a micro venture capital fund for small innovations, in collaboration with the National Innovation Foundation (NIF), at Ahmedabad, with a commitment of Rs.10 crore as its contribution towards the corpus of the fund. NIF is under the Union Department of Science and Technology. This will meet the needs of early stage risk capital to technological innovative projects being set up at various incubation centres and technology parks.

National Venture Fund for Software and IT Industry (NFSIT)

Though the state level funds would take care of small size firms and grass roots projects, a need was felt for launching a similar fund at the national level as the second - tier programme which would help in up scaling the activities of these grass root successful firms, and devote to promoting projects and products with high technical inputs. Accordingly, SIDBI promoted Rs.100 crore close-ended National Venture Capital Fund for Software and IT Industry (NFSIT) in collaboration with the Union Ministry of Communications and Information Technology (MCIT) and IDBI. NFSIT was launched in December 1999 to meet the requirements of software and IT companies in the SS Sector to enable them to achieve rapid growth, and maintain a competitive edge in the domestic and international markets. Being an All India Fund, NFSIT can earmark funds for incubation projects with high risk and high return profile including software products for international markets. The national fund would also have international linkages which state level funds may not be able to provide. The Fund can also access international networking and co-investment from international venture capitalists. Further, the success of units assisted by this Fund would have a demonstrative effect to kick start software activity in other states where it is at a nascent stage.

NFSIT became operational during 1999-2000, and it completed its first full year of operation in 2000-2001. SIDBI has set up two subsidiaries, viz., SIDBI Venture Capital Limited (SVCL), to act as Asset Management Company (AMC) for the Fund; and SIDBI Trust Company Limited as a Trustee Company for the VC funds promoted by SIDBI. SVCL carries out the business of setting up, advising and managing VCFs; and has been acting as Investment Manager to NFSIT. For the corpus of NFSIT, Government of India's contribution is Rs.30 crore, SIDBI's Rs.40 crore; and the balance is expected from other institutions, to make the total as Rs.100 crore. SVCL raised the entire committed corpus from the contributors by March 2004. NFSIT assists projects offering potential for attractive growth and earnings. The Fund's primary focus is on unlisted small companies set up as private or public limited companies in the growing info-tech sector, software industry and related businesses, such as e-commerce, networking, multi-media, data communication, and value added communication services. The extent of investment will depend on the size, nature and stage of the project, its expected growth rate, etc. The minimum investment would preferably be above Rs.50 lakh per enterprise. Assistance from the Fund will be structured on a case-to-case basis, and will include equity and / or equity - related instruments. The Fund will also consider co-investing with other VC funds, including international funds. The Fund will divest its shareholding preferably through IPO (Initial Public Offer). The Fund may consider buy back of shares by promoters at a price which may be mutually settled. Besides financial assistance, SIDBI Venture Capital Ltd's role as investment manager of the Fund is to help the entrepreneur in a number of areas to manage his business more effectively; and achieve rapid growth in the internationally competitive environment.

Under NFSIT, SVCL sanctioned VC assistance during 2003-04 aggregating Rs.20.90 crore (6 companies) as compared to Rs.16.50 crore (7 companies) in 2002-03, Rs.15.20 crore (6 companies) in 2001-02, and Rs.29.24 crore (13 companies) in 2000-01. The cumulative sanctions (net of cancellations) at the end of March 2004 aggregated Rs.59.89 crore (25 companies), compared to Rs.54.89 crore (24 companies) at the end of March 2003. Disbursement during 2003-04 was Rs.7.63 crore (4 companies) as compared to Rs.7.47 crore (4 companies) in 2002-03, Rs.6.81 crore (3 companies) during 2001-02, and Rs.15.46 crore (9 companies) in 2000-01. Cumulative disbursements since inception of the Fund up to March 2004, aggregated Rs.37.72 crore (21 companies), compared to Rs.30.09 crore (17 companies)at the end of March 2003. Slow growth in sanctions and disbursements during the recent two years is due to the cautious approach followed by SVCL in line with similar domestic VC funds on account of depressed market conditions in the last two years. In order to spread risk, SVCL has created a diversified portfolio to cover a wide area of IT industries, such as products, services, internet - related businesses, IT training, and IT enabled services. In view of the high growth prospects of BPO / ITES units, NFSIT has increased its stake in these areas during 2002-03. In the present scenario, NFSIT and state/regional funds promoted by SIDBI have emerged as a major source of VC funds for the SME sector.

Considering the present trend, SVCL has set up a second national fund, *viz.*, SIDBI Growth Fund, with a corpus of Rs.100 crore which would focus on small units in pharma, bio-tech, light engineering, software, IT and other growth-oriented knowledge based industries. It is proposed to raise the corpus to Rs.500 crore in due course. This fund is in addition to the already established National Fund for Software and IT Industry, with a committed corpus of Rs.100 crore.

International Strategy

Further, as the third-tier programme for IT and software industry, SIDBI has planned to set up an International Dollar Denominated Venture Capital Fund in collaboration with In-tech Venture Group (IVG), Mauritius. The Fund will be located in the Silicon Valley in USA to help Indian small scale IT companies to access the international markets, setting up global scale capabilities, buying out small technology companies, and setting up joint ventures, particularly in USA and European Union (EU) countries. The main objective of the Dollar Denominated Fund would be to help Indian SSI units to enhance the business opportunities which in turn would increase the foreign exchange earnings for the country.

Constraints Experienced by VCFs and Suggestions

There are over 70 operating offshore VC funds focusing on India as a country in 2002. It is estimated that over 80 per cent of them are dollar funds, and the rest are rupee funds. The total cumulative assets under management are over US $5 billion. The investments in various sectors in 2000 alone are placed at around US $1 billion. This has given tremendous boost to IT sector from 2000. The total venture capital/ private equity investments have touched $1 billion during 2003-04 from $600 million in 2002-03. VC/PE funding in the calendar year 2003 was in the $500-600 million range, a sharp drop from $1.1 billion in 2002 and $900 million in 2001.

"Post Dot com" bust, the VC industry has started its recovery. The initial push has been provided by BPO and ITES. The BPO has shelved itself at the top position in the VC portfolios. However, the focus of investments is slowly shifting from IT, Software and BPO to other sectors as well such as retail, power and infrastructure, and in manufacturing industries where India has become globally competitive.

During 1999-2003 (5 years) the private equity investments have grown at an astounding rate of 82 per cent of compound annual growth rate (CAGR) while the runner up, Sweden did not give much competition, and managed to achieve a CAGR of 57 per cent. However, in 2003, more than 60 per cent of private equity flow was invested in non-technology sectors like Banks, FMCG (fast moving consumer goods), pharmaceuticals, and telecom. In the years to come, real estate, BPO, entertainment, retail and consumer sector, and manufacturing industries like textiles, auto ancillaries and pharmaceuticals sectors will attract investments from VCFs.

VC industry has thus begun to come of age in India, given the increased investments and successful exits by private equity funds during 2002-04. Though the investments in the initial stage or start-up financing have more or less been stagnant, there is increased momentum in the late-stage financing. Certain regulatory facilitations and the prospering economy are expected to act as a healthy breeding ground for the VC industry.

Very slow growth of rupee funds in VC industry in India is due to lack of knowledge on venture capital and angel investing by investors as well as specific regulatory issues. To ensure greater participation of the corporate sector, banks, and high net worth individuals, there is a strong case for tax deduction of amounts invested in VCFs up to Rs.10 lakh per annum. On the regulatory side, Indian funds must be allowed to be invested globally, for instance, in a U.S. structured entity. This will result in investing in highly scalable enterprises. This will also fetch enormous capital gain inflow into India as and when venture capitalists disinvest in the invested companies.

Some of the venture capital funds promoted by NRIs with investment banking experience in large private equity funds have pointed out a few hindrances in the Indian system of VCFs. First, there is the additional cost of being routed through Mauritius. There is no reason why India cannot set up a similar zone, say in Goa or Pondicherry. The second is remunerating the fund managers, which is a global practice. Fund managers must be allowed to receive remuneration in the form of capital gains at the time of divestment. The third is the issue of liquidity within India. The local stock markets need to have more depth, and greater flexibility. Government must pass a set of regulations encouraging offshore fund managers to set up a shop in India.

A proper regulatory framework for structuring the funds on the lines of Limited Partnership Act and Venture Capital Trust Act should be created. SEBI may take a lead role in evolving the guidelines. Eligibility for registration as VC funds should be neutral to firm structure. The Government should consider creating new structures such as limited partnerships, limited liability partnerships, and limited liability corporations. Internationally, these are accepted practices. A limited partnership is defined as a partnership formed by two or more persons, having as members one or more general partners, and one or more limited partners. The general partners are personally liable for the debts of the partnership; have the power to act on behalf of the partnership; and have control over the partnership. On the other hand, the limited partners, generally do not participate in control; do not have the power to act for the partnership; and are not personally liable for the debts of the partnership. While there are several variants of limited partnership, the generally accepted alternatives are outlined by the Chandrasekhar Working Group on Structure of VCFs. Banks should provide working capital on the basis of assessment made by VCF companies rather than their own norms. At present, many VCFs end up providing working capital funds. Recommendations of the R.H. Patil Committee on Opening up of Capital Markets to SSI Units, and the Chandrasekhar Working Group on Structure of VCFs need to be acted upon expeditiously to create a conducive environment for domestic and offshore VCFs for increasing the tempo of investment in all the potential sectors. Incentives created for VCFs should be on par with mutual funds, if not more; as VCFs involve greater risk. Pension funds, insurance funds and funds from corporate bodies should be permitted to be invested in VCFs. Mutual funds may also be permitted to invest in VCFs up to 5 per cent of their corpus.

The regulatory, tax and legal environment should play an enabling role. Internationally, venture funds have evolved in an atmosphere of structural flexibility, fiscal neutrality and operational adaptability. Resource raising, investment, management, and exit should be as simple and flexible as needed, and driven by global trends. In view of the increasing global integration and mobility of capital, it is important that Indian VCFs as well as Venture finance enterprises are able to have global exposure and investment opportunities. Apart from large investments flowing into prospective areas, adequate attention needs to be paid to SMEs planning to commercialise R & D know-how through innovative approaches, and also other SMEs with high growth potential offering opportunities.

Prospects

Information technology, and software development, biotechnology, food and agro-processing industries, pharmaceuticals, and service enterprises including health care, telecom, media, communications, wireless, entertainment, tourism, etc. should be pursued as focus areas for VC activity. The VC industry is still in the nascent stage in terms of practices and operations. With greater encouragement given to professional entrepreneurship, adoption of innovative technologies and an integration of Indian business with the global market; industry and service sector in particular offer bright prospects for venture capital industry in the country. Chandrasekhar Working Group envisaged US $10 billion assets under VC management by 2005 in the country. Attempts should be made to surpass this target.

REFERENCES

1. Bhushan, Dewan (2001), *E-Commerce*, New Delhi, S. Chand and Company, Chapter 10 - Venture Capital, pp. 87 – 110.
2. National Productivity Council (NPC) (1999), *Productivity* - Special Issue on Venture Capital, 40(3), October - December, published by New Age International (P) Ltd. - Journals Division, New Delhi for NPC.
3. Pandey, I.M. (1996), *Venture Capital: The Indian Experience*, New Delhi, Prentice Hall of India Private Limited.
4. _______ and Shantanu Dutta (1999), Venture Capital Development in India, *Productivity*, 40(3), October - December, pp. 392 - 404.
5. Pandey, I.M. et al. (2003), Colloquium on Entrepreneurship and Venture Capital, *Vikalpa*, 28(1), January - March, pp. 99 - 112.
6. Renuka Ramnath (2005), Venture Funds: Activity Gains Momentum, in *The Hindu Survey of Indian Industry 2005*, Chennai, Kasturi & Sons Ltd., pp103-106.
7. Securities and Exchange Board of India (SEBI) (2000), *Report of the Working Group on Structure of Venture Capital Funds* (Chairman: K.B. Chandrasekhar), Mumbai.
8. Singhvi, L.K. (1999), Venture Capital Industry in India - an Agenda for Growth, *Productivity*, 40(3), October - December, pp. 374 - 379.
9. Sudhir Sethi (2001), Venture Capital - Sustaining the Momentum, in *The Hindu - Survey of Indian Industry 2001*, Chennai, Kasturi & Sons Ltd., pp. 83 & 85.

10. Varshney, Vishnu (2001), Venture Finance - Highlights, in Small Industries Development Bank of India (SIDBI) (ed.), *Technology for Small Scale Industries - Current Status and Emerging Needs*, New Delhi, Tata McGraw-Hill Publishing Company Ltd., pp. 627 - 655.

11. ________(2003), Nurturing a Venture: A Venture Capitalist's Perspective, *Vikalpa*, 28(2), April-June, pp. 83 - 87.

2

ROLE OF FINANCIAL INSTITUTIONS AND DEVELOPMENTAL ORGANIZATIONS IN PROMOTING RURAL NON-FARM SMALL ENTERPRISES

Dr. D. Nagayya*

In the context of liberalisation, rural non-farm small enterprises as well as small enterprises in urban areas have been adversely affected due to severe competition. Moving away from the pre-liberalisation era of protection, small scale sector has been steadily reorienting itself to face the challenges posed by increased competition, domestically and internationally, in the phased programme of integration with the global economy. Small enterprises with their dynamism, flexibility and innovative spirit will have to adapt themselves to the fast changing needs of the market-driven economy, where government acts as a facilitator and promoter; no longer as a regulator.

Presentation of the paper is in four sections: (A) Rural industrialisation - concept and coverage, (B) National programme for rural industrialisation (NPRI), (C) Institutional efforts at rural industrialisation, (D) Conclusion. As part of the NPRI, key areas being pursued are ; technology upgradation/ modernisation, and export promotion, with emphasis in recent years on integrated approach through an action plan for each cluster. Cluster identification in different product lines is an important aspect of the programme. Role

---

* Consultant on Small Enterprises at Guntur; and former Director(Industrial Development), National Institute of Small Industry Extension Training (NISIET), Hyderabad.

played by NABARD and SIDBI in stimulating rural industrialisation, and in promoting SHG-bank linkage for supporting self help groups (SHGs) through micro finance is another significant direction. NABARD is operating the Micro Finance Development Fund (MFDF), and SIDBI is operating the SIDBI Foundation for Micro Credit (SFMC) to bring about holistic approach for the development of the micro finance sector. Involvement of commercial banks in financing small enterprises promoted under all the above mentioned programmes is quite substantial. This speaks of the role of the banking sector at the field level in particular. Enhancing competitiveness of rural micro, tiny, small and medium scale enterprises is the major thrust of various programmes at present to enable the enterprises to withstand global competition. The new trade regime offers opportunities for market expansion. These need to be pursued vigorously by rural enterprises. Formation of consortia, cluster associations, and strategic alliances with enterprises and associations in other countries, technological linkages, and financial tie-up are important directions to derive benefits from the competitive environment.

Introduction

Rural Industrialisation–Concept and Coverage

For facilitating policy direction, connotation of the term 'rural industries' as widely popularised in the country is given here. This is mainly based on the recommendation and viewpoint of the Study Group on Rural Non-Farm Sector constituted by National Bank for Agriculture and Rural Development (NABARD) in collaboration with Swiss Development Cooperation (SDC) as brought out in its *National Report on Rural Non-Farm Sector in India* (1994) released from New Delhi. A few other study teams including the National Committee on the Development of Backward Areas of the Planning Commission (Chairman: B. Sivaraman) in its *Report on Village Industries* (1981) released from New Delhi, have brought out similar views.

The term 'rural industries' can be used in a broad sense to cover enterprises and artisanal units which could be classified as small, tiny, micro, village and household units involved in manufacturing, processing (including processing of agro-based products), preserving, storing or marketing of goods, and those engaged in industry-related services which could be considered as capable of generating employment opportunities to the rural work force without a major shift in their habitat. Typically, rural labour may secure employment in nearby growth centres endowed with critical minimum infrastructure. This definition may encompass marketing, research and development or other linkage activities related to the above enterprises irrespective of their location. The idea of a growth centre is well recognised at the national level. Under the circumstances, the Study Group on Rural Non-Farm Sector constituted by NABARD and SDC, has indicated that all villages and small towns with population up to one lakh may be covered under the rural industries programme of various organisations, with the exception of activities having linkage effects with rural industries, which should be considered for assistance irrespective of location. For the sake of clarity, agriculture and allied activities as defined by NABARD for coverage under Farm Sector are excluded from the definition. Focus of rural industrialisation programmes has thus to be on rural areas and small towns, facilitating rural-urban linkages, and integration between the two. As per the present definition, all SSI units with gross investment in plant and machinery up to Rs. one crore, and in case of specified export-oriented product lines up to Rs. five crore, can be treated as rural industries, if they fulfil the location criterion. In the context of globalisation, medium enterprises are gaining importance. Enterprises with investment in plant and machinery ranging between Rs.one crore and ten crore fall in this category. Small enterprises are being referred to as small and medium enterprises (SMEs) at present. SMEs can, thus, form part of rural industrialisation strategies.

Rural Non-Farm Sector (RNFS) as emphasised by NABARD and Union Ministry of Rural Development covers a wide spectrum of highly variegated activities using different materials, technology and inputs, and catering to different sets of consumers. Activities in the category of manufacturing and processing, no doubt constitute the single largest segment of RNFS. For all India in 1991, out of 18 per cent of employment in the non-agricultural sector in rural areas, manufacturing activities account for 6.3 per cent. Over one-third (35%) of RNF employment is in the manufacturing activities. But at least two other sectors, namely, trade and construction, are also significant segments of RNFS. Trade accounts for 18 per cent, and construction for six per cent of RNF employment. Services–

community, social and personal – account for 34 per cent, but over one-half of it is in the public sector. Transport and communications contributing seven per cent is another important sector.

Obviously, all these sectors are important in themselves as well as in relation to each other for the development of the entire RNFS, and for diversification of the occupational base of rural areas. Even if manufacturing is regarded as the centre-piece of rural non-farm development, development of other sectors such as transport, trade, construction, and services, electricity generation, and finance constitutes a necessary concomitant of rural industrialisation. Development of all these sectors in rural areas, is closely integrated with agricultural development, though the present discussion is confined to non-agricultural activities.

For purposes of refinancing by NABARD, all eligible investments in RNFS located in rural areas as defined in NABARD Act, 1981, and modified thereafter, cover all villages irrespective of population size, and towns with population not exceeding 50,000. However, investments made for agro-industries, sericulture and marketing of RNFS products are exempt from the location criteria.

Khadi and Village Industries Commission (KVIC) adopted a formal definition for village industries coming under its purview in 1987, taking into account the recommendations of the Khadi and Village Industries Review Committee (KAVIRC) (1987) of the Union Ministry of Industry (Chairman: M. Ramakrishnayya). This was modified in 1994. As per the present position, any industry located in a rural area, village or town with population not exceeding 20,000, and per capita investment in fixed assets excluding land not exceeding Rs.50,000, is considered a village industry for coverage under the KVIC programme. The modification was effected based on the recommendation of the High Power Committee on Khadi and Village industries (Chairman: P.V. Narasimha Rao, the then Prime Minister). Village Industries covered by KVIC at present number 119. The number has increased over years. KAVIRC has suggested substantial modifications in the KVIC pattern and programmes, whereas the High Power Committee focussed on employment generation through specific programmes, emphasising the role of Khadi, in particular. There is need to broad-base the coverage of rural industries under the umbrella of KVIC, beyond the product lines already notified. Service activities have rightly been included in the KVIC coverage. The list needs to be further enlarged.

National Programme for Rural Industrialisation (NPRI)

In the rural industrialisation programme, integrated approach is being pursued at present by a number of organisations by identifying clusters of industries. The package of measures can include the following: credit, technology upgradation/modernisation, design development, marketing including export marketing, wherever practicable, infrastructure development, common services, supply of raw materials, training of entrepreneurs and workers, etc. In respect of existing clusters of rural industries, through a study of individual enterprises, requirements of the group are being finalised taking into account the long-term perspective of growth of the industry in the context of liberalisation in consultation with all the stake holders.

From 1999-2000, National Programme for Rural Industrialisation (NPRI) is planned through clusters by a number of institutions to develop 100 rural clusters annually over a five-year period (1999-2004) to give boost to rural industrialisation for the benefit of rural artisans and unemployed youth in rural areas to reduce rural-urban disparities, and slow down migration of rural artisans to towns and cities. Out of the 500 clusters to be developed over the five-year period; in the first year, the distribution of 100 clusters among various agencies was as follows: Khadi and Village Industries Commission (KVIC) in 50 clusters, Small Industries Development Bank of India (SIDBI) in 25 clusters, National Bank for Agriculture and Rural Development (NABARD) in 15 clusters, and the Small Industry Development Organisation (SIDO) through Small Industries Service Institutes (SISIs) to develop 10 clusters. KVIC is, thus, responsible for developing at least half of the total number of rural clusters planned for development. In the first year, KVIC initiated work in 18 clusters, and also identified 60-65 clusters for development in the coming years. SIDBI initiated work in 25 clusters, and SISIs in 10 by conducting motivational campaigns and entrepreneurial training along with skill upgradation of artisans and prospective entrepreneurs in rural areas. A few clusters from Andhra Pradesh are also included in the centres selected for the first year. SIDO has been implementing technology upgradation programme, earlier known as UPTECH. This has now been linked with cluster development and enhancing competitiveness to face the challenges of the present industrial environment.

To coordinate and synergise the efforts being made by various ministries / departments / organisations and state governments so as to have a concerted effort towards setting up of rural clusters, an inter-ministerial committee has been set up at the Centre under the Chairmanship of Secretary (Small Scale Industries, and Agro and Rural Industries). It is planned that an amount of Rs.5 lakh will be utilised per cluster for creating the environment for the development of the cluster. This includes extending financial support for conducting a diagnostic study of the cluster, demonstration and development of modern tools and kits, and various other technical inputs including design, market linkages, hiring of a consultant for conducting a technical gap study, etc., training and strengthening of the NGO/cluster change agent, setting up of a common facility centre, organising seminars / workshops, entrepreneurial / managerial programmes, study visits, etc. This amount is meant for gap filling exercises, and not for the development of the cluster as such. In the early years, mainly diagnostic studies are planned to be taken up to identify the interventions required for the development of the cluster. In the subsequent years, implementation interventions will also be taken up. During the 10th Plan period, outlay for the NPRI schemes proposed is Rs.13.5 crore for the development of 350 clusters, on an average about Rs.4 lakh per cluster. Up to March 2004, 109 clusters have been taken up for development by KVIC, NABARD, SIDBI, SIDO and state governments.

NPRI is designed to improve the quality of the product by introducing new tools and processes, to reduce raw material wastage, and to impart skill development training to artisans in the cluster. Another intervention which has been supported under NPRI seeks to set up a design development centre for the benefit of artisans in the zari work cluster at Howrah in West Bengal. In the first place, skill development programmes were supported in the cluster. In case of mango jelly cluster in East Godavari district of Andhra Pradesh, critical gaps in three areas, *viz.*, manufacturing process, packaging and marketing network, were identified and remedial measures introduced. Consequently, the products have become more hygienic and eco-friendly.

NABARD proposes to develop 50 rural clusters in a phased manner over five years (1999-2004). 65 clusters have been identified up to March 2004 in 18 states, and promotional programmes were launched in 55 clusters. Activities covered under these clusters are mainly artisan-based, including handicrafts and handlooms.

This programme is estimated to benefit 16,000 artisans and small entrepreneurs. A grant assistance of Rs.1.55 crore has been sanctioned up to March 2004 for supporting various interventions in clusters. A field study conducted by NABARD in ten selected clusters to assess the impact of the programme (Box 1) revealed that NABARD as a facilitator in coordinating with participating agencies, and other promotional interventions resulted in social empowerment, skill upgradation, improving market access, employment generation and group formation, thereby leading to enhanced access to credit.

Box-1: Impact of Development of Industrial Clusters on Rural Economy

Results of a field study carried out by NABARD in ten clusters promoted under its sponsorship in different states ...

- Attitudinal changes in the beneficiaries who are now motivated to bring about socio-economic development of the cluster
- Awareness about opportunities for furthering activities in the cluster
- Gender equity and social empowerment
- Formation of artisans' associations in most of the clusters, and recognition of the power of collective bargaining
- Formation of 100 SHGs, majority of which were linked to formal banking system
- Disbursement of bank credit to the tune of Rs.2 crore
- Promotional efforts resulting in the setting up of 2,000 new units
- Technology and skill upgradation, and improvement in the quality and range of products
- Additional employment for 3,400 persons created

- Revival of handicrafts as a profitable source of employment
- Arresting migration from rural clusters to urban areas
- Elimination of middlemen, direct marketing, and exposure to the latest trends
- Increase in income of the cluster members by 50 – 100 per cent
- Repayment ethics inculcated among beneficiaries
- Export of cluster products and participation in international exhibitions.

Source: NABARD (2004), Annual Report 2003-04, Mumbai, p. 35.

Out of the 25 clusters planned by SIDBI, a few of them in which work was initiated by selecting suitable implementing agencies are eco-cluster development at Binsar, Almora (Uttaranchal) with Mahila Haat as the implementing agency, zari work in Howrah (West Bengal), mat diversification and improved designs in Midnapore (West Bengal), stone carving in Sikri (Rajasthan), and handicrafts in Phalodi (Rajasthan).

Small Industry Development Organization (SIDO) in collaboration with United Nations Industrial Development Organization (UNIDO) identified 11 clusters in Andhra Pradesh for technological upgradation. Some of the important ones selected are: food processing industry in Krishna district, ceiling fans, bulk drugs and foundry clusters in Hyderabad, mango fruit pulp cluster in Chittoor district, and foundry cluster in Vijayawada. They are receiving priority attention. Some of the others under consideration are: graphite crucibles at Rajahmundry, wooden toys at Kondapally near Vijayawada, brass and bronze items at Srikakulam, gold covering ornaments at Machilipatnam in Krishna district, lace manufacture at Palakol and Narsapur in West Godavari district. These clusters need technological upgradation, product development, quality improvement, marketing and financial support for enhancing their competitiveness, and to face the challenges of the present era. It is planned to conduct an indepth study in each cluster, and evaluate the needs of the industry in that cluster with the active cooperation and participation by the industry associations and the units themselves. Based on the findings of the study, steps will be taken to evolve a mechanism for developing these clusters, covering technological ugradation and modernisation, and other related areas.

Institutional Efforts at Rural Industrialisation

SIDBI has been pursuing rural industrialisation programme (RIP) in a few districts based on an integrated approach for promotion of tiny industries in rural areas. The number of districts covered under this programme is increasing every year. This is essentially a five-year effort in a district to accelerate rural industrialisation, and to provide impetus to rural development by creating sustainable industrial and service enterprises in rural areas, leading to higher employment generation and effective utilisation of local skills and resources. By the end of March 2004, the programme has been in operation in 67 districts of 24 states through 37 implementing agencies. Cumulatively, around 13,650 enterprises were promoted under RIP including around 2,800 units during 2003-04. In order to assess the impact of RIP, and suggest mid-course correction, a national convention on RIP was organised by the Bank in May 2003 at Lucknow. Suggestions finalised during the convention included the following: (a) need for building competitiveness among implementing agencies, (b) focus on vertical growth of units already set up under RIP, and (c) improved technological content of the programme.

SIDBI established five Regional Development Centres, one in each region of the country, to outsource professional expertise for monitoring as well as providing interactive management support to the implementing agencies. The Bank continued its capacity building exercise of RIP implementing agencies. For rural service providers, a certificate course has been organised. Reorientation training programmes on Rural Industries Programme have been organised for personnel of implementing agencies, including non-governmental organisations (NGOs).

Another programme in which SIDBI has been involved in providing financial assistance is integrated infrastructure development centre (IIDC) scheme of the Union Ministry of Small Scale Industries, in which for identified locations for developing infrastructure for the benefit of tiny and small industries, investment envisaged is Rs.5 cr. per location. Out of this, up to Rs.2 cr. is given by the Centre as grant, up to Rs.3 cr. by SIDBI as loan; the proportion being 2:3 between the

Centre & SIDBI. Cost of land is the contribution of the state government. In the Northeastern region, the proportion is 4:1 between the Centre and SIDBI. Among the locations identified, at least 50 per cent are planned in rural and backward areas. Focus is on tiny sector as well as women promoted enterprises. Other than the IIDC scheme, SIDBI provides funds for developing industrial estates and industrial areas to state level corporations, and any other agency likely to be associated with the development of industrial infrastructure. Infrastructure development including common services, research and development, and testing facilities, common effluent treatment facilities, constitutes an important aspect of the rural industrialisation programme.

NABARD has taken up credit intensification drive for rural non-farm enterprises, initially in five districts, including Kurnool in Andhra Pradesh from 1993-94 for a period of seven years up to 2000-01. District Rural Industries Project (DRIP) of NABARD was extended to 9 districts in 1999-2000, 8 districts in 2000-01, 20 districts in 2001-02, 18 districts in 2002-03, and 16 districts during 2003-04, taking the total number of districts covered up to March 2004 to 76. It is planned to cover 100 districts in a phased manner over a period of five years. The objective of DRIP is to generate sustainable employment opportunities by providing adequate credit support together with promotional measures.

Apart from organisations directly involved in the rural industrialisation programme in the small scale and decentralised sectors, a number of other ministries of Government of India and their specialised institutions at national and state levels have been making their contribution to diversification of the rural occupational base for promoting rural non-farm sector enterprises. Banks and development financial institutions with the overall support from NABARD have been involved to a substantial extent in encouraging individual entrepreneurs and groups of entrepreneurs or registered institutions and NGOs to take up this role. Union Ministries of Rural Development and Urban Development have been engaged in non-farm sector development by supporting weaker sections in particular under various self employment programmes. These include Swarnjayanti Gram Swarozgar Yojana(SGSY) (integration of six rural development programmes including IRDP, TRYSEM and DWCRA from 1999), and Swarn Jayanti Shahari Rozgar Yojana(SJSRY). Union Ministry of Social Welfare is implementing programmes for women through Central and state Social Welfare Boards. Self Help Group (SHG) approach with micro finance made available by commercial banks through NGOs and Self Help Promoting Institutions has become popular in some of the states. High level of performance recorded so far is in the Southern and Western states, with Andhra Pradesh alone accounting for nearly half of the country's total in terms of groups formed, and also in terms of institutional finance availed so far. NABARD and SIDBI have developed separate funds for channelling micro finance through refinance facility, and to a limited extent as direct finance.

NABARD has set up the Micro Finance Development Fund (MFDF) in 2000 with a start-up contribution of Rs.100 crore - Rs.40 crore each from NABARD and RBI, and Rs.20 crore from 11 commercial banks identified by RBI. The Fund is being utilised for scaling-up various micro finance (MF) initiatives with special focus on capacity building under the SHG-bank Linkage Programme. NABARD has decided to replenish the entire expenditure from MFDF during any year from its profits, which enables the opening balance of the Fund to be retained at Rs.100 crore each year. During 2002-03, Rs.3.66 crore and during 2003-04, Rs.7.05 crore was utilised from the Fund for various initiatives taken by NABARD for promotion and development of micro finance in general, and up-scaling of SHG-bank linkage programme in particular. The MFDF was also used for providing loans of Rs.1.51 crore during 2002-03, Rs.3.22 crore during 2003-04 in the form of revolving fund assistance to NGOs and micro finance institutions (MFIs).

SIDBI Foundation for Micro Credit (SFMC) was set up in January 1999 for channelising funds to the poor with a start-up contribution of Rs.100 crore. SFMC's mission is to create a national network of strong, viable and sustainable Micro Finance Institutions (MFIs) from the informal and formal financial sector to provide micro finance services to the poor, especially women. The Bank has formulated a multi-pronged strategy for holistic development of the micro finance sector. SFMC has sanctioned financial assistance of Rs.70.84 crore during 2003-04 compared to Rs.38.51 crore during 2002-03. Sanctions included loan assistance and capacity building grant, transformation loan assistance, and liquidity management support. During 2003-04, total disbursements stood at Rs.66.31 crore as against Rs.31.04 crore during 2002-03. The outstanding loan portfolio as at end-March 2004 was Rs.90.94 crore compared to Rs.54.76 crore as at end-March 2003. The cumulative assistance disbursed since inception of the operations of the Fund up to end-March 2004, aggregated Rs.232.08 crore disbursement through 192 MFIs, benefiting approximately 10.41 lakh poor, mostly women.

The National Micro Finance Support Programme is being implemented by SFMC in collaboration with DFID (Department for International Development) of U.K., and IFAD (International Fund for Agricultural Development), Rome. A mid-term review (MTR) of the project was jointly undertaken during December 2003. The MTR concurred with SIDBI's decision to take the MFI route to serve the poor as a step in the right direction. It has been acknowledged that the parenting role taken up by SIDBI has been well performed, and the sector acknowledged it as major service extended by the Bank to the micro credit sector. Further, SIDBI has been able to successfully mainstream micro credit and bring focus to the sector. The MTR concluded that SIDBI has built a very strong foundation for organised growth of MFIs, and also highlighted some operational areas requiring attention by SFMC.

Khadi and Village Industries Commission (KVIC) through its REGP (Rural Employment Generation Programme) has been contributing to development of village industries with focus on sustained employment generation in productive ventures. REGP of KVIC is applicable to rural areas and towns up to 20,000 population, with per capita fixed investment excluding land of an artisan/entrepreneur/worker not exceeding Rs.50,000. Except Khadi and Polyvastra, all other viable schemes covered by KVIC, numbering 119 at present can be considered under this scheme. Product lines listed under negative list of KVIC cannot be considered. The following categories of persons and institutions can be covered under the programme: individual entrepreneurs, self help groups, institutions, cooperative societies, trusts, and public limited companies of the state/central government. Individuals can take up projects up to Rs.10 lakh investment. Institutions/cooperative societies/trusts can take up projects up to Rs.25 lakh investment. By adopting the project approach, credit is made available by scheduled commercial banks to enterprises, for which 25 per cent of project outlay would be the tail-end grant that can be given after observing the satisfactory performance of the enterprise. In respect of advances above Rs.10 lakh, margin money is at 25% of project outlay up to Rs.10 lakh, and at 10% for the balance amount. For weaker sections, and in the hill, border and tribal areas and other.designated backward areas such as the northeastern region, Sikkim, Andaman and Nicobar islands, and Lakshadweep, margin money will be at 30% of project cost up to Rs.10 lakh, & above this amount up to Rs.25 lakh, it will be 10% of the remaining amount. Project cost will include one cycle of working capital. Promoters' contribution needed is at 10% of the total cost of the project for general category, and 5% in case of others for categories mentioned above including the northeastern region and other areas listed above. Out of a target of 25 lakh, additional employment opportunities to be created in the 10th plan under REGP, employment generated is 9.4 lakhs during the first two years (2002-04), and the target for 2004-05 is 5.25 lakhs.

Under Prime Minister's Rozgar Yojana (PMRY), self employment ventures are promoted in urban and rural areas. Experience of recent years shows that it is more urban oriented, as the response is better there; and awareness in rural areas, and among weaker sections and women is still limited. Ventures promoted can be in industry, services, businesses, and agro-related activities. The scheme is under the Union Ministry of Agro and Rural Industries, and implemented through the Commissioner of Industries at the state level, and district industries centres at the district level. Project outlay can go up to Rs.2 lakh for activities other than businesses; and Rs.1 lakh for business enterprises. Subsidy component is at 15% of project outlay, subject to a maximum of Rs.7,500 generally, and Rs.15,000 in case of northeastern region and Sikkim. Subsidy and promoters' contribution together should total 20% of project outlay. Eligibility conditions are stipulated in terms of age, education, length of stay in the place from where loan is to be obtained, and family income level. Two to five persons can join for promoting a venture, in which case total project outlay and subsidy amount will be multiples of the amount admissible to an individual, based on the number of persons joining. Self Help Groups (SHGs) are also eligible for PMRY assistance. There is no upper limit on the loan sanctioned for SHGs. SHG may undertake common economic activity for which loan is sanctioned without resorting to onward lending to its members. Loan may be provided as per individual eligibility taking into account requirement of the project. SHG may consist of 5 – 20 educated unemployed youth fulfilling the eligibility criteria of PMRY. Subsidy may be provided to the SHG as per the eligibility of individual members, subject to a maximum of Rs.15,000 per person. Required margin money contribution (subsidy and margin brought by the promoter to be equal to 20 per cent of the project outlay) should be mobilised by the SHG collectively. In the 10th plan period, employment generation target through PMRY is 16.5 lakhs, out of which 5.44 lakhs have been created during the first two years (2002-04), and target for 2004-05 is 3.75 lakhs.

Conclusion

Exposure of rural non-farm enterprises to the impact of liberalisation is placing a huge demand on the part of development institutions and government to equip the working poor and micro-enterprises with skills, knowledge, access to credit, technology and all other requisite resources to enable them to operate, compete and survive in the competition against the large players. Development support for this sector has to be reviewed and redesigned in this context. This also requires large scale state investment for modernisation and expansion of infrastructure in terms of power, transport, communications, cold storage facilities, etc. This is necessary to equip these industries with the requisite capability to face international competition. There appears to be no alternative for the government but provide a level playing field for the rural micro enterprises in the period of transition. This level playing support in terms of fiscal as well as tariff measures has to become one of the core elements of the national strategy for economic development whose priorities are removal of poverty, generation of productive employment, and contribute to the livelihood security of majority of the population.

The key challenge during the Tenth Plan(2002-07) for the small and medium enterprise (SME) sector is remaining competitive while continuing to ensure employment intensity of operations. Review of implementation of a few thrust areas followed in the recent years to enhance the competitiveness of small-scale sector reveals that the sector has intrinsic strength to withstand global competition. It has been readapting itself to the emerging needs. The process of liberalisation has not only created new vistas, but has also thrown up new challenges for the sector. With globalisation and WTO environment, the sector has to face intense competition in the years to come. The new trade regime offers opportunities for market expansion to small enterprises, and also provides a number of protective devices, which can be legitimately used to extend relief, at least temporarily, against increasing imports in response to elimination of quantitative restrictions, and lowering of tariffs. SSIs can gain through product innovation, diversification and strategic diversion from slow growth traditional products to high value added growth products, and adoption of aggressive marketing strategies. Formation of consortia, cluster associations, and strategic alliances with their counterparts in other countries, technological linkages, and financial tie-up can maximise the growth potential of SMEs in the country. Special attention needs to be paid to promote research and development, innovation and incubation. Extensive application of information technology tools can improve the performance of the SME sector in a number of directions. A strong surge of export-led growth in labour-intensive manufacturing activities can come about if key policy ingredients are put in place. Another important direction of SME growth is environmental preservation through treatment of effluents and wastes, and use of cleaner and eco-friendly technologies and materials. This is gaining popularity.

3

CHALLENGES FOR INDIAN BANKING INDUSTRY

Dr. M.S. Narayana* and **Prof. G.N. Brahmanandam****

There has been a paradigm shift in the Indian banking industry with cash credits and demand loan being slowly phased out and marketable debt papers are coming in. Using this process, banks have greater flexibility in passing on the credit rise to the market and using the funds generated for other lendings, allowing them to cater to a larger number of clientele. Disintermediation has been on the rise with more and more corporates approaching the debt market for raising funds rather than approaching banking system for direct loan. The international experience has also been that around 70% of revenues of banks are coming from fee-based activities, disintermediation and treasury business. However, this raises a serious concern, as commented by R.B.I. How long will the banks rely on retail banking and treasury operations to boost their profitability? What are the other challenges ahead for Indian Banks? How equipped are the Indian banks to deal with these challenges? The present paper is an attempt to identify the challenges for the Indian banking industry and to offer pertinent suggestions to face these challenges.

Introduction

The banking industry has moved through various stages of transition. Most of the commercial banks were born out of the entrepreneurial initiatives of the either big business houses or distinct

* Reader and Principal, DonBosco PG College, Guntur.

** Dean, Faculty of Commerce and Management Studies, Acharya Nagarjuna University, Nagarjuna Nagar.

communities and were geographically local in nature. Post Independence saw the banks spreading their networks and growing in size. The two rounds of nationalisation of banks gave a further imputes to the urge for growth. These were the times when size was considered synonymous with quality. The indiscriminate expansion and the ills of mass social lending pushed the banks to a situation where the NPA levels were high and the business itself was under threat. Legislation was all pervasive including the rates at which a bank could take a deposit or lend money.

In the early 1990's fresh licenses were given in the private sector for new commercial Banks, which were to offer international quality service, while being able to identify with their Indian counterparts. These banks had an advantage of starting with a clean slate, adequate capital, lean staffed and technology driven. After the advent of new private sector banks, the competition in the industry increased and forced the public sector as well as the foreign banks to have a relook at their business models. The customer has now a wide variety of products and services to chose from at competitive pricing. Most of the banks now offer tailor made end to end solutions to all the financial needs of the clients.

Depending on the economic cycle, the banks are active in various sectors or segments at any point of time. It is not that, banks would ignore other segments, but they may be focussing more on the ones that show greater promise. Banks, are after all, accountable to stakeholders and given the capital constraints have to necessarily optimize its use depending on the return vis-à-vis-risk. Even over the last few years, when the global economy was undergoing a recessionary phase. Indian banks have turned to the retail side for credit growth. Since the size of retail is insignificant, it may not reflect in the overall credit growth. Banks left with surplus liquidity have to turn to alternatives, which in the Indian context was the debt market.

Financial results of Scheduled Commercial Banks

Indian banks put forth an outstanding performance during the last couple of years. This is commendable given the fact that credit offtake remained poor. The high profitability of the banks was due to gains from their treasury operations.

The fiscal year 2002-03 was the most happending year for the Indian banking industry. The industry was able to post extraordinary results on multiple fronts–higher incomes and lower expenditure, profitability growth, declining NPA levels, improved return on assets, successful IPOs of PSBs, and high valuations to banking stocks. During the year, the income of Scheduled Commercial Banks (SCBs) rose to 14.1%, higher than the average growth rate of 12.1% for the period 1997-2002. At the same time, the expenditure of the SCBs stood at 11.4%, lesser than the average annual growth of 11.7% for the period 1997-2002. The net profits have witnessed an increase of 47.5% (Rs. 17,007 cr from Rs.11,576 cr in 2001-02). The return on assets has also risen significantly to 1%, which is the highest in the last six years. On account of all these factors, the valuations of bank stocks have also soared high in the stock markets.

Select Financial Sector Indicators: 2001–02 Vis-a-Vis 2002–03

Indicator	*2001-02*	*2002-03*
Scheduled Commercial Banks		
Growth in Major Aggregates (%)		
Aggregate Deposits	14.6	13.4
Non-food Credit.	13.6	18.6
Investment in Government Securities	20.9	27.3
Financial Indicators (as percentage of total assets)		
Operating Profits	1.9	2.4
Net Profits	0.8	1.0
Spread	2.6	2.8
Non-Performing Assets (as percentage of advances)		
Cross NPA	10.4	8.8
Net NPA	5.5	4.4
Urban Cooperative Banks		
Growth in Major Aggregates (%)		
Deposits	15.1	9.1
Credit	14.1	4.5
Financial Indicators (as percentage of total assets)		
Operating Profits	1.5	1.3
Net Profits	-0.9	-1.1

(Contd...)

Spread	2.2	2.1
Non-Performing Assets (as percentage of advances)		
Gross NPA	21.9	21.0

Source: RBI Report on Trends and Progress, 2003

Challenges for Indian Banks

According to the Reserve Bank of India's (RBI's) recently released 'Report on Trends and Progress of Banking 2003', "Financial intermediaries are witnessing significant changes all over the world under the impact of deregulation, technological upgradation and financial innovations. Indeed, the traditional face of banking is no longer as it was even a few years ago. The way financial services are provided is changing dramatically. In many countries banks are now providing services that do not come under the domain of traditional banking. The old institutional demarcations are getting increasingly blurred. Consequently, increased competition from non-bank intermediaries has led to a decline in traditional banking, wherein banks only accepted deposits and made advances that stayed on their books till maturity. The business of banking has been moving rapidly in recent years to a 'one-stop shop' of varied financial services. This process of transformation is particularly striking in emerging market economies like India.

The apex bank in its recently published report, while acknowledging the economic condition and the transformation which the Indian banks are undergoing, expressed concerns over the shift to retail and boost in profits by way of treasury operations. According to the report, banks have been neglecting their primary function of credit creation in favor of short-term goals and termed this phenomenal shift as 'Narrow Banking'. In India, the term 'narrow banking is being used for the alleged propensity of the banks to place their liquidity in government papers rather than resort to lending. In other words, here the term connotes reluctance of banks to lend. In the more developed countries, the term stands for the opposite phenomenon; the propensity of the banks to lend far too easily, since at a crunch they can always promptly bankrupt the borrower."

One of the risks of narrow banking is that it concentrates on treasury operations and neglects the productive sectors of the economy. Thus, the growth of the manufacturing sectors gets impaired on account of poor credit allocation. Notwithstanding the fact that recovery in industrial production is on the way, credit offtake has remained poor. In fact, if the banks are reluctant to lend to corporates and SMEs for a long period of time, the momentum that is getting built in the manufacturing sector can be lost and thus, impact the GDP growth adversely. In fact, while the bank rates have come down to 6%, the median lending rate on term loans still hovers in the range of 11.5-14%. For the GDP growth to reach the targeted levels, it is important that the banking system reaches the desired sectors.

A comparison of interest of advances during the last five years reflects the true picture of falling core income. During the comparative period 1996-97 and 2002-03, interest on advances grew by 10.4, while the income from treasury operations recorded an annual compounded growth of 17.4%. While the mid-year economic review predicted a GDP growth of 7%, the banking indicator- credit offtake does not reflect the belief. Non-food credit offtake stood at 5.7% much lower than that of last year, which stood at 7.3%.

Basel II Measures

By 2006, Indian banks are required to adhere to the international standard of capital adequacy norms under the new capital accord, Basel II, the RBI is confident that the Indian banks are geared up to meet the challenges. The RBI, in its report commenting on the preparedness of Indian banks said, "The Reserve Bank has already taken steps to implement two major components of the second pillar of Basel II i.e., risk-based supervision and Prompt Corrective Action (PCA). The PCA Framework has already been put into operation, on an experimental basis, by the Reserve Bank. Further a pilot-run of risk –based supervision has been introduced in October 2003."

However, according to a survey conducted by the Federation of Indian Chambers of Commerce and Industry, Indian banks are not adequately geared up to implement the stringent Basel II norms including capital adequacy and non-performing assets. The survey also concluded that the implementation would be delayed at least by two years, taking the deadline to 2008. The implementation of Basel II norms will have two implications on the banking system. First is the ability of the banks to measure the risks they bear. Although banks are now having adequate risk management practices in place, the existing systems may not be able to support the banks in meeting the stringent norms. This calls for additional investment in information technology and information sharing systems.

Second is the challenge of meeting the adequacy norms by providing more capital towards reserves. Banks have to look out for funds to back the identified risks and then earn income to service that additional capital requirement. If banks are not able to meet the reserves criteria, then the ability of the banks to lend further will be limited. This can have a negative impact on their income. However, the Indian banks are confident that the additional capital requirements can be met easily, especially with the enactment of the securitization law in India, which can unlock the resources for banks. In future, the usage of securitization route and spreading the risks will be on a higher side.

RTGS–The Upcoming Challenge

Another important challenge for the Indian banks will begin from June 2004, when the RBI will introduce the Real Time Gross Settlement System (RTGS). Under the new online payment system, banks and customers will be receiving funds with certainty, enabling them to use funds immediately.

Since RTGS would affect the settlement of funds on a real time basis, finance managers of companies can manage their cash flows much better and they would be in a position to take away a part of the cost-free deposits. This in turn will affect the banks, as the huge float funds (the interest-free deposits that customers maintain with banks to meet payment obligations) enjoyed by banks would become history. This is especially true with nationalized banks. The free float funds are used by the banks to meet either their statutory reserve requirements or investment needs. In the absence of these funds, banks have to look for other sources of capital.

Conclusion

The Indian banking system has come of age. The banking system has gone from mass banking to personal banking. The future would be in mass customization of services. RBI is slowly freeing up the banking sector and encouraging self-regulation. RBI has been progressive in taking views from the market participants before formulating policies. In this environment, market transition would be smooth for heralding new products and services comparable to those in the advanced economies. A multitude of risk hedging instruments, structured products (assets as well as liabilities) and derivatives will be seen. Educating the customers would have to go concomitantly with the introduction of these products. Banks would have to be at the cutting edge of technology to ensure process delivery. Banking in India is poised for exciting times ahead.

4

HRD PRACTICES IN BANKING SECTOR
AN ANALYSIS

L. Srinivas* and **Dr. G.V. Chalam****

The banking sector has been an instrument for the economic development of any nation and its role in a developing nation like ours is of vital importance. Globally, the banking activities are undergoing rapid diversification. In order to maintain their status in the present competitive environment, banks have to concentrate in developing their human resource. Human Resource Development (HRD) is an essential process for every organisation, for the optimum utilisation of its human resource, involves both the parties for their mutual benefit consequent to the attainment of the organisational objectives.

Since the State Bank of India is the premier bank Central Bank with wide network of several branches, it has been chosen as a sample organisation for the study. In this paper a research survey is conducted to elicit information about general climate, HRD mechanisms and attitudes of the employees of the selected bank. This paper is an attempt to review the HRD practices in the Indian banking sector taking place in the aftermath period of the new competition emerged with the arrival of new private banks and foreign banks through the process of liberalisation.

* Research Scholar, Dept. of Commerce and Business Administration, Acharya Nagarjuna University, Nagarjuna Nagar-522 510

** Head, Dept. of Commerce and Business Administration, Acharya Nagarjuna University, Nagarjuna Nagar-522 510

Certain statistical tools have been applied while analysing the position of the bank with respect to the HRD systems. The findings of the study are helpful to several banks and individual professionals who are keen on implementing HRD practices and want to be ahead of their competitors.

Introduction

The banking sector has been an instrument for the economic development of any nation and its role in a developing country like ours is of vital importance. The banking activities worldwide are undergoing rapid diversification. Technological changes have become the very essence of the banking sector and the Indian Banking Sector is also prone to these changes. In order to maintain their status in the competitive environment, banks have to concentrate in developing their human resources. In any organization, the quality and amount of productivity mainly depends on the skill and interest of its employees. Therefore, every business organization should take the lead for upgrading the skills and knowledge of its employees for the mutual benefit and progress. In this direction "Human Resource Development (HRD)" is an essential process for every organization in order, to optimally utilize its human resource and in turn to attain its designed objectives.

Like any other industrial organization, banking sector is also highly dependent on the quality of HRD practices for the motivation of its employees. An effective implementation of HRD activities would result in excellent organizational climate for the people to be competent and productive. Nevertheless, it is not only the implementation of HRD practices but also their review from time to time helps the banking institutions maintain their status in the competitive environment.

With this background, an attempt is made in this paper to investigate whether the HRD practices followed in the State Bank of India are in line with the contemporary developments in the Indian Banking Sector. The existing literature leaves many gaps and stimulates the need for conducting this kind of extensive study in the field of Human Resource Development. In this study a survey research technique is adopted to elicit the data about general climate, HRD mechanisms and attitudes of employees of the selected bank. While choosing the sample respondents, different levels and categories of employees adequate in number are administered with a structured questionnaire in order to get facts and figures regarding HRD climate and systems apart from the secondary data. For the purpose of the study there is a single hypothesis formulated and it has been tested reasonably by applying various statistical techniques.

Importance of HRD in the Present Environment

In India managing a commercial bank is unique and challenging as compared to any other economic activity. Banking activities are highly regulated both by the social value systems and monetary considerations. It appears that the complexity of the task has increased manifold, making the management of banks more and more difficult and challenging in the years ahead, than over the past. The crucial factor in the management of commercial banks is human resource development. It is very important for a bank to develop their personnel in order to cope with increasing and changing demands in banking. It has become inevitable for the banks to concentrate seriously on setting up systems for suitable human resource development.

Human Resource Development seeks to bring about overall development of employees by enabling them to improve their knowledge, skill and behaviour. It also helps them develop better awareness about their roles in the work situations and contributes to the process of integration of the employees with organization. Also, the need of HRD is more in service organizations like banking sector. An efficient and effective commercial banking activity is the result of effectively motivated employees. A banking institution is said to be functioning efficiently, if its objectives are achieved effectively. However, these objectives can be achieved fully, when the employees are trained, committed and motivated. Thus, the efficiency and effectiveness of commercial banking will depend upon how best the management has taken care of the development of their employees in these institutions. It has been widely recognized that improving human skills through well-tailored HRD programs can enhance the productivity of any organization.

HRD assumes significance in view of the fast changing organizational environments and need of the organization to adopt new techniques in order to respond to the environmental changes. The vitally of human resource to any industry including banking industry depends upon the level of its development. Organizations should be dynamic, growth-oriented and fast changing to develop their human resource. It is needless to say that organizations possessing competent human resource grow faster, can be dynamic and steer the hearts of the public. Any organization that is interested in improving its services and effectiveness needs to develop its employee competencies to perform the tasks required to bring about such improvement.

In the wake of deregulation, liberalization and globalization of the Indian economy, the banking system is also getting gradually internationalized. The process of globalization of Indian economy has become irreversible and will be further intensified. In such an environment, Indian commercial banks have to equip themselves to meet the challenges of competition within the country as well as outside. And as they proceed to do this, they have to ensure that their human resource remain sound in order to face such challenges. The image of the bank and its overall effectiveness to a large extent depends upon the performance level of its employees. It is only through the implementation of HRD programs; performance of employees is increased. The more the implementation of HRD programs the higher the performance of employees.

Banks are revamping their procedures and methods of work for economic and technological reasons. Also, job designs are reviewed to suit automation and changing characteristics of new groups of recruits. Staff will need to learn new skills and knowledge to cope with changing work technology. In the period of rapidly changing technology and increasing competition, the banks should be conscious of the development of its human resource in order to achieve standards of excellence through the development of human resource. The foregoing discussion makes it clear that the banks need to concentrate more on HRD practices to sustain themselves in the competitive environment. It is assumed that there are threats to the banks from inside and from outside for which they are required to redefine and redesign the HRD systems to overcome those situations. Therefore, an attempt is made to undertake a comprehensive investigation to review the HRD policies and practices in the selected public sector bank.

Need of HRD in the Banking Sector

The need of HRD for an organizaion's growth arises mainly due to the following reasons.

(i) The dearth of capable managerial manpower and a greater need in the future increase the competition for available talent.

(ii) The continued growth and development of business, coupled with increased complexities such as the problems of size, technology and competition, add further pressures.

Similarly, the need of HRD is more in service oriented institutions like commercial banks. An efficient and effective banking system helps the process of economic development of any nation as per its priorities. It functions as catalytic agent for bringing economical, industrial and agricultural growth and prosperity of the country. A banking institution is said to be functioning efficiently, only when the objectives of sound banking system are achieved effectively. These objectives can be achieved only when the employees of the bank are trained, satisfied and motivated by the management for the contribution towards productivity and overall effectiveness of the bank. Thus, the efficiency and effectiveness of commercial banking would depend upon how best the management has taken care of the development of its employees working in their institution.

The need of the HRD in the banking institutions has continuously grown because of the effective role they are called upon to play in the task of socio-economic development and rehabilitation of especially those people who were hitherto neglected and deprived. There are also high expectations of the society from the banking system, which cannot be met without the development of the integrity, efficiency and behavioral pattern of those who are working in the banks. Besides, the clientele of banking is not only growing with large increase in population but also getting widely diversified.

Thus, HRD in the context of banking would mean not only the development of new knowledge and skills of the employees but also developing capabilities to meet the needs of both internal and external environment, attaining self-confidence and motivation for public service". HRD also aims at giving more and more thrust on the human resource to encourage creativity for the better customer service. HRD efforts in banks focus on building a strong character of honesty, integrity and truthfulness. Such efforts try to culminate in enhancing the banks' renewal capabilities through competitiveness, innovativeness and creativity. HRD efforts crystallize the values that are goal supportive and contribution oriented. It emphasizes the functional style, ethos, culture and work ethics, which are built around people, manifesting a concern, and is sensitive to the needs of the organization. The entire philosophy of developing an employee in banks rests on 'building a holistic person by framing his personality, character and way of life".

The HRD policy in the banks has to act as an effective instrument to encourage employees, to show creativity, to reach for excellence and finally to render better customer service. Thus, the objectives of HRD in banks can be listed as:

- creating a climate of openness and trust;
- building a collaborative culture whereby everyone is an important member of an effective team;
- preparing individuals for technological competence;
- psychological preparedness for willing to participate in change-implementation;
- promoting human capabilities and competencies in the organization;
- facilitating to build a strong character of honesty and integrity in performance;
- helping the individual to develop his potential, realize his power so that he will be able to achieve his self-goals while contributing to the success of organization;
- improving quality of work life;

HRD Practices in State Bank of India: An Analysis

This paper is focused on the examination of the basic activities of HRD viz., job rotation, training, performance appraisal, rewards, career planning and development, feedback and counseling, potential development, human resource information systems, organization development, etc. State Bank of India has a great story in the field of Human Resource Development. It has a well-structured HRD set-up and a wide spectrum of HRD activities. The training system of SBI is now recognized as one of the best systems in the country.

It is found that the employees of State Bank of India are very sincere and committed. It is observed during the time of the survey that in several branches of the bank, often, they are required to remain in their offices even after the closure of the business hours. This situation further implies that the working hands in case of officers level is inadequate, and also not in proportion to the workload assigned to them. Consequently, they are overburdened, and this condition led to the frustration of this group of employees in the bank. Obviously, this tendency communicates that an atmosphere of exploitation of human resources is prevailing in the bank.

It is further observed that the employees who are not allowed to go on VRS are greatly dissatisfied towards the management attitude. They felt that the action of the management with regard to VRS is self-seeking. In addition, they believed that lot of work has been imposed on their shoulders in the aftermath period of VRS in the bank. The prevailing circumstance consequent to the implementation of VRS is very rigid. Thus, the employees of the bank have been overloaded due to the excessive work and the bank branches looked like manufacturing units.

The survey also identified that the off-the-job training is not a continuous process in the bank, which speaks that the training function is irregular. It is also reported that the assessment of training need is also done irregularly in the bank and hence the evaluation of training needs is not a continuous process in the bank. Further, it is also found that most of the learning in the bank is facilitated when the tasks are performed and the employees familiarize most of the work procedures during their on-the-job-training. On the other hand, it is well known that the job rotation is a regular phenomenon in the bank. It is observed that employees are frequently subjected to internal transfers within the same branch and thus they are exposed to multifarious functions existing in the bank. This helps the employees to acquire knowledge and skills and therefore, job rotation is facilitating employees' development in the selected bank.

The majority of the respondents revealed that they are fully aware of the work rules and procedures of the bank. This implies that the employees in the bank strictly comply with the code of conduct framed by the management and thus it forms the basis for union-management relationship. In this context, a large group of respondents opined that they are greatly satisfied with their affiliation to the bank and with their present job. The data further revealed that the senior management cadre is highly satisfied with the training and development system. Among the three cadres of employees in the bank, the senior cadre is very well pleased with respect to the HRD system. However, it could be disclosed that the other two cadres of employees have shown a minute dissatisfaction towards the training and development system. Further, it is observed that the junior management cadre is highly favourable to the system of 'recognition and reward'. It is also unveiled that all the three cadres of employees are comfortable with the existing 'security' system. Every respondent felt that he is highly secured with respect to his employment. The majority of the respondents from the two cadres' viz., clerical cadre and junior management cadre are optimistic with respect to relationships in the bank. Very few respondents from the senior management group opposed this view. This indicates that there is a microscopic gap existed between the senior management and the other two cadres of employees as far as the working relationships are concerned.

The survey also identified that an average OCTAPAC culture is observed in the bank. It is found from the study that the managers in the bank are not keen in supporting their subordinates' development continuously. The survey further revealed that the managers are providing mere support to their subordinates to accomplish the tasks of the latter. Through the analysis of the data it is noticed that the top management efforts with regard to the identification and utilization of the potential of the employees is simply at the middle of the road. It is further brought to light that 'employee development' in the bank is quite inferior to the other elements in the general climate. It is also found from the analysis that majority of the respondents have a high degree of response in favour of the overall HRD climate in the bank. More specifically, it is the junior management cadre, which exhibited a high degree of satisfaction about the overall HRD climate. This category is the more satisfied one among the three groups of the employees in the bank. On the other hand, very few interviewees have unfavourably responded. To sum up, it is clear that extraordinary climate responses are not seen with respect to any dimension in the bank, which indicates that the bank has an average climate with regard to Human Resource Development.

Suggestions

The following measures are suggested by the researcher for an effective functioning of the HRD practices in the selected bank.

The perception of junior management and clerical cadre employees of the bank on the dimension 'training and development' is at low degree. Therefore, the management has to provide equal training opportunities to all the employees depending upon the need.

The bank management has to take care of the employees who are unfavourable to the overall HRD climate. In this direction the management is required to carry out surveys from time to time within the bank in order to comprehend the percentage of people who are against the climate and the drawbacks of the system. This kind of surveys help the management to know the degree of HRD climate frequently.

The employees irrespective of their cadres should be equally treated with respect to the dimension 'recognition and reward'. The bank managers should not be partial in determining the good performers. Recognition should be dispassionate and rewards stand by contribution. In this context, the management of the bank should devise the ways to recognize the virtuous performers by rewarding the employees as and when they innovate. This move can motivate the employees for higher achievements.

The bank management has to strive to fill the gap that exists between the senior management cadre and clerical cadre employees with respect to the dimension 'relationships'. The misconception among the employees of the bank creates menacing situation and therefore, the management has to encourage teamwork by eliminating disparities among different categories of employees in the organization. Further, the authorities of the bank should give access to improve the OCTAPAC culture vigorously in the bank. This would further help employees build enthusiasm and liberty at the work place. Hence, the bank management should bear in mind that OCTAPAC culture is essential for facilitating the HRD in the organization.

In the light of growing business it is not be possible for the bank to reduce the workload. Yet, the bank management can go for increasing the manpower with respect to the officers' category so that the burden would be lessened. Besides, the bank management has to proportionately distribute officers to the existing branches according to their work arrangement. In this context, the bank branches with minimum amount of business may be allotted the minimum number of officers and whereas the branches with the more amount of business may be allotted more number of officers. Thus, a rational adjustment of manpower should be facilitated for effective functioning of the bank.

In case of VRS, though it is a sensitive issue, it is the responsibility of the management to disclose the reasons why an employee has not sanctioned the VRS. This would eliminate certain gaps between the management and the employees. The employees who are not permitted VRS should be placed in such a setting that they would be optimistic even at the stage of increased burdens.

Further, the management of the bank has to initiate measures to improve off-the-job-training facilities. As the workload is increasing day by day the management should prefer to conduct meditation classes in order to ease the employees from stress and strain which arise out of imbalances in the assignments. Also, Meditation classes help employees enhance their psychological attitudes. Certainly, this aspect of guiding employees spiritually would impart dual advantage, serving the purposes of both the parties.

It is more important that a separate department for HRD could be set up in the State Bank of India for enabling management to exercise full-fledged Human Resource Development practices. The existing personnel and HRD department is merely concentrating on personnel matters and as well as matters pertaining to HRD viz., training, rewards management, performance appraisal and job rotation. This may not adequately support the HRD climate in the bank. The personnel and HRD department is supposed to promote OCTAPAC culture and implement other HRD mechanisms vigorously in order to have a good overall HRD climate conducive to the development of individuals. But this is not happening in SBI, where the personnel and HRD department is overburdened with the personnel matters. Therefore, it is better to separate HRD from personnel function in the bank for faciliiating a complete Human Resource Development climate in coordination with the personnel department.

Finally, the bank has to reveal the statistics pertaining to the HRD activities carried with regard to its employees and the resulting progression through huge displays at the respective branches. This would help the customers of the bank sustain faith about the future prospects of their bank.

REFERENCES

1. Mani R.S.S., HRD for OD, *The Hindu Speaks on Management,* July 21, 1994, p. 164.
2. Rohmetra Neelu, *HRD in Commercial Banks in India,* Ashgate Publishing, Aldershot, 1998, p. 20.
3. Prabhu, N.D. 'Human Resource Development - The Canara Bank Experience' in Khandelwal, A.K.(ed.), *Human Resource Development in Banks*, Oxford and IBH, New Delhi, 1988.

5

THE BALANCE SHEET OF LIBERALISATION

A STUDY OF THE BANKING SECTOR

Dr. Tessy Kurian*

Chronology and content of economic reforms and banking sector reforms in particular are presented in the article of analyze the balance sheet of liberalization. Beginning with the serious balance of payments situation in 199-91, the main landmarks are recalled. Structural reforms of early 1990s covered areas of industrial licensing, foreign trade, exchange rate management, and the financial sector. Apart from banks, the reforms in the financial sector covered term lending institutions, non-banking finance companies, mutual funds and insurance companies. Reform process made Indian banks conform to the international prudential standards, and simultaneously impart a greater element of competition in the financial system. The first phase laid the base for a sound and viable banking system. The slowing down of the reform process from mid-1990s causes concern. Corrective measures need to be taken speedily as prospects of future growth of the banking system and the Indian economy crucially depend upon the accelaration of the reform process towards achieving an open and stable economy.

Introduction

The economic crisis which India had to encounter in the 1990s contained in itself a God-sent opportunity to investigate the maladies of the economy. The policy makes were forced to take a long and

* Assistant Professor in Development, Debub University, Awassa, Ethiopia

hard look at the regime of protective policies that the country had been following. It was only then that the revelation dawned on the powers – that instead of fuelling growth, the policies being pursued by the successive governments that had ruled the country since its independence had actually hampered it, albeit unintentionally.

An analysis of the Indian economy revealed many shocking realities to the planners. In 1991, the fall in the rate of growth of the GDP was a common feature in all comparator countries (except China which could buck the trend) but nowhere was it as steep as in India. Rate of growth of the Gross Domestic Product of our country had, as a rule, been among the lowest in the peer group and in 1991, it has plumbed abysmal depths.

The serious balance of payments position India faced in 1991 due to the abnormal increase in oil prices in the wake of the Iraq-Kuwait war exacerbated the situation when the current account deficit of the country touched the level of 3.2 per cent of the GDP in 1990-91. That this level was comparable, in percentage terms, to that of some fast-growing economies was small comfort because, given the magnitude of India's. GDP, it was quite high in absolute terms. Being a net importer of oil, the burden was huge: in just one year, the bill increased from USD 3.7 bn to USD 6.0 bn and India had to draw down the bulk of the foreign exchange reserves in order to meet the higher landed cost of the crude-oil. So, a vicious circle was set in motion-the drawing down of the reserves, downgrading of the rating and inability to finance the deficit. All this aggravated the already grim scenario.

There was increasing recognition that the overall pace of economic development had fallen short of the aspirations of the people. The crisis brought forth unsustainability of the expansionary policies under a regime of restrictive and inwards-looking policies that hampered growth and encouraged an inefficient, production structure' it was, in fact, argued that the policies that existed had rewarded and provided generous incentives, putting a premium on inefficiency. The crisis highlighted the inadequacy of the financial and other support systems in the country. It was clear that the absence of policies aimed at stabilization was what was ailing the country.

Once the problem was identified, it did not take long for the government to initiate corrective steps. The objective was to dismantle the restrictive barriers and to gradually open up the Indian economy. Prudential regulations had to be adopted, the quality of supervision improved and the seeds of competition sown aimed at generating healthy competition. Greater participation by private sector and technical and financial collaboration with entities abroad were to be permitted. 'Financial Sector reforms not only contribute to economic growth, which is the most important way to reduce poverty, but they can lessen the severity of financial crises, says Frank Polman, Resident Director of ADB in India.

It was recognized that stabilization by itself would not be adequate unless structural reforms were introduced and recurrence of such problems prevented. Obviously, structural reforms could not be attempted without attaining some degree of stabilization. That was why India had to put in place, simultaneously, a set of policies aimed at both stabilization and structural reforms.

It was strongly felt that 'we can achieve our development objectives much more efficiently provided we prune the role of the state and give greater leg-room to market forces; change over to fiscal controls instead of mandatory controls; adopt general and transparent regulations instead of the notorious case-by-case approach; and insulate the economy from populist tendencies as well as influence-pedlars. This, then, constituted the goal and the process of structural reform, which, it was expected, would lead to a faster rate of economic growth, high-wage employment growth and self-reliance through international competitiveness in time.

Treading a new path, the reform covered numerous aspects of the economy. In the yeas since 1991, India has thus migrated away from a closed economy and is slowly maturing into a liberalized one. Though the central government has changed many times since 1996, each government voted to power has supported and hastened the reform process, sending an encouraging signal to the investors, particularly the foreign investors. The governments that ran the country in the later years have also appreciated that continuation of the reform process is crucial for the future growth and attainment of an open and stable economy and maintained the thrust. Therefore, the common thread running through the policy is the objective: improvement of the efficiency of the system. Taken together, these reform measures in the various areas constitute an important break in India's economic policy. The structural reforms introduced in the early nineties broadly covered the areas of industrial licensing, foreign trade, exchange rate management and the financial sector.

For the development of an economy, money is essential and the finical sector provides the mirror image of the underlying real economy. Toning up of the financial sector would, therefore, be an essential ingredient of the reforms and the organization and conduct of financial markets should be such that they reflect the underlying fundamentals of the economy. India had built a vast network of financial institutions and market over time. The mandate of the financial sector reform in India was to usher in a 'strong and efficient financial system to attain the avowed objectives of creation a market-driven productive and competitive economy and to support higher investment levels and accentuate growth. Apart from banks, the reforms in the financial sector covered term lending institutions, Non-Banking Finance Companies, Mutual Funds and Insurance Companies. The financial sector reforms were subjected to on-going and periodical reviews.

An important issue which generated a lot of debate on the content and the timing was Capital Account Convertibility. The Tarapore Committee report on the subject released in June 1997, recommended a three-year time-frame for complete capital account convertibility of the rupee. The Committee set out the following preconditions for full convertibility:

- Reduction of the fiscal deficit to 3.5 percent of GDP by 1999-2000;
- Average inflation rate of 3-5 percent for the period 1997-2000;
- Complete deregulation of all interest rates in 1997-98;
- Reduction in the cash reserve ratio (CRR) to about 3 percent;
- Reduction in the level of banks' non-performing assets from an estimated 13.7 percent of total loans in March 1997

(actual NPAs were 17.8 percent of total loans) to 5 percent in 1999-2000; and

- Adoption of a transparent exchange rate policy by 2000.

India's Banking Sector

Driving the economy of India, as in the case of any other country, is the banking system. Therefore any reform of the financial sector had to necessarily impact the banking sector. It is therefore hardly surprising that financial sector reforms are, in essence, coterminous with the reform of the banking sector. And rightly so: ever since the nationalization of fourteen major banks in 1969, the state of the financial sector in India had been precarious. True, the expansion in the coverage of the banking system was spectacular, with a seven-fold expansion in the total number of bank branches from 8,262 in 1969 to 60,190 in 1991, but this was not without the problems that came with it.

Six more banks were nationalized in 1980, bringing nearly 85% of the business within the folds of public sector banking. The major impact of nationalization was that it took banking to hitherto unbanked and underbanked areas. More than 50% of the bank branches were located in rural areas. Public sector accounted for about 85% of the banking business of India. All banks were called upon to disburse 33 1/3% (Later enhanced to 40%) of its credit to the priority sectors so as to correct the skewed pattern of credit dispensation.

Implementation of the schemes was not without its faults. Efficiency was judged by social policy considerations. Organizational effectiveness, operational efficiency etc. were relegated to the background. Gross profits constituted only 1.1% of the working funds of banks in 1989-90. A few banks did not generate enough gross profits to take care of the provisions and were on the brink. To quote from the Narasimham Committee Report, 'The deterioration in the financial health of the system has reached a point where unless remedial measures are taken soon, it could further erode the real value of and the return on the savings entrusted to them (banks and financial institutions) and even have an adverse impact on depositor and investor confidence). Target-oriented loan melas at one end of the delivery-chain, which was indeed one of the major contributors to the situation, at the other we had the then newly-announced policy of waiver of dues. Non-recovery halted the process of recycling massive amount of funds locked up in sticky accounts, leading to erosion in the profitability of banks. Added to these maladies was the attempt to window-dress the balance sheets, aided and abetted by the fact that transparency was not a virtue in the existing scheme of things. Reforms in the financial sector were aimed at Indian Banks conforming to international prudential standards and simultaneously imparting a greater element of competition in the financial system.

The measures adopted in the process fall into categories represented as under :

- Bank norms were liberalized and banks were given the freedom to decide levels of holding of individual items of inventories and receivables.
- Ceiling on term loans was raised to Rs.10,000 million for projects. Involving expansion/modernization of power generation capacities.
- Banks were allowed to set their own interest rate on post-shipment. Export credit (in Rupees) for over 90 days.
- Interest rates on loans over Rs.2000.00 against term deposits and on. Domestic deposits with maturity periods over two years were deregulated.
- Banks were freed to fix their own foreign exchange open position limit, subject to RBI approval.
- Guidelines were issued to banks to ensure qualitative improvement in their customer service.
- Loan system was introduced for delivery of bank credit.

Depending on the extent of the compulsions to boost exports in order to tackle the problem of adverse balance of trade/payment situation, the Reserve Bank of India provided refinance in varying degrees. Banks found that new dimensions were added to their functioning, as they were to conform to the internationally accepted norms of stringent classification of assets, income recognition, provisioning and capital adequacy. Consequently, a few of the supposedly 'solid' banks posted losses in their initial years of the post-reform period, creating turmoil of sorts in the banking system. Banks with a capital base of Rs.1000 million and foreign banks were allowed to be set up, ushering in new banks with the support of high technology which in turn triggered keen competition, particularly in metros, cities and large towns. While the monolithic public sector banks were rudely awakened from their slumber by these developments, it was a shot in their arm for most of the old private sector banks, which came back on the scene with renewed confidence and started making their presence fell.

Liberalization Policy: Implementation

Adoption of the international standards of accounting in India did cause tremors in the beginning. Apart from facilitating comparison of the figures and performance of banks, uniform accounting standards and transparent disclosure norms have cleaned up the balance sheets to a great extent. Barring two, all public sector banks had been able to achieve the minimum capital adequacy ratio, sixteen of them with capital adequacy ratio over 10%, and five between 9 and 10%. The first phase of financial reforms has thus laid the base for a sound and viable banking system. The reforms brought out structural changes in the financial sector, eased external constraints in their working, introduced transparency in reporting procedures, restructuring and re-capitalization of banks and have increased the competitive element in the market'. In the second phase of reforms, success will depend primarily on the organizational effectiveness of banks for which initiatives will have to come from the banks themselves. The core issue in the next phase of reforms will be competitiveness.... which could provide lasting solutions to the sluggishness in the economy and finance vital to withstand the risks of volatility.

The dividing line between commercial banking, is increasingly getting blurred. Commercial banks have entered into merchant banking, leasing, infrastructure financing, trading in investments, etc. which belong in the domain of other players.

This arrangement has to be examined it is necessary that the regulators avoid the temptation to over regulate and breathe down the neck of banks. In a dynamic and ever changing scenario, if not on going, review of the structure, operations and working is essential. The concept of voluntary retirement scheme was a step in the right direction, but it went awry in its implementation, with those targeted under the scheme staying on and a large chunk of top quality man-power leaving the system.

Problems and Challenges Ahead

The preparedness of the banks to face the challenges of liberalization would no doubt depend upon the speed with which the establishment responds and the extent of the intervention in the following areas:

Self-governance in interest rates,

Harnessing of appropriate technology to eliminate routine work

Human resources management

Costing and pricing

Fee-based income

Different challenges stare at banks in their face. All public sector and old generation private sector banks need to gear up to the demands of technology up gradation. With the norms regarding foreign investment in banks having been eased, the prospects of such events taking place are getting brighter. At least some of the new generation banks too, it is apprehended, might fall sown on the wayside in the ensuing shakeout, if they are not merged or taken over by then. Term lenders like IDBI are looking at the possibility of similarly becoming universal banks.

The Balance Sheet of Liberalization

Going by the standard criteria of growth rates in national income and per capita income, the Indian economy has done well since liberalization, despite politica uncertainities and a difficult external environment. Betweel 1992-93 and 1998-99, the average annual growth rate was 6.55%, higher than the 6.04% achieved between 1985-86 and 1989-90. The growth rate of per capita income went up from 3.4% in the eighties to an average of 4.7% between 1992-93 and1998-99. The foreign exchange reserves of the country had recorded a remarkable growth from USD 5.5 bn in 1991 to USD 32.5 bn by March 1999. The gross domestic savings rate of the economy had remained at 24% on an average the nineties and the rate of inflation had shown a perceptible fall.

Conclusion

There are certain areas of concern. The signs of the slowing down in the economic reform efforts by the mid nineties need to be addressed squarely as the prospects of future growth depend crucially upon a continuation of the reform process towards achieving an open and stable economy. To conclude, every cloud has a silver lining; and the economic crisis that Indian economy faced in the 90s paved the way for a strong & steady balance sheet for the banking sector of the country.

6

THE MENACE OF NON-PERFORMING ASSETS

CHALLENGES AND REMEDIAL MEASURES

Dr. P. Niranjan Reddy* and **Prof. N. Kamaraju Panthulu****

The high level of non-performing assets (NPAs) in banks has been a matter of great concern in the country in view of its implications for the economy as a whole. To move towards the internationally accepted norms for asset classification and income recognition, Reserve Bank of India has tightened the definition of NPAs in a phased manner. Up to 1993, assets were treated as non-performing if due beyond four quarters of a year. From end-March 2004, the period is reduced to beyond 90 days. Magnitude of NPAs of public sector, private sector and foreign banks is given up to 2003. After presenting an outline of measures taken by Government of India and RBI, the article makes a forceful plea for stern measures to be initiated in the near future. The article stresses the need for monitoring the early warning signals in relation to NPAs in the assisted units, and appropriate measures to be taken to speed up recoveries from the defaulting enterprises.

Conceptual Clarification

The high level of NPAs in banks has been a matter of great concern and anxiety not only to the banks, but to the economists and policy planners as well, since credit acts as a catalyst to the economic growth of a country and any obstacle, such as threat of NPAs, is

* Associate Professor, Rayalaseema Institute of Information and Management Sciences, Tirupati.

** Dean, School of Social & Behavioural Sciences (Retd.), Sri Venkateswara University, Tirupati.

bound to have adverse consequences not only on the health of banking system, but also on the economy as whole. The cost of financial intermediation by banks is high partly because of the cross subsidization of non-performing assets. NPAs are an inevitable burden on the banking industry. The success of a bank depends upon methods of managing NPAs and keeping them within tolerance level. Of late, several institutional mechanisms have been developed in India to deal with NPAs and there has been also tightening of legal provisions. Perhaps more importanatly, effective management of NPAs requires an appropriate internal checks and balances systems in a bank. The profitability of the financial institution largely depends upon the level of income generated by optimum use of the assets after paying the cost of funds for acquiring them and other administrative costs involve therein. Once the assets cease contributing to the income, they are termed as non-performing assets, which not only have cost of funds involved but also requires to be provided as per prudential norms. An asset, including the a leased asset becomes non-performing when it ceases to generate income for the bank. A non-performing asset can be defined as a credit facility in respect of which the interest and/ or installment of principal has remained 'past due' for a specified period of time. The specified period was reduced over the years in a phased manner.

With a view to move towards internationally accepted norms for asset classification and income recognition, Reserve Bank of India has tightened the definition of NPAs in a phased manner. Thus, from the norms of classifying those assets as non-performing which are four quarters past due, which was applicable until 1993, Reserve Bank of India moved to the norm of three quarters past due in 1994 and then to two quarters (180 days) past due in 1995. In 2001, RBI tightened this further by removing the "past due" concept. As a result, NPAs are to be recognized 30 days earlier than they were to be before 2001. RBI has now advised banks to move to the 90 days norm for recognizing loans as non-performing, with effect from March 31, 2004.

With effect from 31st March 2004, an advance will be classified as an NPA where in the case of :

(i) Term Loan-the interest and/or installment of principal remain overdue for a period of more than 90 days,

(ii) Overdraft/Cash Credit (OD/CC)-the account remains out of order,

(iii) Bills purchased and discounted-the bill remains overdue for a period of more than 90 days,

(iv) Advance granted for agricultural purposes-interest and/or installment of principal remain overdue for two harvest seasons but for a period not exceeding two half years, and

(v) Other accounts-any amount to be received remains overdue for a period of more than 90 days.

The Volume of NPAs in Indian Financial Sector

As stated already the volume of NPAs in the Indian financial sector particularly in banking sector have been continuously increasing. As on 31st March 2003, net NPAs in the public sector banks has been in the order of Rs.2,49,632/- millions; in the private sector banks; the net NPAs on 31st March 2003 have been computed at Rs. 38,253/- millions. In the foreign banks; Rs.9,148/- millions and in the financial institutions Rs.1,42,980/- millions.

The details of the size of NPAs in Indian financial sector have been provided in the table 1.

Table 6.1: Size of NPA Portfolio of Indian Financial Sector

Particulars	*Gross NPAs 31 March 2002*		*Net NPAs 31 March 2002*		*Gross NPAs 31 March 2003*		*Net NPAs 31 March 2003*	
	Rs. Million	*%*	*Rs. Million*	*%*	*Rs. Million*	*%*	*Rs. Million*	*%*
Public Sector Banks	5,65,070	60	2,79,580	59	5,40,871	55	2,49,632	57
Private Sector Banks	1,16,720	12	66,680	14	1,17,042	12	38,253	9
Foreign Banks	27,260	3	9,200	2	29,662	3	9,148	2
Financial Institutions	2,40,000	25	1,17,540	25	2,92,000	30	1,42,980	32
Total	**9,49,050**	**100**	**4,73,000**	**100**	**9,79,575**	**100**	**4,40,013**	**100**

Source: IBA Bulletin , January 2004, Page 63.

Factors influencing the growth of NPAs

There are several factors that contribute to the growth of NPAs in the banking sector in India. All these factors can be broadly classified under two headings. 1. Internal Factors and 2. External Factors.

Some of the important factors contributing to the growth of the NPAs in the Indian Banking Industry and as a matter of fact, in Indian Financial Sector itself can be summed up as follows:

Diversion of funds for expansion/diversification/modernization; taking up new projects; helping/promoting associate concerns; time/cost overrun during the project implementation stage; business (product, marketing, etc.) failure; inefficiency in management; slackness in credit management and monitoring; inappropriate technology/technical problems; lack of co-ordination among lenders; recession; input/power shortage, price escalation; exchange rate fluctuation; accidents and natural calamities etc.; changes in government policies in excise/import duties; pollution control orders etc. Apart from these there are some more factors contributing to the growth of NPAs in Indian banking industry i.e. liberalization of economy/removal of restrictions/reduction of tariffs; lax monitoring of credits and failure to recognize Early Warning Signals; over optimistic promoters; direct lending; highly leveraged borrowers; funding mismatch; high cost of funds; willful defaulters; strained labour relations; inappropriate technology; helping/promoting associate concerns; time/cost overrun during the project implementation stage etc.

What has been done so far to Contain NPAs?

Several measures have been undertaken in recent times to minimize the size/volume of NPAs in banking sector in our country. For example : enlarging the credit base through careful selection and booking quality assets; improving appraisal skills through training intervention; vigorous physical, financial, legal follow-up towards upgradation; resorting to restructuring/rehabilitation; forming committees for expeditious settlement through compromises; and expediting technical write-off. Apart from what is stated above, there are a number of other measures adopted in the recent years as suggested by Reserve Bank of India to minimize the incidence of NPAs in banking sector/financial sector:

(i) specific guidelines were issued to public sector banks by RBI for one time non-discriminatory settlement of NPAs in small sector;

(ii) Lokadalat institutions help banks to settle disputes involving accounts in "doubtful" and "loss" category with outstanding balance of Rs. 5 lakhs for compromise settlement under Lokadalat;

(iii) Debt recovery tribunals (DRT) have been set up in all major centres of the country in order to enable the banks/ financial institutes to recover the debts;

(iv) a separate legislation has to be enacted for this purpose;

(v) the Reserve Bank of India has put in place a system for periodical circulation of details of willful defaults of borrowers of banks and financial institutions. This serves as a caution list while considering for new or additional credit limits from defaulting borrowing units and also from the director/proprietor/partner of the enterprise;

(vi) the Reserve Bank of India has advised to examine all cases of willful default of Rs.1 Crore and above and file criminal cases for willful defaults. The board of directors have to review NPAs of Rs. 1 crore and above with special reference to fixing the staff accountability;

(vii) an Asset Reconstruction Company (ARC) with an authorized capital of Rs. 2000 crores and initial paid-up capital Rs.1400 crores has been set up as a trust for undertaking activities relating to asset reconstruction. It would negotiate with banks and financial institutions for acquiring distressed assets and develop markets for such assets. The Government of India has already initiated the legal reforms to facilitate an effective functioning of the mechanism of ARC;

(viii) Corporate Debt Restructuring (CDR) mechanism has been also institutionalized in 2001 to provide a timely and transparent system for restructuring of the corporate debt of Rs.20 crores and above with the banks and financial institutions. The CDR process would also enable viable corporate entities to restructure the dues outside the existing framework and reduce the incidents of NPAs;

(ix) Institutionalisation of the information sharing arrangements through Credit Information Bureau of India Ltd (CIBIL) set up by Reserve Bank of India is another important measure undertaken in recent years to minimize NPAs, and

(x) the most important step which Government of India has taken in recent times in reducing the magnitute of NPAs is by issuing SAROFA (Securitisation and Reconstruction of Financial Assets) ordinance 2002. This ordinance conferred necessary powers on the banks to summarily proceed against willful defaults and effect recoveries without intervention of courts/tribunals.

What is yet to be Done?

We should not be complacent with various measures that are undertaken so far either by Government of India or Reserve Bank of India or some of the leading financial institutions or leading banks. All the laudable objectives of various measures enunciated so far have not been achieved totally. It is true some of the measures are partially successful. Hence, it is high time the Government of India in collaboration with Reserve Bank of India and leading financial institutions and individual banking organizations should evolve and implement some more measures effectively and tackle the problem of NPAs and strengthen the viability of banking industry and financial sector as a whole.

The exiting systems and procedures for NPA identification and resolution have to be reinvigorated. For this purpose the following steps have to be taken;

(a) Designating relationship manager/credit officer for monitoring accounts;

(b) Preparation of 'know your client' profile;

(c) Credit rating system;

(d) Identification of watch-list/special mention category accounts;

(e) Monitoring of early warning signals can be broadly classified under the following heads:

1. Financial warning signals
2. Management related warning signals
3. Banking related warning signals
4. Operational warning signals
5. Signals relating to external factors

Some of the leading banking organizations and financial institutions have already initiated a number of activities in these directions. The recent amendments to Companies Act vested powers for revival and rehabilitation of companies with the National Company Law Tribunal (NCLT) in place of Board for Industrial and Financial Reconstruction (BIFR). With modifications to address weaknesses experienced under Sick Industrial Companies Act (SICA). As per the latest amendment to company Law, NCLT will prepare a scheme for reconstruction of any sick company and there is no bar on the lending institution of legal proceedings against such company. The bill to repeal SICA is currently pending in parliament and the process of staffing of NCLTs has been initiated. This is expected to make recovery procedure faster.

Let us hope some of the suggestions made above will contain the menace of NPAs and its impact on the sound functioning of the banking sector of India. Containing NPAs is a continuous problem. A constant monitoring and review of NPAs and evolving and implementing effective measures to contain NPAs is an exercise to be undertaken with utmost caution, vigilance, alertness and earnestness by all the concerned parties in the financial sector in our country.

REFERENCES

1. R. Venkatkrishna 'Performance of Public Sector Banks in NPA management; A critical Evalaution', *State Bank of India monthly review,* Vol. 42, No.3, March 2003.

2. S. Vijayulu Reddy, B. Sakunthala and B. Ramachandra Reddy 'Non-performing Assets in Public Sector Banks – An Analysis'. *The Business Review,* Vol. 7, No. 1 & 2, 2001.

3. T.P. Misra 'Managing Non-performance Assets – A Professional Approach', *IBA Bulletin* Vol.25, No.1, January, 2003.

4. K. Mohan Chandran 'Handling of NPA : Lessons From East Asia', *IBA Bulltein*, Vol.24, No.8, August, 2002.

5. PricewaterhouseCoopers 'Management of Non-performing Assets by Indian Banks', *IBA Bulletin*, Vol. 26, No.1, January, 2004.

6. Gopal Singh and Manjula Tyagi 'Magnitude and Management of Non-performing Assets in Banks, *Southern Economist*, Vol.41, No.2, March 1, 2003.

7. Indira Rajaraman, Garima Vasishtha 'Non-performing Loans of PSU Banks' *Economic and Political Weekly*, Vol. 37, No.5, February 2002.

7

CREDIT DISBURSEMENT BY COMMERCIAL BANKS AFTER SECOND GENERATION REFORMS

Y.V.S. Prasada Rao* and **A.V. Aruna Kumari****

This paper has endeavoured to present recent trends in the banking sector with regard to lending pattern after the second generation reforms from 1998 to 2001. The banking industry gathered greater momentum after the liberalization process. With the advent of modern private sector banks and foreign banks, it has led to healthy competition and customer sovereignty.

Business prospects and banking growth always go together because bank credit is the life-blood of modern economies. This is evident, that out of total bank credit, industrial loans always stood at more than 44% of total bank credit. Further, it is also shown that private companies and government companies account for more than 65 per cent of total credit. However, it can also be noticed that though personal loans bear lesser proportion, it is steadily increasing during 1998-2001, from 10 to 12 per cent, it makes clear the potentiality of credit to individuals and its emergence as a prospective sector. However, still the short-term home credit plays a dominant role with more than 50 per cent of total bank credit but short-term foreign credit occupies only about 15 per cent.

* Lecturer, P.G. Dept., T.J.P.S. College, Guntur - 522 006.

** Lecturer, Dept. of Bank Management, Theivanai Ammal College for Women, Villupuram, Tamilnadu.

A few recommendations can be suggested to make bank credit more effective and socially justifiable. Firstly, the policy makers, must initiate to improve the share of rural areas by training the entrepreneurs in agriculture and allied activities under the small scale sector and self-help groups. Secondly, foreign trade seems to be the need of the hour during the present era of globalization, but foreign trade credit is not showing the good upswing. Hence, necessary steps must be taken to boost up foreign trade and foreign credit. Finally, it is alarming to note that much bank credit is tied up in the hands of private sector companies. It may lead to further scams; hence, certain measures may be to prevent the misuse of public money.

Introduction

The role of banks as financial intermediaries is emphasized through their primary functions of accepting deposits for the purpose of lending and investment. In India, banks have been sanctified by the State as, "Social Justice Delivery Vehicles". True to the Diktat, so far, banks have rendered their might to the social cause through their priority sector lending. Thus in India bank credit has assumed an unusual and unique role of creating social justice.

Credit is the life-blood of modern economies. Financial institutions have been entrusted with the task of providing funds to industry, agriculture and trade. Bank credit has been known for its capacity to turn around business units and lubricate the wheels of industry by acting as working capital. Bank credit acts as a muscle to the basic structure of the economy in providing the employment opportunities to people, helping business to accept fresh orders and execute current orders as per the schedules. Bank credit saves the face of the business units in times of liquidity crisis and prevents the closure of the units. Bank credit ultimately helps in successful implementation of projects by commercial banks in India.

Credit creation by banks in India : The credit-deposit ratio and the credit-GDP ratio have been presented in Table 7.1.

Table 7.1: Credit creation by commercial banks in India

Year	Credit-deposit ratio	Credit-GDP ratio
1998-1999	51.66	23.09
1999-2000	53.32	25.86
2000-2001	53.51	27.92

Source: CMIE reports.

The above table reveals that the credit – deposit ratio of banks has been slowly rising and the percentage of credit to GDP is also rising indicating increase in the credit created by the banks.

Composition of borrowers – segment-wise : The segment-wise composition of borrowers has been depicted in Table 7.2.

Table 7.2: Segment-wise composition of borrowers from banks in India

(No.of accounts)

Year	Total bank credit	Industrial loans	Personal loans
1998-99	52305456 (100)	47523329 (9)	12570802 (24)
1999-00	54370397 (100)	5354140 (10)	14420051 (27)
2000-01	52364395 (100)	4712767 (9)	16272488 (31)

Source: CMIE reports. Figures in brackets indicate percentage to total credit.

It can be observed from the above table that in terms of number of accounts, personal loans constitute a greater part of borrowers of Indian banks. They stand in the range of 24-31 percent, while the number of industrial loans is in the range of nine to ten percent. This trend is reverse when the outstanding loan amount is compared.

Table 7.3: Segment-wise composition of borrowers from banks in India

(Outstanding Rs. in Crores)

Year	Total bank credit	Industrial loans	Personal loans
1998-99	382425.0 (100)	187946.9 (49)	395899.5 (10)
1999-00	460080.7 (100)	213778.8 (47)	51638.5 (11)
2000-01	538433.8 (100)	236430.4 (44)	65940.1 (12)

Source: CMIE reports. Figures in brackets indicate percentage to total bank credit.

In terms of outstanding loan amount in crores of rupees, the personal loans are of lesser percentage in the range of ten to twelve percent of total bank credit. The industrial loans outweigh the personal loans, standing in the range of 44 to 49 percent.

Table 7.4: Ownership of borrowers

(Outstanding Rs. in Crores)

Year	*Total credit*	*Govt. owned & managed cos*	*Private Cos.*	*Individuals*	*Co-operatives*
1998-99	294143.5	52027.4	141398	26718	4442.7
	(100)	(17.69)	(48.07)	(9.08)	(1.51)
1999-00	357336.0	69858.8	168872.2	33680.4	4827.2
	(100)	(19.54)	(47.26)	(9.43)	(1.35)
2000-01	432139.6	90252.6	196338.9	463.41.7	6719.5
	(100)	(20.89)	(45.43)	(10.72)	(1.55)

Source: Compiled from published reports.

Figures in brackets indicate percentage to total bank credit.

A further analysis of the ownership of borrowers – government owned and government managed companies, private companies, individuals and cooperative sector reveals the relative financial assistance they have been receiving from the commercial banks in India. The private sector has been the single largest recipient of credit from banks in India, followed by the government companies. No drastic changes have been observed in the ownership of credit recipients of commercial banks in India over the period selected for the study. The cooperative sector has been receiving the lowest quantity of financial support from the banks in India over the period selected for the study. The cooperative sector has been receiving the lowest quantity of financial support from the banks in India. Reason may be the few number of ventures in co-operative sector and low level of operations requiring lesser amount of finance from the banks. The units under government sector and individuals have been increasing their share in the bank finance, while the private sector companies have recorded an opposite trend.

Bank credit by Type of Borrowing

The period for which banks are lending tells about the speed of rotation of bank funds. It also explains the purpose for which bank loans are used. Table 7.5 gives the type of credit sanctioned by banks in India.

Table 7.5: Bank credit by type

(Rs. in crores)

Type of credit	*1998-1999*	*1999-1990*	*2000-2001*
Short term- home trade	154906.3 (52.66)	191813.4 (53.68)	232469.3 (53.80)
Short-term- foreign trade	51643.2 (17.56)	57461.2 (16)	65554 (15.16)
Medium term	26555.3 (9.03)	29908.1 (8.37)	37489.6 (8.68)
Long term	60859.8 (20.69)	78153.3 (21.87)	96626.9 (22.36)
Total credit	294143.5 (100)	357336.0 (100)	432139.6 (100)

Source: CMIE reports.

Figures in brackets indicate percentage to total credit.

Commercial banks in India have been catering mainly to the short-term needs of the economy. On the whole, 69-71 percent of the bank credit is in the form of short-term loans, of which 54 percent is to finance the domestic trade. A small change is observed in the long term, loans – they are on a raise. The domestic trade is financed through the cash credit, overdraft and demand loans. The export and import trade is financed through the packing credit export trade bill purchases, export trade bill discounting, advances against export trade bills and inland bills purchase and advance against import bills and foreign currency loans. The trend has to be improved and exporters should get a higher share of bank credit.

Bank credit by size of credit

It is quite interesting to find the amount of credit sanctioned by the banks according to different slabs.

Table 7.6: Bank credit by size of credit

(Rs. in crores)

Size of credit	*1998-1999*	*1999-2000*	*2000-2001*
Less than 25,000	38285.0 (10.01)	36408.7 (7.91)	37816.3 (7.02)
25,000-200,000	49996.6 (13.07)	66336.1 (14.42)	68477.9 (12.72)
2,00,000-5,00,000	22427.9 (5.86)	28602.01 (6.22)	37170.1 (6.90)
5,00,000-10,00,000	11532.6 (3.02)	14552.6 (3.16)	17812.7 (3.31)
10,00,000-25,00,000	16139.3 (4.22)	19471.5 (4.23)	21577.3 (4.01)
25,00,000-50,00,000	16829.3 (4.40)	181250 (3.94)	21474.8 (3.99)
50,00,000-100,00,000	199.03 (5.20)	21654.2 (4.71)	22714.5 (4.22)
1,00,00,000-4,00,00,000	51812.0(13.55)	56414.3 (12.26)	60897.1 (11.31)
4,00,00,000-6,00,00,000	19605.6 (5.13)	21793.3 (4.74)	23989.8 (4.46)
6,00,00,000-10,00,00,000	24508.2 (6.41)	27906.3 (6.07)	31500.3 (5.85)
Above-10,00,00,000	111385.6 (29.13)	148816.7 (32.35)	195003.0 (36.22)
Total credit	382425.0 (100)	460080.7 (100)	538433.8 (100)

Source: CMIE reports. Figures in brackets indicate percentage to total credit.

The findings of the above table are – the share of all other categories except above ten crore slab has been decreasing. The share of above ten crore slab has been increasing. This may be due to the fact that private companies are the single largest recipients of bank credit. And short-term credit forms the major chunk of credit sanctioned by commercial banks in India.

Credit by Range of Interest

Another important feature to be observed in bank credit is the rate at which the banks lend in India.

Table 7.7: Bank credit by Range of interest

Range of interest	*1998-1999*	*1999-1990*	*2000-2001*
1	*2*	*3*	*4*
Less than 6%	697.9 (0.27)	786.1 (0.25)	704.3 (0.18)
6% - 10%	9674.5 (3.71)	3291.3 (1.03)	2162.8 (0.56)
10% - 12%	8663.9 (3.33)	25451.8 (7.96)	65741.0 (16.06)
12% - 14%	53095.3 (20.38)	85571.2 (26.75)	110882.0 (28.61)

(Contd...)

1	2	3	4
14%-15%	25280.6 (9.70)	36758.0 (11.49)	48660.2 (12.55)
15%-16%	36508.5 (14.01)	57179.2 (17.8)	60847.9 (15.70)
16%-17%	52545.4 (20.17)	54603.3 (17.07)	54762.7 (14.13)
17%-18%)	34024.8 (13.06)	27498.3 (8.60)	20299.9 (5.24)
18%-20%	27356.7 (10.50)	19877.2 (6.21)	15748.7 (4.06)
20% and above	12656.7 (4.86)	8834.9 (2.76)	7810.8 (2.02)
Total credit	260504.2 (100)	319851.4 (100)	387620.3 (100)

Source: CMIE reports. Figures in brackets indicate percentage share in total credit.

Commercial banks in India have been reducing their lending rates over the three-year period selected for study. 20 percent of the total bank credit was at two-interest ranges – 12% - 14% and 16% - 17% in 1998-99, while 27% and 29% of the loans were in the 12-14% interest range. Two factors are obvious from the above table. One is differential rates of interest are charged by banks in India and the other is most of the bank loans fall in 19-12% to 16-17% interest rate range.

Bank Credit by Population

The disbursement of bank credit over various regions with varying population is studied in Table-8.

Table 7.8: Bank credit by population

(Outstanding Rs. Crores)

Population	*1998-1999*	*1999-2000*	*2000-2001*
Rural	53908.6 (14.10)	59425.8 (12.92)	68881.9 (12.79)
Semi urban	54820.0 (14.33)	64790.5 (14.08)	71105.9 (13.21)
Urban	70716.7 (18.49)	79590.5 (17.30)	95302.9 (17.70)
Metropolitan	202979.7 (53.08)	256274.0 (55.70)	303143.1 (56.30)
Total credit	382425.0 (100)	460080.7 (100)	538433.8 (100)

Source: CMIE reports. Figures in brackets indicate percentage to total credit.

The pattern of lending of commercial banks by population reveals an interesting phenomenon. The share of rural, semi-urban and urban areas in bank credit has been coming down. The share of urban area has slightly picked up in 2000-2001 while the metropolitan areas raced far ahead of all others by grabbing 53-56 per cent of total bank credit. The growth in sunrise industries, development of high tech cities and townships for the software business and BPO operations can be stated to be reasons behind this phenomenon. The growing population concentration in certain places may be shrinking the number of rural and urban places. A clue from the above table for the policy makers is that by encouraging self-help groups and small-scale industries in rural and urban areas, the share of such areas can be raised.

Credit Disbursement by Bank groups

All the more important, is the group-wise performance of the commercial banks in India. This has been presented in Table-9.

Table 7.9: Bank group-wise performance

Year	*Bank group*	*Total credit Rs. Crores*	*Percentage share in total credit*
1998-99	SBI & Associates	107544.6	28.12
	Nationalized banks	188109.0	49.19
	Foreign banks	31331.6	8.19
	RRBs	11278.6	8.19
	Other scheduled banks	44161.3	11.55
1999-00	SBI & Associates	127146.6	27.64
	Nationalized banks	224236.2	48.74
	Foreign banks	38694.4	8.41
	RRBs	13126.1	2.85
	Other scheduled banks	56877.4	12.36
2001-01	SBI & Associates	144100.5	26.76
	Nationalized banks	261329.7	48.54
	Foreign banks	45355.4	8.42
	RRBs	1635.6	3.04
	Other scheduled banks	71296.6	13.24

Source: CMIE reports.

A macro study of bank credit has been done in tables 1 – 8 by its size, range of interest, population, ownership of borrowers. Table-

9 presents the credit disbursement of banks by its group. The share of other scheduled banks has been increasing in the total credit disbursed by the banks in India. The regional rural banks have been lagging behind in the race. The scale of operations of the regional rural banks is very small while foreign banks are of recent origin. Nationalized banks are well ahead of all other banks. The State Bank of India and its associates are the second largest in the disbursement of credit.

Conclusion

The credit disbursed by banks in India is very impressive after the post liberalization period. Banks are lending more at lesser interest rate. Private companies and metropolitan areas are the largest beneficiaries of bank credit in India. Eventhough the nationalized banks are undoubtedly the biggest creditors in India followed by the SBI group, the share of the other scheduled banks and foreign banks is steadily growing.

A few recommendations can be suggested to make bank credit more effective and socially justifiable. Firstly, the policy makers, must initiate to improve the share of rural areas by training the entrepreneurs in agriculture and allied activities under the small scale sector and self-help groups. Secondly, foreign trade seems to be the need of the hour during the present era of globalization, but foreign trade credit is not showing the good upswing. Hence, necessary steps must be taken to boost up foreign trade and foreign credit. Finally, it is alarming to note that much bank credit is tied up in the hands of private sector companies. It may lead to further scams. Hence certain measures may be taken to prevent the misuse of public money.

8

FINANCIAL SECTOR REFORMS AND THEIR IMPACT ON BANKS

P. Sriram* and **Dr. Talluru Sreenivas****

Financial sector reforms may have encouraged banks to go in for innovative measures, develop business, earn profit and benefit shareholders; however, the social content of banking has suffered continuous neglect. 60% of India's population including the weaker sections of society is without banking facilities. The financial sector reforms form a part of the real sector. Reform introduced since the second half of 1999 to bring about a major change in the economic development policy. The reforms emphasized the "Commercial Character" of the banking system and helped the banks to stand on a firm footing. In the reality of banking, the RBI, prima facie, appears to be moving away from the social content of bank. This paper is an attempt to identify the impact of financial reforms required and suggestions made to strengthen the Bank System in India.

Introduction

The Indian Bank System has witnessed a significant transformation in recent years. Indian banks, before the institution of financial sector reforms, operated in a highly regulated environment with regard to different parameters, such as branch location, deposit and lending rates and deployment of credit to mention a few. Further, in view of the social responsibility placed on the banking sector,

* Lecturer, P.G. Dept. of Business Administration, P.B. Siddhartha College of Arts and Science, Vijayawada - 520 010.

** Reader, Department of Management Sciences, R.V.R.& J.C.College of Engineering, Guntur-522 019, A.Ps profitability was not considered as an important concept of their performance. From the time of the nationalization of 14 major scheduled commercial banks in 1969 till the early 1990s, the main thrust of Banking Operations was on social banking. Hence, the emphasis was placed on enhancing the branch network in rural and semi-urban areas. Moreover, banks had to undertake several other responsibilities, which included financing the fiscal deficit and facilitating the development of certain specific sectors as reflected in high and increasing prescriptions of SLR and directed lending.

With the institution of financial sector reforms, competition among the banks has increased. Efficiency and profitability have, as a result, become critical objectives to be aimed at. Besides, the increased openness of the economy and improved freedom to operate in different financial markets and to effect portfolio shifts have necessitated positioning more stringent supervisory norms on the times of international practices to ensure banking soundness. However, the different segments of the banking system do not seem to be operating at the same levels of efficiency and profitability because of some built-in structural characteristics of individual banks.

By the very nature of ownership, the constraint faced by the public sector banks (PSBs) has been large, generating the problems of a level playing field. In terms of banking skills, however, there may not be significant differences among different bank groups, but in terms of general functional styles and environment and the ability to adopt quickly to emerging situations, PSB may not have the type of flexibility that is possessed by Indian Private Sector banks and foreign banks operating in India. In fact the face of the new competitive pressures, interactive rigidities in PSBs to enhance their overall efficiency pose serious challenges. Against this background, it is necessary to ask as to what has been the impact of financial sector reforms on the Indian Banking System. An attempt is made in this paper, to raise this issue in the context of financial sector reforms and its impact on the Indian Banking System.

Policy Administration

Indian Banking has witnessed a big change in recent years, reflecting the onset of deregulation, financial market liberalization and disintermediation. The measures aimed at deregulation have facilitated the much needed operational flexibility. While traditional activities continue to occupy a dominant position, an important development is the set of initiatives taken by banks to diversify into new financial services such as hire purchase, mutual funds, leasing, etc. to ensure growth on non-fund-based activities.

The major objectives of the financial sector reforms could be broadly discussed under three categories.

(i) Policy changes aimed at enhancing the competition which included permitting new banks and allowing more foreign banks.

(ii) Measures aimed at improving the financial health and soundness of banks by introducing appropriate prudential norms and

(iii) Measures aimed at providing more freedom to the banking system. Interest rate deregulation, reduction in SLR etc.

The financial sector reforms measures focused on reforms in ownership and control, reforms to increase competition, and reforms in regulation and policy environment. With regard to ownership and control, PSB have been permitted diversified ownership subject to 51%, holding by the Govt. of India; with a view to enhancing the overall efficiency. To enhance competition, entry of new private sector banks has been permitted. Furthermore, the policy with regard to entry of foreign banks in India has been eased to some extent. In one of the recent measures the Government has announced its decision to amend the laws to reduce its equity participation. Total effective pre-exemption of banks resources on account of cash reserve ratio and statutory liquidity ratio has been brought down from 63.5% in the early 1990s in stages to less than 35% at present. For a long time interest rates in India remained administered and were determined by the RBI from time to time.

However, in recent years, measures have been taken to gradually deregulate the interest rates. Banks have the freedom to determine interest rates on term deposits. Similarly, the lending rates for different categories of loans which were earlier prescribed by the RBI have been abolished and banks have been given considerable freedom. Banks had limited freedom regarding branch expansion programmes. At present banks have been provided with more freedom to determine their branch location.

With a view to meeting international standards, prudential norms have been introduced. Measures have been varied and related to areas such as capital adequacy ratios, risk weights in respect of investment in Government and other approved/non-approved securities, norms relating to income recognition, asset classification etc. Prudential norms and ratios have aimed at bringing out the true picture of a bank's loan portfolio and facilitate in arresting its deterioration, if it is considered bad. These ratios are designed to classify assets according to risk, define bad loans and ensure adequate provisioning for them.

Furthermore, transparency and income recognition norms have also been enhanced to meet international standards. In terms of accounting standards, income from non-performing assets cannot be taken to profit and loss account unless the income has been realized. Further, there have also been efforts to enhance transparency norms through additional disclosure requirements, i.e., regarding current performing assets. Initializors have also been taken to increase the efficiency of credit delivery system and to provide greater freedom to banks in matters relating to credit. Priority sector lending's has been made more flexible by enlarging the number of eligible activities. Measures have also been taken to strengthen the recovery process by setting up debt recovery tribunals. Amendments have also been introduced to related legal provisions. Likewise banks have also been encouraged to set up settlement advisory committees for compromise settlement of chronic NPAs of the small scale sector. The sharp changes in the policy environment concerning the operation of the banking system have direct and indirect implications for the performance of banking sector.

Reform Measures

The Reforms introduced at the beginning of the 90's breathed fresh air in the banking sector. Deregulation and liberalization encouraged banks to go in for innovative measures, develop business, earn profit and benefit the shareholders. The reforms emphasized the 'Commercial Character" of the banking system and helped banks to stand on a firm footing.

The reforms measures can be classified into three different groups.

(a) Liberalization measures

(b) Prudential Norms

(c) Competition–directed

Liberalization Measures

Statutory Liquidity ratio (SLR) was gradually reduced from 38.5% to 25% of net demand and time liabilities (NDTL). U/S 24 of Banking Regulation Act, 1949, banks are required to maintain in the form of cash, gold, current account balances with notified banks and investments in Government and other approved securities an amount equal to 25% of their NDTL. In Indian banking, the SLR is viewed as the second line of defence, the first line of defence being the cash reserve ratio (CRR) which is a cash deposit with RBI. CRR has also been reduced, in stages, from 16.5% to 5.5% at present. The medium terms goal is to bring it down to the statutorily prescribed minimum of 3% of NDTL. The reduction in the SLR and CRR has released substantial funds for deployment in the corporate and business sectors. Unfortunately, however, in the absence of demand for credit, as also due to the over-vigilant attitude of the controlling authorities, banks continue to maintain a high level of SLR which ranges between 36-38% of NDTL. The interest rates on deposits have been almost entirely freed except those on savings bank deposits on which RBI prescribes 4.5% interest. Similarly, interest on advances have also been deregulated except in respect of

(a) loans up to Rs.2.00 lakhs which have to be provided at PLR, and

(b) credit at 2.5% below PLR. The 4% differential interest rate scheme has not been officially withdrawn but since there is no monitoring of the achievement of the target the prescription is observed more in the breach.

(c) The 40% target of directed credit (Priority Sector Credit) continues but the concept has been diluted considerably by including subscriptions to bonds and debentures of the infrastructure and development organization.

The sub-targets in the priority sector of 10% to the weaker sections and 60% credit-deposit ratio in the rural and semi-urban areas have been conveniently forgotten both by the banks and the regulatory authorities. Selective credit controls have been totally abolished, thus giving the banks the freedom to lend even in the sensitive sectors.

Prudential Norms

As per the Basle Committee norms, RBI introduced capital adequacy ratios in a phased manners. At present, commercial banks are required to maintain a minimum of 9% capital to risk asset ratio. Banks were advised to recognize income only on actual receipt basis and to classify asset into 4 categories viz.

(a) Standard

(b) Sub-standard

(c) Doubtful and

(d) Loss asset

In addition, Banks have been advised to make their balance sheets transparent with maximum "disclosures" on the financial breadth of the institutions. Elaborate instructions about the disclosure of NPA including their movement and provisioning have been laid down.

Competition Directed

Reforms also prompted competition to activate the "animal spirit" in banks to constantly improve quality to serve and attract customers. After nationalization of banks in 1969, opening of new commercial banks was prohibited. Under the reforms, for the first time, the establishment of new bank was permitted. These banks with their up-to-date technology have been providing good competition to the PSB and old private sector banks. The number of foreign banks in the country also went up substantially during the 1990s (24 in 1991 to 42 in 2000). Competition has awakened banks to the need to introduce technology, improve efficiency and provide qualitative service.

Concluding Observations

The setting up of a new competitive environment has resulted in new challenges for the PSB to retain their share. Ongoing changes in the structure of Indian Banking shown; the new private sector banks have succeeded in enhancing their position. The foreign banks have been facing stiff competition from the new private banks. In the face of the growing competition, the policy changes and the operational environment in respect of the Indian banking system, there has been an increased focus on profitability although other social objectives continue to be important. Interest rate spread has exhibited a decline over the years in the case of PSB. The spread was the lowest in the case of new private sector banks and the highest in respect of foreign banks. These findings have once again force the policy makers to think afresh on the basics of banking, sooner than later banking policies may once again shift towards society-oriented development

9

VOLUNTARY RETIREMENT SCHEME
IMPACT ON BANKING SECTOR

Dr. B.K.S. Prakasha Rao* and **Professor G. Prasad****

Today, the entire world is undergoing transition. The fall of soviet union, the merger of East Germany with West Germany amply proves the same. Another important aspect of this transition is that, various economies in the world are moving towards capitalism either from their present communism or socialism. During this transition process, structural distrubances naturally take place resulting in severe losses to the economies concerned. Besides this, various countries in the world started reform process during the late eighties. India also in tune with the global trends, undertook reform processes, popularly known as liberalization, privatization and Globalisation in the early nineties with the introduction and implementation of these reforms, the Indian industries and in particular the public sector banks have been witnessing keen competition from private sector banks. It is estimated that, out of the 8.83 lakh employees in 27 PSBs, 2.5 lakhs are surplus. The federation of Indian chambers of commerce and Industry, stated that the banking industry was over staffed by 35%. The Govt's own estimate put the figure at around 30%. Hence, the major options before the PSB's are retrenchment or VRS. But the policy of retrenchment has practical limitations and more painful due to the fact that, prior consent of the appropriate authority provided in the Industrial Disputes Act is a must. According to many, VRS is the only option as it offers attractive package of benefits. It also enables a

* Reader, Dept. of Management Sciences, RVR & JC College of Engg, Guntur

** Dept. of Commerce & Business Admn., Acharya Nagarjuna University, Nagarjuna Nagar

firm to rationalize labour, strength, attain cost effectiveness and go well into strides once again. In this paper. We would like to highlight the impact of VRS on Public Sector Banks in India.

Introduction

Today, the entire World is undergoing transition. The fall of Soviet Union, the merger of East Germany with West Germany amply proves the same. Another important aspect of this transition is that, various economies in the world are moving towards capitalism either from their present communism or socialism. During this transition process, structural disturbances naturally take place resulting in severe losses to the economies concerned. Besides this, various countries in the world started reforms process during the late eighties. As part of reforms process the developed and developing nations like – USA, Canada, Japan, India etc. opened up their economies to the market forces resulting in free flow of trade among the countries. India also is in tune with the global trends and undertook reforms process which is popularly known as Liberalization, Privatization and Globalization in the early nineties. With the introduction and implementation of these reforms, the Indian industries in general and the public sector banks in particular have been witnessing keen competition from private sector banks. For instance, competition for the public sector banks come mainly from the new private sector banks, while the SBI group has been able to hold on to its market share, but the nationalized banks have not been able to withstand the aggressive onslaught from private sector banks. The nationalized banks have seen their market share declining from 48.5% to 46.9% in advances and from 53.8% to 53.6% in deposits between March 1999 and 2001. During the same period the private sector banks raised their share from 10.7% to 12.3% in deposits and from 7.8% to 8.1% in advances. So, the real challenge to the PSB's market share comes from the new private sector banks most of which are going retail and are in a major expansion mode. In terms of net profit also, public sector banks as a whole has declined by 16% from Rs.5116 crores to Rs.4316 crores.

As per the recommendations of the Narasimham Committee, the banks have authority of redeployment of staff, cut in operating cost and reduction of manpower. It is estimated that, out of 8.83 lakh employees in 27 public sector banks, 2.5 lakh are surplus. The

Federation of Indian Chambers of Commerce and Industry, also announced that the banking industry was over staffed by 35 percent. The Government's own estimate put the figure at around 30 percent. Hence, the major options before the PSBs are retrenchment or Voluntary Retirement Scheme (VRS) as a measure of cost reduction. But, the policy of retrenchment has practical limitations and more painful due to the fact that, prior consent of the appropriate authority as provided in the Industrial Disputes Act is a must. Hence, some have thought of a less painful strategy, which may prove more acceptable to all the employees resulting in the adherence to VRS choice rather than retrenchment. In a nutshell, PSB's are resorting to a strategy of VRS to downsize the work force so as to adjust the manpower as per the needs of the organizations.

According to many, VRS is the only option as it offers attractive package of benefits. It also enables a firm to rationalize labour strength, attain cost effectiveness and go well into strides once again. More than 1.25 lakhs (see Annexure-1) employees of PSB's including SBI group opted for the scheme availing benefits to the tune of Rs.15,000 crore. Exgratia payments alone amounted to about Rs.7500 crore. For this purpose, the Government created a National Renewal Fund (NRF) to provide employees an opportunity to seek voluntary retirement and also to train and retain the existing workforce in the emerging high-tech areas so as to absorb them more productively. But the benefits of VRS will be visible from 2001 onwards. While on one hand it would trim down the growth rates in operating expenses, on the other hand banks will be presented with an opportunity for smoother transition towards a technology savvy organization.

The scheme brought into force with certain accounting issues relating to booking of VRS related expenditure such as ex-gratia payment and other terminal benefits. Consequently, the accounting treatment of VRS expenditure was specified in consultation with the Institute of Chartered Accountants of India (ICAI). In particular, the banks were advised that unless expenses in the same period, the entire ex-gratia amount as a result of VRS could be treated as an extra-ordinary item and as Deferred Revenue Expenditure (DRE) and in view of the extra-ordinary nature of the event, VRS related DRE would not be reduced from tier I capital. The banks are required to disclose in the balance sheet the accounting policies followed in respect of VRS expenditure. The DRE would be restricted to a maximum period of five years.

Round one VRS has led to major benefits for the bank's balance sheet. For instance, a study of Business India finds employees cost in banks have largely fallen after VRS. The highest reduction in employees cost was shown in 2001-02 by Dena Bank, which clocked by 25.76 percent in such costs, with the outgo declining to Rs.322.57 crores from Rs.434.50 crore in 2000-01. The next steep fall came from Bank of Maharastra, which recorded a 20.77 percent decline. The third slot was taken by Bank of India, which showed a 19 percent decline and SBI showed a healthy decline of 14.29 percent in employee costs.

While some bankers agree that it is difficult to arrive at a direct relation between a decline in employee costs and an increase in profitability, they concede that the fallout of VRS had a major role in posting the higher profits by a number of banks. For example, Dena Bank recorded a hefty 104 percent jump in net profit, making a huge turn around from a loss of Rs.266.12 crore to a profit of Rs.11.36 crore in 2001-02. Bank of Maharastra, on the other hand recorded a steep rise in net profit, which grew 222 percent, while SBI was up by 52 percent.

The advanced nations have adequate social security measures including unemployment insurance. As such their voluntary retirement schemes have a smooth sailing. Further, in these countries, greater transparency is clearly visible in the implementation of VRS. But in developing countries like – India, the above stated elements are absent due to various reasons and also due to the special circumstances prevailing here. Even the VRS Schemes are lopsided and more generalized and not in tune with the specific needs of the organization. This is because, systematic studies were not carried out about the number of surplus employees and workers in various branches of PSB's. All the same, there is no specific way to segregate the talented from the untalented. Consequently, instead of getting rid of the dead wood in public sector banks, qualified and talented officers and employees are leaving the banks. However, some CEOs and HRS Chiefs believe that once VRS is implemented, it trims the fat thereby the rest of the people will work as a cohesive team.

Challenges and Realities of VRS to Developing India

1. A review of the utilization of NRF clearly points out the fact that it is used only for the purpose of VRS rather than achieving the duel objectives of VRS plus training and retaining the workforce resulting in negative effect on productivity and efficiency. In other words, NRF instead of chopping of the dead wood is cutting off the live plants also. For instance, in Indian Tourism Development (ITD) all qualified and skilled Managers and Cooks left it availing VRS in a short span of three months leaving Waiters and Servers to run its group of hotels. All the same, around 1100 talented Scientists and Managers of IDPL left the organization leading to the grinding halt of the R&D activities as well as the Management of the Organization. The same story was repeated in State Trading Corporation (STC) when it gave an option to its entire staff to avail the VRS scheme. Consequently, the young and highly efficient Managers and staff left the organization to take-up senior positions in the private sector export-import houses. To overcome the problem STC upgraded the redundant staff to higher positions causing severe loss to the organization.
2. There are divergent views about the VRS scheme and its implementation. Some trade union leaders favourably view it while some others oppose it. However, some trade union leaders insist that bilateral consultation should be a necessary condition before the VRS scheme was formulated and implemented. According to Mr. K. Ashok Rao, President, National Confederation of Officers Association – the PSUs are paying Dowry in the form of VRS to enable the qualified staff of PSUs to hop to the private sector.
3. Some experts in the field of labour economics and industrial relations strongly feel that instead of relying on adhoc assessment, the size of redundant manpower should be worked out by systematic industrial engineering study and VRS should be implemented accordingly in phases. They advocate that complete transparency should be ensured so that through prior consultation with workers could be taken into confidence. This would make the implementation of VRS to be smooth and effective.

4. A Mumbai based consultant – Hemendra K.Varma stated that VRS should be the last option and not the first choice. According to him, VRS is not the panacea to all the problems. He believed that, a number of problems other than VRS should be tackled first and set right. Even after solving these problems, if desired results are not obtained then only VRS should be undertaken. He also believed that VRS will give short term and illusory benefits which will soon get neutralized by the continuance of other problems.
5. In the words of G.M.Bhakey, President of the State Bank of India Officers Association 22,000 rural branches of PSBs have to be merged or closed down in favour of a satellite branch which will operate just once a week. If these fears come true, rural India may be the biggest victim of VRS and it ruled out the basic objective of banks nationalization.
6. According to Tarakeswar Chakraborthy, General Secretary, All India Banks Employees' Association "We have repeatedly stressed proper manpower planning and redeployment, but it was not taken care of". Prof.Ashis Bhattacharya, IIM, Kolkata, said that "The VRS in banks appears to have been based on overpayment and was therefore bad". Prof.Sunil Kumar Maheswari, IIM, Ahmedabad said that "In Indian conditions, VRS acceptance will remain the last resort with employees unless it is extremely attractive".
7. RC Agrawal of the Central Bank Officers Association agrees, "No work is the biggest punishment, our Society looks upon VRS as a stigma, they feel that something must be wrong with the person. Moreover money is never retained, your special contacts ensure that it is spent," stated Agarwal. VRS is not quick fix for today's ailing organizations – the truth is there are not quick fixes. Only organizations like PSBs that are willing to go the long haul by firm, tough, bold and honest management practices will survive.

Why the Panic Rush for VRS?

When the country's public sector banks began drawing up their voluntary retirement schemes to bring down the industry's total workforce from the hefty 8.8 lakh figure, they did so with some trepidation. Why the rush to exit from PSU banks? One of the reasons, clearly, is the attractive package being offered by the banks with many other benefits. Another reason is the fear of the retirement age being reduced from 60 to 58, which has led to the older among the bankers seeking to quickly exit at a price.

Also, the fact that the cabinet has just decreed the reduction of Government Equity in PSU banks to 33 percent has also played its part. Many people, particularly the good performers, start looking for openings elsewhere and leave at the first opportunity. Another problem according to Bhakey, President of SBI Officers Association, "They are transferred anywhere, are held accountable in case of problems in rural areas and do not get residential accommodation".

Conclusion

Some bank Chairmen are already suggesting that VRS should be an annual feature and a sizable portion of the staff have welcomed the idea. Perhaps VRS is the way forward if the Public Sector Banks are to convert themselves. VRS is designed to address the need of an organization to remove excessive and unproductive staff from amongst its ranks and enable it to reorient itself into a leaner and meaner organization. The VRS design should take into account. It is essential to build a generic profile of the employee before designing the scheme. Before designing a scheme, one needs to consider whether the payments should be made in one lump-sum or as a form of annuity, or a mix of both. It can succeed only if there is a special stimulus enabling the employee to decide in favour of taking the VRS. Counseling should focus on providing the requisite guidance to the worker to enable him/her to focus on building a future career and being productive again. Again it should provide financial counseling to ensure reasonable and sustainable deployment of VRS payments, in terms of investment options and savings planning for the future. Both Pre-VRS and Post-VRS counseling sessions require counsellers who would be able to address the psychological needs of the worker and provide mental support. One good way to do a VRS is to follow some practices (i) giving advance notice (ii) helping them to identify their present skillsets (iii) nominating them for skill development programmes and (d) helping them in getting jobs by internal advertisement of the requirements. The VRS has now become a basic

component of the labour adjustment strategy of public sector banks to weed out inefficiencies and make the industry more competitive and cost effective under the new economic set-up. The organizations have not only spent huge amounts of money as compensation but also lost a good number of highly efficient people. If this trend continues, it will end-up in a problem of greater dimension than the present one of excess labour force without taking proper care while implementing the VRS.

REFERENCES

1. Dalbir Sing,Chairman, IBA and CMD, Central Bank, Dealing with Surplus, *Business India,* July, 22 – Aug, 4, 2002.
2. B.S.Srinivasulu Reddy, Banks Discount Life After VRS, Warts and All, *Financial Express*, 27-07-2002.
3. Dnyanesh V. Jathar, Officer's Choice, The Week, April,1, 2001.
4. S.R.Sen Gupta, Voluntary Retirement Scheme in PSB – A Retrospect and a Challenge, A Study report, June,2001.
5. Corporate News, More Companies Join the VRS fray in Quarter2, *Capital Market*, Feb.4-17,2002.
6. Editorial, VRS Story, *Economic and Political Weekly*, Jan.20, 2001.
7. Aloka Majumdar, Rush for the Exit, *Business India*, Nov. 27, Dec.10, 2000.
8. Financial Express Banking Bureau, VRS not Favourable for SBI, May Dilute Shareholder Value, *The Financial Express*, June 20, 2001.
9. Tushar K.Mahant, VRS Helped Banks Shed Their Flab, not Wage Outgo, *Economic Times*, May 13, 2001.
10. Hemendra K.Varma, Chief Executive, A Consultancy Firm, Mumbai, VRS the New Quick Fix Indian Management, April, 2000.
11. E.T. Political Bureau, Bold VRS Proposal is Actually a Diluted Version, *Economic Times*, Feb.7, 2002.
12. B.P. Gupta, VRS in Indian Industries, *Indian Journal of Industrial Relations,* Jan., 1996.
13. K.P. Muralidharan, Implementation of Voluntary Retirement Scheme – Some Issues, *Productivity*, Vol.37, No.2, July-September, 1996.
14. Tamal Bandyopadhyay, Why the Bank VRS worked or Did it? *Indian Management*, April, 2002.
15. Ashis Battacharya, IIM, Kolkata, VRS will be the Rule Rather than the Exception, *Indian Management,* April, 2002.
16. Sunil Kumar Maheswari, The Focus is Shifting from Production to Productivity, *Indian Management*, April, 2002.

Name of Bank	O	VRS optees	%	C	VRS optees	%	S	VRS optees	%	Total Strength	VRS optees	%
1	2	3	4	5	6	7	8	9	10	11	12	13
State Bank of India	60536	19295	31.87	117184	12948	11.05	59784	3137	5.25	237504	35380	14.90
State Bank of Travancore	3150	560	17.78	7023	370	5.27	2964		0.00	13137	920	7.00
SB of Bknr & Jaipur	3400	400	11.76	6887	850	12.34	4113		0.00	14400	1250	8.68
SB.of Mysore	2530	600	23.72	4377	765	17.48	2256	400	17.73	9163	1765	19.26
SB of Indore	2500	161	6.44	4300	545	12.67				680	706	10.38
SB of Hyderabad	4263	632	14.83	7185	1284	17.87	3318	882	26.58	14766	2798	18.95
SB of Saurashtra	2100	378	18.00	6130	530	8.65	2070	222	10.72	10300	1130	10.97
SB of Patiala	3200	310	9.69	6876	640	9.31	3124	235	7.52	13200	1185	8.98
Allahabad Bank	9558	908	13.24	10620	463	4.36	4867	200	4.11	22345	1571	7.03
Andhra Bank	5153	1200	23.29	7011	417	5.95	2439	176	7.22	14603	1793	12.28
Bank of Baroda	14020	3254	23.21	23125	2564	11.09	9909	944	9.53	47054	6762	14.37
Bank of India	12412	2800	22.56	28217	3700	13.11	11333	1100	9.71	51962	7600	14.63
Bank of Maharashtra	3957	897	22.67	8544	1510	17.67	3597	390	10.84	16098	2797	17.37
Canara Bank	16652	4511	27.09	26380	3701	14.03	12432	354	2.85	55464	8566	15.44
Central Bank	15279	4450	29.12	21601	2850	13.19	11380	1200	10.54	48260	8500	17.61
Corporation Bank	3388	No. VRS offered		5054		0.00	1740		0.00	10182		
Dena Bank	4160	1396	33.56	6774	1609	23.75	3612	529	14.65	14546	3534	24.30
Indian Bank	8898	2525	28.38	13177	1289	9.78	3860	174	4.51	25935	3988	15.38

(Contd...)

1	2	3	4	5	6	7	8	9	10	11	12	13
Indian Overseas Bank	8337	2283	27.38	15058	1400	9.30	4952	305	6.16	28347	3988	14.07
Oriental Bank	4917	440	8.96	6170	120	1.94	3314	80	2.41	14398	640	4.45
PNB	16903	2835	16.77	35302	2245	6.36	13500	730	5.41	65705	5800	8.83
Punjab & Sind Bank	4879	1472	30.17	4953	385	7.77	2360	215	9.11	12192	2072	16.99
Syndicate Bank	8846	2701	30.53	19496	3940	20.21	5541	516	9.31	33883	7157	21.12
UCO Bank	8078	2783	34.45	16448	2064	12.55	6697	632	9.44	31223	5479	17.55
Union Bank of India	9580	2433	25.40	15141	1424	9.40	6113	464	7.59	30834	4321	14.01
United Bank of India	5701	1395	24.47	11022	1000	9.07	5034	405	8.05	21757	2800	12.87
Vijaya Bank	4268	1353	31.82	7281	1032	14.17	2871	192	6.69	14420	1582	17.91
TOTAL	**243961**	**61977**	**25.40**	**441336**	**49645**	**11.25**	**193181**	**13482**	**6.98**	**878478**	**125084**	**14.24**

Note: O = Officers C = Clerical cadre S = Staff

10

EMERGING CHALLENGES OF ELECTRONIC BANKING

Dr. K. Jayachandra[1], Dr.B. Ramachandra Reddy[2], Dr. M.Venkateswarlu[3] and **B.Yuvaraja Reddy[4]**

In India electronic banking is of fairly recent origin. The traditional model for growth has been through branch banking. Only in the early 1990s there has been a start in the non-branch banking services. The new private sector banks and the foreign banks are handicapped by the lack of a strong branch network in comparison with the public sector banks. In the absence of such networks, the market place has been the emergence of a lot of innovative services by these players through direct distribution strategies of non-branch delivery. All these banks are using "home banking as a key "pull" factor to remove customers away from the well entrenched public sector banks.

Credit cards have found wide spread acceptance in the 'metro's and big citities. Credit cards are gaining popularity for on line payments. Credit card transactions result in immediate overnight payments to the merchants. This rapid payment can reduce the merchant's requirements for financing inventory.

Introduction

Liberalization of the Indian economy has fuelled the growth of wide- spread banking network in our country. Consequently, the revolution in information technology has brought about sea changes in the way banking transactions are carried out. From the traditional banking, which involved voluminous and laborious paper work, the

1, 2, 3 Faculty Members, Dept. of Commerce, S.V. University, Tirupati.

4 Research Scholar, Dept. of Commerce, S.V. University, Tirupati.

banking network in India has been slowly transforming into online banking or what is popularly called as e-banking in its attempt to ensure a fast and sophisticated service to the customers. In this online banking all the services performed earlier with laborious paper work, have been reduced to a few click of the mouse. Also, the physical movement to the banking premises for performing various banking activities has become a thing of the past. In on-line banking, various services can be accessed with equal ease almost anywhere in the developed world. Yet another possibility and advantage worth mentioning is the wide network in operation without regard to national boundaries. So, on-line banking is transactional in character.

Online or e-banking services include conducting bank transactions sitting at home or office using a telephone and a personal computer. Some of the transactions performed through on-line banking include opening new account, reviewing transactions details, checking various account balances, transfer of funds, payment of bills, reconciliations, applying for loans, funds transfer from one account to another, etc.

Evolution of Electronic Banking

In its evolutionary history, a start had been made in electronic banking as early as the 1920s. But this technology or this form of banking did not get a widespread acceptance till the 1960's. It required almost a complete generation before this form of banking found popularity with a sizable group of consumers and bankers.

The effectiveness of electronic banking system was inhibited by three main factors.

1. Communication Technology was in its infancy and inadequate for local or global coverage.
2. Most companies and banks had incompatible systems sometimes even different branches of the same bank had different systems.
3. Computer manufactures were unable to agree on the development of technology standards which would permit data exchange directly between computer systems.

After 1960 electronic banking and its use recorded a quantum jump. In the year 1991 this form of banking took a great leap by which home, office and telephone banking was made more effective and efficient as a means of selling and delivering products. At the same time, the rapidly rising costs of operating a physical branch network particularly in terms of staff and premises, are making the traditional channel less attractive.

Electronic Banking in India

In India electronic banking is of fairly recent origin. The traditional model for growth has been through branch banking. Only in the early 1990s has there been a start in the non-branch banking services. The new private sector banks and the foreign banks are handicapped by the lack of a strong branch network in comparison with the public sector banks. In the absence of such networks, the market place has been the emergence of a lot of innovative services by these players through direct distribution strategies of non-branch delivery. All these banks are using "home banking as a key "pull" factor to remove customers away from the well entrenched public sector banks.

The Catalyst in initiating Electronic Based Delivery System

Credit cards : Credit cards have found wide spread acceptance in the 'metro's and big cities. Credit cards are gaining popularity for on line payments. Credit card transactions result in immediate overnight payments to the merchants. This rapid payment can reduce the merchant's requirements for financing inventory.

Debit card: Debit card have also started becoming popular in the last two years only with Master Card and visa tieing up with Indian and foreign banks.

Tele-banking : Tele-banking is available with a foreign and private sector banks, offering this service through the technology called interactive Voice Response Service (IVRS). It has moved into the domain of mobile phones as well as service that is being marketed as mobile commerce (m-commerce).

ATM: ATM trade their first appearance in the early 1990s started by Citi Bank, and Hong Kong Bank. By the end of 1990 even Indian Private banks and Public Sector banks have come up with their own ATM networks. Under the initiative of the Indian Bank Association (IBA) in Mumbai, a pilot project to link up 165 ATMs of 31 member banks has come up in the form of 'SWADHAN' a shared payment network system which has a card base of 1,00,000 with 30,000 transactions per month. Master Card and Visa are also following suit to offer shared ATM network.

Internet Banking: Internet banking has made its debut with ICICI banks product called Infinity and Citi Bank being the pioneer in this field. This is now being offered by some selected banks as well. This seems to be the latest growth area.

Indian Private Sector Banks

In the 1990s the private sector banks have been aggressively following a mixed approach for enhancing their reach. They have no restrictions in opening branches. This explains the reason why Times Bank, Centurion Bank, Global Trust Bank and HDFC Bank have been setting up new branches at a fast pace. Very recently HDFC Bank and Times Bank have merged and created India's largest private bank under the umbrella of HDFC bank. These branches are very small and operate at Front Office Sales and Service points only. No back room accounting or processing activity happen here. Back rooms of these branches are centralized in regional locations, and serve multiple branches. Therefore, the approach of these private banks has been the best mixture of ATM driven electronic Banking and Sales and Service driven branches as distribution points.

Indian Public Sector Banks

Despite the compelling business case for restructuring their distribution channels, the public sector banks have not given too much priority to non-branch delivery. Also, the customer profile for the public sector banks is probably not the right fit for electronic banking services, because of their social obligations to provide banking services for the masses. Electronic banking products require a certain sophistication that may prove to be a hurdle on the way of smooth absorption of the technology by the client profile of the public sector banks. Therefore, there is not much focus on electronic banking services here, even though exceptions are there like Bank of Baroda and Stae Bank of India, who have aggressively pushed their credit cards. Bank of Baroda has credit card brand of its own called the BOB Card which is India's one and only proprietary card. SBI has tied up with multinational GE Capital to provide it VISA credit cards. It has already become the second highest issuer of credit card in India within just three years.

Many of the other banks like Allahabad Bank, Vijaya Bank, Central Bank, Canara Bank, Andhra Bank etc. have issued credit cards as well, in collaboration with either Visa or Master card. Some of these banks also have ATM's which are mostly attached to their branches and can be used by customers of that particular branch only. Though they have plans of networking them in future, it become evident while talking to their personnel that this is not a key area of focus yet.

Barriers of e-Banking

1. Lack of proper commercial and legal systems for doing business through the web.
2. Lack of strong national telecom, hardware and software infrastructure which will also give fast, reliable access to the Internet at a lower cost.
3. Lack of policy from the banks regarding the conduction of business electronically.
4. Lack of secure payment system.
5. Lack of system that allows cross border e-commerce transactions.
6. Lack of awareness among users about the importance of e-commerce and its benefits.

The Future of Electronic Banking

The future holds a wide vista in terms of the possibilities that could be enabled by technology, including the following scenario:

1. *Smart Card*: Technology has already introduced as an improvement on commonly prevalent technology i.e., magnetic media by the use of micro chip. This technology offers new products for product differentiation and expansion that cannot be achieved with the existing magstripe technology. Chip technology is viewed as the future platform for the card industry.

2. The concept of an electronic purse as a global reality has already commenced with the introduction of Mondex. This is a smart card which functions as an electronic wallet. There are no credit limits and the customers wallet is loaded up front by the issuing bank and can be spent and reloaded at designated terminals.
3. Customer identification is increasingly going to migrate to more sophisticated forms like biometric identification e.g. Finger print/Palm scanning, voice recognition etc.
4. 'Internet' is fast growing as an innovative means to reach clients and potential customers literally at their finger tips. This is now the latest version of home banking and currently is very popular for targeting Non-resident Indians. This medium provides on line banking service and could be used to generate fee income recognized as a growing share of bank profits due to the pressure on interest margins.

Conclusion

Evolution of technology is taking place at an enormous pace and the approach to automation in banking must have an element of healthy "opportunism". A rigid approach could be non-functional and an excessively flexible approach would result in loss of control over the strategy : Just the right combination would help to achieve the desired objectives at optimum cost. Though the Indian consumer at large is still not completely comfortable with technology as a way to do banking, the affluent middle class is becoming more familiar. The younger generations have started using computers from a very early age and this is the generation which would be the consumer of the future.

The safety and soundness of e-banking procedures are intended to complement traditional procedures in evaluation of specific activities, such as lending, deposit-gathering and non-deposit activities. Therefore, efforts should be made to coordinate reviews of written policies, internal controls and other related functions. Currently the e-banking in India is exposed to a lack of trust, hackers threat, lack of communication, infrastructure and inadequate security. However, India is gifted with skilled manpower wealth. We should build a strong secured communication network in order to become electronic banking a popular one.

REFERENCES

1. The journal of Indian Institute of Bankers.
2. Business line.
3. Computer today
4. E-commerce by Ravi Kolakota
5. The Chartered Financial Analysis
6. E-World

The internet and e-commerce by James Brien.

11

INFORMATION TECHNOLOGY IN BANKS

L. Esther Sujana* and **K. Suguna****

From the past 50 years, computer technology all over the world either in the U.S. or in China is in forefront. Technology has improved the importance of information. The back bone of any successful industry is INFORMATION and if it is provided faster, accurate and in time the industry success. The success of the IT service industry in India, coupled with availability of manpower and arbitrage has led to fast development of IT enabled industries.

Introduction

One of the necessary preconditions for economic development of developing counties like India is a well-developed banking system because it mobilizes financial resources for industrial growth from the savings of public. Customer care service has contributed the most to the growth of the industry in India. As a result there has been an explosive growth of call centers and contact centers. Now many companies are focusing on back office operations like payroll, claims etc. The requirement of major banking services is technological support in customer interaction services, back office operations, legal database and web site services. These parameters are becoming mandatory for the success in these organizations.

Technological developments would render flow of information and data faster leading to faster appraisal and decision-making. This would enable banks to make credit management more effective

* Faculty Members, J.B. Institute of P.G. Courses, Tirupati.

** Faculty Members, J.B. Institute of P.G. C

besides leading to an appreciable reduction in transaction cost. To reduce investment costs in technology, banks are likely to resort more and more on sharing facilities, such as ATM networks. Banks and financial institutions will join together to share facilities in areas of payment and settlement, back office processing, data warehousing and so on. The advent of new technologies could see the emergence of new players doing financial inter mediation .The conventional banking system may undergo changes due to technological changes.

The above-mentioned reasons are enabling the banking system to implement the required technological up gradation. The banking system should follow the ACE MODEL (Adoption, Collaboration and Evaluation). Our study justifies the requirement and implementation of this model.

The economic reforms initiated a decade ago by the Indian government have influenced all the sectors of Indian economy. The ongoing developments in Indian industry and government and integration of India with global market are also offering opportunities in all the sectors. Technological advances, a sense of acceleration, atomized market and economic shocks are affecting the business today and also the scenario shifted to micro segmentation, multiple competitors and short product life cycles. The banks are under an unprecedented pressure to perform and therefore this is the right time to repair the roof when the sun is shining. So some of the activities to be carried out to meet these changes are continuous R & D, responsiveness to change, and TQM and process improvement.

Service industries are known as tertiary industries. Transport, communication, banking, finance etc., are part of the tertiary sector. Over the past decade the service sector has expanded in the world. In advanced economies service sector is the key sector which contributes to about two thirds of total economy. Since the high average level of real income per head is always associated with a high proportion of working population engaged in tertiary industry the share of tertiary sector in macro variables, namely, GDP, employment and investment depicts the level of development of a country. Among these variables of tertiary sector the banking sector's contribution is relatively high in the economic development. During the 18th and 19th century the growth of commercial banks in EUROPE has lead to industrial revolution. Rate of capital formulation is one of important determinants of economic development. Thus the presence of sound banking system would create healthy atmosphere for the promotion of savings and hence capital formulation.

India has an extensive banking network in both urban and rural areas. In the process of economic development of our country banking system in India has been playing a dominant role. If it is so, are our Indian Banks doing enough to respond to changing times? Under these circumstances what are the key traits required to be improved which would directly impact the organization growth? In Indian scenario it is mainly the MNC's driven, by their global process that are directing the business. So these aspects should be taken into the consideration and implemented by the Indian banks.

Financial Intermediaries In India

Structure of Financial Markets

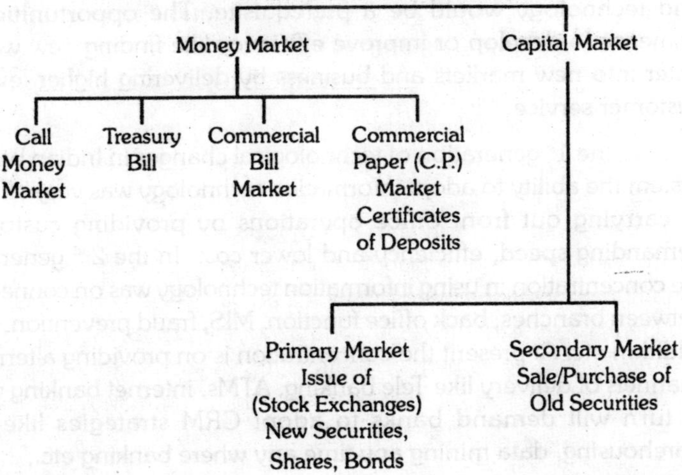

Source: Banking and Financial Systems, Dr.A.V.Ranganadha Chary and Dr. R.R.Paul

As a consequence of Liberalization, Privatization and Globalization (LPG) a large range of services, availability of funds and ownership patterns of banks will be affected. Now these LPG factors have made the customer very powerful and their demand of wanting the goods to be delivered can be met in an innovative and cost effective manner by exploiting the prevailing technological advancements with increase in operating efficiency improvement high quality banking service. The aspiration levels, life systems, cultural changes of Indian customers are changing hence, banking sector should tune to these changes.

The customer requirements are endless in physical plane and his plans are made from the birthday to the end of his life. This has lead to the increasing requirements of customer viz., a bank account, credit card, finance for children education, home loan etc. The endless customer requirements have to be turned into good prospects by the banking system in India and this paper explores some strategies in this direction.

Changes in Indian Banking Sector

The Indian banking sector is facing some structural changes like alignment with global developments, sub optional in size and scale etc. There fore high level sophistication in information systems and technology would be a prerequisite. The opportunities are immense to develop or improve efficiency like finding new ways to enter into new markets and business by delivering higher levels of customer service.

In the 1st generation of technological changes in Indian banking system the ability to adopt information technology was very effective in carrying out front office operations by providing customer's demanding speed, efficiency and lower cost. In the 2nd generation, the concentration in using information technology was on connectivity between branches, back office function, MIS, fraud prevention, value addition etc. At present the concentration is on providing alternative channels of delivery like Tele banking, ATMs, internet banking which in turn will demand banks to adopt CRM strategies like data warehousing, data mining any time any where banking etc.,

The present Indian scenario is mainly revolving around the MNC's which in turn are driven by their global process that is driving the business. An evolving business environment and technological innovations are reengineering the system together with long term changes in customer needs and profiles. Companies are working in an environment where they have to interact with numerous other participants in the market. With this increasingly competitive environment coupled with rapid technological advancement the corporate sector is confronted with the issue of achieving high growth rates with an inherent risk.

The major key areas to be concentrated for development

1. Innovation
2. Responsiveness to change
3. Total quality management
4. Process improvement
5. Organization values

Even though the world class competition has challenged the very survival or existence of Indian companies, some organizations for example ICICI, HDFC, reliance, Wipro, DRL, Infosys, Hero Honda have been gearing up to face the competition. Innovation is one of the key factors of success. Many Indian companies are focusing on innovation through design or the R&D route. Responsiveness to change is another key area of success. The organizations in future especially in developing India should concentrate on special insights into the need of the customer. The strategies should be based on a customer value; improvement on quality commitment at all levels, continuous up gradation and innovation of products and process by depending on facts and feedbacks of the customer.

Indian banks should work towards having an enhanced retail delivery system, which should have transformed branches, telephone services and leading edge Internet banking functions. This can be enabled by an integrated Customer Relationship Management system. Further the banks also need to develop internal control systems, MIS and early warning triggers. The major trends alerting the banking industry are:

- Consolidation
- Globalization of operations
- Development of new technologies
- Universalization of banking
- The banking sector had already underwent so many changes during the post decade. It had witnessed

- Deregulation of lending and deposit rates
- Entry of new private sector banks
- Extensive use of technology
- Emergence of retail banking
- Stricter provisioning and asset classification norms
- Raising capital adequacy
- Requirement of better risk management
- Increased transparency

Apart from the above changes the Indian banking sector should foresee many more changes for facing global competition.

Challenges of Banking Sector

"Around the world the banking industry has undergone major transformation in the present decade." Increased penetration, consolidation and international integration are the primary driving forces behind this transformation.

In India the process of banking sector reform began in July 1991. The global players entrance had brought introduction of new instruments, reduction in interest rates, relaxation of rules and regulations etc. Since Nov. 1994 the RBI had undertaken supervision of the commercial banks, financial institutions and HDFCs. All these changes slowly showed upward profitability trend and also demanded continuous upgrading, monitoring and controlling of the issues like customer orientation, sophisticated product risk management, MIS, diversification etc., So the banks are upgrading their knowledge base to meet the sophisticated clients demands like well informed reactive and responsive banks. So they are trying to differentiate among the factors like CRM, product differentiation, brand equity and technology.

With the above-mentioned changes, the challenges that the banks are facing are

(i) Changing needs of customer with special emphasis on

 (a) High expectation

 (b) Diminishing loyalty

(ii) Coping with regulatory reforms

(iii) Thinking speed

(iv) Maintaining high quality assets

(v) Keeping pace with technology upgradation

Key Areas To Be Considered For Business Excellence

1. CRM
2. Technological upgradation
3. Marketing strategies

1. Customer Relationship Management

Customer satisfaction is the success mantra of an organization. Special insights into customer needs should be practised. For example, the Bank of Baroda, employees are visiting organizations for fixed deposits and recurring deposits to be invested in their banks. This shows that resistance to change is slowly vanishing and customer is being identified as the king. Various examples and further this concept is evolving and getting digested in the minds of employees. New generation entrepreneur is coming with real change in the market with new options. A super market named BUY AND SAVE is offering reduction in price of every product by reducing its profit margin and providimg customer value, which is at present the best strategy. Major achievement of ICICI bank is money transfer without any transactional charges and in seconds the money gets transferred which is again a customer value strategy.

In India we have two types of customers for banks. They are:

Anchor channel customers: Anchor channel customers are those who depend only on Branch banking that is teller, ATM etc

Multi channel customers: Multi channels customer, who demands continuous service provision without long wait, inconsistent information. So they prefer to use all channels.

- Phone banking
- Branch banking
- Internet banking

Phone banking usage means using call centers, interactive voice response etc. Wireless, browser, personal computer come under

Internet banking. So multi channel customers will use all of these banking channels. The following are the customer's expectations which are growing vastly.

- Swift service with minimum response time
- Efficient service delivery
- Tailor made products
- Value added products
- Hassle free procedures
- Minimum transaction cost
- Pleasant and personalized service

2. Marketing Strategies

1. *Cross Selling:* A sales promotion technique in which the manufacturer attempts to sell the related products to the customer using a prime product. Add on card for the credit card holder is the best example for cross selling.
2. *Retail Banking:* Retail consumers are those who have specific needs. Banks have a lot of potential with retail consumers having requirements like personal loans, home loans, vehicle loans etc. Businessmen and Transport operator's require timely and hassle free credit.
3. *E-Banking (Internet Banking):* The emergence of e- banking has enabled the banks to offer real time transactions and integrate all the customer related functions. Information management is one of the major advantages of e- banking. Individual monthly account statements, tracking of cheque status etc can be done on a single portal now. In treasury management usage of online trading channels by corporate provide the access to more transparent channels of information with out the level of intermediation. Internet based cash management solutions help corporate sector to make vendor payments or collections. E-mail is serving as a means to communicate between corporate and bank with regards to exchanging of financial information and also for showcasing the new products of the bank.

A Summary of the Key Offerings of Internet Banking

Accounts	**Trade Services**
Account statements	LC issuance
Deposit schedules	BG issuance
Loan account schedules	Advices
Online balances	View LC Status
Today's transactions	View BG Status
Status of cheques lodged in clearing	View details of bills purchased / discounted
Stop payment	View details of outstanding forward contracts
Request for e-mail statements, chequebooks, opening of fixed deposits.	
Fund Transactions	**Other Services**
Single Transfers	Cash Management collection reports
Bulk Transfers	Treasury Solutions
Interbank transfers	Investment Solutions
Bill Payments	Market Information
Bill Payment with external site linkages	Debt Trading
Request for Demand Drafts and Pay Orders	Online book building for bonds
	Equity Trading
	Research reports

Source: Product And Technology Group ICICI Bank, "Corporate Banking: Using Technology In Transactions", ICFAI Reader, Jan 2004, P: 75.

4. *Mobile Banking:* Instead of going to an Internet center for any financial the transaction information (through wireless communication) with every detail can be made available on the mobile telephone.

5. *Institutional Banking:* This is considered as a separate customer segment for managing relationship with institutional clients like mutual funds, co-operative banks, foreign banks etc.

6. *Customer Focused Approach:* By using new technology development using CRM one can transform the technique of cultivating loyal customer base, which can further develop a resource intensive business. Now the concentration has shifted to customer focused approach rather than product-focused customers.

7. *Marketing of Information Systems:* The critical success of marketing factors will encompass good management of branch based distribution, minimal response time, pro active and polite service empowered staff with good product knowledge, ability to address customer queries, better cross selling of various products to the existing clients, effective lead management system for tracking prospects through staff, tele sales, direct mails, local campaigns and customer referrals which can be achieved only through a marketing information system.
8. *Narrow Banking:* This type of banks concentrate their primary function in favour of only long-term goals especially treasury operations for boosting up their profitability.

3. Technological Advancement

The developments in technology are the key devices of business in banking. The key devices such as computers and telecom have revolutionized the financial industry and banks by using net. Tele banking, Internet banking, remote access and ATM etc are some activities of banks on net. The market is very vast and the requirements are also more, hence to capitalize on this situation the usage of technology is a prerequisite and the only solution to meet all the demands also.

Due to the technological changes, service delivery would become active, which would influence the business by reducing costs of delivery and transaction therefore the concentration can be on acquiring new customer and maximizing the available opportunities in present Indian banking system. Technology would change its position from enable to driver of business by computerization of banks with improved operational efficiency and customer service. The organization today is being influenced by numerous forces like atomization of markets and demand, a sense of acceleration, economic shocks, deconstruction of business etc., which has changed the scenario to micro segmentation, multiple competition and short product life cycles. So the business is under tremendous pressure to perform. The key to performance lies in anticipating the future and working towards it.

The technological revolution has made banking transactions more convenient. The different services that are going to be offered are online loan application, opening an account online, corporate Internet banking, balance enquiry and funds transfer and in view of this banks are being considered to be technological leaders with developed customized solutions. Now corporate are able to transact salary payments etc., on line. One of the life insurance corporate is making commission agent payments on Internet. Dealer payment, dealer collections are also some of the services demanded by the corporate through on line banking.

All the above-mentioned CRM and marketing strategies can be implemented through technological advancements. Without technological updation the above-specified tasks would not be possible. Therefore technological up-gradation becomes a strategic tool in order to cope with corporate vision which bring competitive advantage. So at the core, a need to cultivate a culture to adopt the latest technological tools and techniques for higher end use is fast pressing. The employees must collaborate and work in teams with faster and beneficial planning and implementation which will lead to a well-developed process having constant in-built monitoring and evaluation.

As there is a close linkage to the strategy that is responding to the dynamic business environment, a synchronization between them can be achieved by having a well established set of processes to carry out, continuously practiced mechanisms to identify its weakness and which ensures the contribution to the business goal.

In spite of realizing the importance of implementation of technological advancement, majority of the developed systems are not coming up to the expectations. Some of causes of such situations may be organizational changes, strategic problems, supply problems, poor management, user skills, techno phobia, lack of participation, poor control system etc.,

So without the user participation, involvement and ownership of systems technical aspects are useless. Therefore inter and intra organization levels collaboration is very important to achieve the best out of such investments and continuous evaluation has to be done to support business goal achievement.

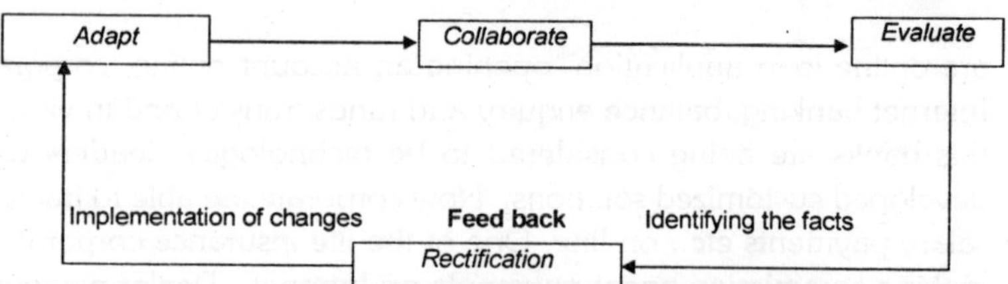

To meet all the above-specified requirements to improve the efficiency and effectiveness of the organization it must undergo all the three stages specified above by implementing the three environments detailed below.

Adoptive Environment: Banks must be an early adopter so that it can fastly respond in a competitive environment. The environment can be made fertile by adopting technology innovations and applying of technological paradigms.

Collaborate Environment: In spite of adapting the technological innovations, banks are not meeting the expectations due to reluctance to change, user poor management skills, techno phobia and lack of participation. To reduce such problems banks should reduce authoritative roles at senior level to much involvement of bureaucracy and encourage lower levels to participate by getting training and to establish the collaborative environment.

Evaluative Environment: To measure the performance against the well-defined standards a well-established procedure is required to evaluate. To solve the bottlenecks and to identify the failures a constant feedback mechanism is required. Even to check the effectiveness of adoptive and collaborative environments of organization evaluation mechanism should be implemented.

Conclusion

In the post-liberalized era, Information Technology is an inevitable resource to be considered to ensure an effective and competitive environment, which is adaptive and collaborative to change. Hence, the technological advancement in banking sector can be made effective when a simple, flexible and modular approach is considered and implemented.

REFERENCES

1. K.V.Kamath, S.S.Kohli, P.S.Shenoy, Ranjana Kumar, R.M. Nayak and P.T.Kuppuswamy N.Ravichandran(co-coordinator) *"Indian Banking Sector: Challenges and opportunities" Vikalpa*, July-Sep 2003, Vol: 28, No: 3, P: 83-99
2. Kamna Malik and D.P. Goyal *"Organizational Environment And Information Systems", Vikalpa*, Jan-Mar 2003, Vol: 28, No: 1, P: 61-73
3. Suresh Rajpal and Ravi Raj Sagar *"Business Excellence In Indian Scenario"* Vikalpa, Vol:28, No:4. P: 77-81
4. Product and Technology Group ICICI Bank, *"Corporate Banking: Using Technology In Transactions"*, ICFAI Reader, Jan 2004, P:71-76
5. Full text : 'Tying the Knot : IT Systems in a Merger', The Mckinsey Quarterly 2003, No: 4 "Merging IT Systems", ICFAI Reader, Dec. 2003, P; 15
6. Dr.A.V.Ranganadha Chary and Dr. R.R.Paul *"Banking and Financial Systems"*, Ed: 2003, Kalyani Publishers
7. Chandrasekar *"Indian Banking: Challenges Ahead", Chartered Financial Analyst*, Feb 2004, P: 27-34.

12

RELATIONSHIP BETWEEN STOCK PRICES AND EXCHANGE RATES

Dr. K. Chandrasekhara Rao* and **S. Syed Ahamed****

Since Liberalisations, the Indian Industry has been exposed to a variety of global challenges. More specifically, the bottom lines of export oriented/import dependent companies have been influenced by changes in exchange rates in the floating exchange rates regime. The present study is primarily focused on capturing such forex exposure on equity returns of companies with global transactions. Considering a sample of 62 companies, the present study has tried to find the possible existence of *forex beta* in addition to market beta, explored by the traditional CAPM. The results are mixed. Although, the market has not shown any clear premium for compensating the exchange rate exposure, the coefficient is found positive and linear in a two factor CAPM context.

Introduction

The Indian stock market though one of the oldest in the Asia being in operation since 1875, remained largely outside the global integration process until late 1980s. In line with the global trends of reforms, the Indian stock market has witnessed a series of changes since the economy opted for liberalizations presumably due to pressure from IMF on account of external payment crisis. Prior to nineties The Indian financial system was full of substantial rigidities and was under

* Reader & Head, Dept. of Commerce, Pondicherry University, Pondicherry

** Lecturer (Management Area), Arunal Engg. College, Tiruvannamalai, T.N. and Research Scholar, Dept. of Commerce, Pondicherry University, Pondicherry.

severe administrative controls. Administered interest rate structure, thin foreign exchange market, fixed exchange rate mechanism, under-developed secondary markets for equities as well as for government securities, inadequate depth of money and capital markets, inadequate institutional arrangements/framework are the dominant characteristics, resulting in substantial segmentation of financial markets .

Major developments that have taken place during the reform process and which might facilitated for the integration of financial markets are:

(i) Dismantling of various price and non-price controls in financial markets; relaxation of foreign investment restrictions primarily through country deregulation;

(ii) Permission to Indian corporates for issuance of American Depository Receipts (ADRs) or Global Depository Receipts (GDRs) which in turn facilitated the trade of securities on NYSE, NASDAQ, etc.;

(iii) Allowing the exchange rates to be determined by market forces (through, at times, the intervention of Reserve Bank of India) and gradual move towards full convertibility on Indian Rupee which enabled the international investors to invest substantial amounts (about US $15bn) in Indian capital market;

(iv) The two-way fungibility of ADRs/GDRs allowed by RBI has further strengthened the linkages between the stock and foreign exchange markets.

The relationship between a country's stock market and its foreign exchange market has been a subject of theoretical and empirical investigation in International Finance for over two decades. The traditional CAPM tells us that exchange rate risk being firm-specific and nonsystematic and should be diversifiable and hence would not be considered by markets.

However, International CAPM says that the expected excess return on risky asset is a linear function of not only their beta, but also the exchange rate factor. The extension of traditional CAPM to a multi-country context under the assumption of integrated capital markets, must account for exchange rate risk and its co-variance with World market portfolio. Two outstanding issues in extending the pure domestic Capital Asset Pricing Model (CAPM) to the International context are: (a) Whether the global capital markets are integrated or segmented and (b)what would be the Impact of exchange rate on asset pricing. The Asian currency crisis of 1997-98 had revealed a dynamic link between stock prices and exchange rates. During the crisis, the currencies of emerging market's have depreciated, resulting in greater outflow of funds from portfolio investment, in turn lead to the dramatic fall in stock prices.

If stock prices and exchange rates are related and the causation runs from exchange rates to stock prices then crises in stock markets can be prevented by controlling the exchange rates. Moreover, developing countries can exploit such a link to attract/stimulate foreign portfolio investment into their countries. Similarly, if the causation runs from stock prices to exchange rates then authorities can focus on domestic economic policies to stabilize the stock markets. If the two markets/prices are related to each other then investors can use this information to predict the behavior of one market using the information from other market.

Most of the empirical literature on stock price -exchange rate relationship has focused on examining this relationship for the developed countries with very little attention on the developing countries. The results of these studies are, moreover, inconclusive. Some studies have found a significant positive relationship between stocks prices and exchange rates (Smith (1992), Solnik (1987) and Aggarwal (1981) while others have reported a significant negative relationship between the two (e.g., Soenen and Hennigar (1998)). On the other hand, there are some studies that have found very weak or no association between stock prices and exchange rates (Franck and Young (1972), Eli Bartov and Gordon Bodnor (1994)).

The standard definition of exchange rate exposure is a measure of the correlation between real asset values and real exchange rates. Exchange rate fluctuations can have a substantial impact on the profitability of domestic industries. Price changes caused by movements in the exchange rate may (a) change the terms of competition between foreign firms for domestic exporters and import competitors; (b) alter input prices for industries that use internationally priced inputs or firms that import for resale; (c) change the value of assets denominated in foreign currencies. Because of these diverse sets of influences, exchange rate movements affect some industries different from other.

Indian companies are now allowed to tap foreign equity by using GDRs and ADRs. Apart from that, exchange rate regime was liberalized with almost complete current account convertibility since 1994. In this context this paper explores whether share prices in India are likely to get influenced by the changes in foreign exchange rates.

Literature Review

Several studies have examined the effect of changes exchange rates on the stock prices in different markets. Aggarwal (1981) was the first to conduct a study to examine the relationship between stock prices and the floating values of dollars. He found that the value of the US dollar and US stock prices were positively correlated during the period of 1974-1978. Jorion (1990) has explored into that the sensitivity of a firms value to exchange rate exposure of US multinationals. This study observes such relationship as positive and it is largely related to the degree of foreign operations. The study has used the ratio of foreign sales to total sales as a proxy for foreign involvement.

Apte (1997) has examined the exchange rate exposure on Indian stock prices by considering monthly share prices of 143 firms from CMIE corporate database during 1990 to 1997. Considering trade weighted indices of NEER and REER, the study estimated the exchange beta and regressed it with firm specific characteristics like exports ratio and imports ratio. The results obtained from REER and NEER indicate that 32 firms out of 143 report significant exchange rate exposure out of which eight were negative and rest report a positive exposure. This study thus reveals that exchange rate risk is behaving as a systematic risk over and above market risk in case of many Indian companies.

Apte (2001) further investigated the relationship between the volatility of the stock market and that of the nominal exchange rate in India using daily closing stock market indices of BSE-30 and NSE-50 and daily closing USD/INR exchange rates using EGARCH specification proposed by Nelson (1991). The study addressed on the question whether the innovations in stock returns have any impact on the volatility in foreign exchange markets and vice versa. The results reveal that the hypothesis of return innovations in one market support not only on the conditional variance in the same market by also in the other markets.

Yamini and Kawadia (2002) have examined the relationship between sectoral indices and exchange rates by considering sectoral indices like BSE-IT; BSE-CG, BSE-FMCG, BSE-CD and BSE-HC. Their results show that the impact of SENSEX on exchange rate is positive and significant on various indices, viz BSE-CG, BSE-CP and BSE-CP and BSE HC. FMCG and IT sectors do not report any significant exchange exposure.

Nath and Samanta (2003) have tested whether returns in stock market are interrelated with returns in capital market considering a period from March 1993 to December 2002, using daily NSE-50 index price and daily INR/USDs value. The Granger - causality tests are conducted to find the relationship between exchange rate and stock prices with a lag of 5-days suggest that these two markets did not have any causal relationship. If one goes into specific years to see whether the liberalizations in both the markets have brought them together. or not, then also no significant causal relationship is observable between exchange rates and stock prices except for the years 1993,2001 and 2002, during when unidirectional causal influence from stock index return to return in forex market is detected (with corresponding F statistics are significant at 5 per cent level of significance). Very mild causal influence in reverse direction is also found in some years (1997, 2002).

Nath and Samanta (2003) in another paper examined the extent of integration between foreign exchange and stock markets in India during the liberalization era, considering NIFTY index and exchange rate of Indian Rupee to Dollar for a period of 10 financial years from April 1993 to March 2003. The study tried to employ two methodologies, first Granger's causality in Vector Auto Regression(VAR) context and second the Geweke's Feedback measures. The results show contemporaneous relationship between returns in two markets as very strong (statistically significant at 1 percent level) during four financial years, 1998-99, 1999-00, 2001-

02 and 2002-03. The causal impact in reverse direction is detected significant in the years 1994-95 (1 percent level), 1996-97 (5 percent level) and 2001-02 (1 percent level) and 2002-03 (10 percent level). Thus, the tests reveal the existence of mild-to-strong causal relationship (either contemporaneous or lagged) between returns in foreign exchange and capital markets during some years.

Seshaiah, Ganesh and Vuyyuri (2003) have examined the effect of exchange rates as well as inflation on stock returns. The period of study of 1980-81 to 1999-2000 has been subdivided into two parts before and after 1991 to find the effect of liberalizations. Using annual changes in BSE Index, Gold and Silver Returns and inflation rates, the study has estimated stepwise linear regression equations. It was found that the stock returns and exchange rates during pre-liberalization era have no significant relationship. However, during the post-liberalization period the degree of dependence between stock returns and exchange rate movements is found significant at 5 per cent level. This may be due to huge inflow of foreign portfolio investment into Indian capital markets after liberalizations. This means that exchange rate movements and stock return volatility are closely related with exchange flows affecting stock returns.

Yamini Karmarkar and Kawadia(2002) have explored the interrelationship between capital market, forex market and bullion market in India. Considering the indices of BSE-Sensex, BSE National and Nifty as the representatives of capital market, the Rupee Dollar exchange rate as indicator of movements in forex market, the study has estimated the response functions. It was observed that there is price integration between stock prices, bullion prices and exchange rates. The growth in stock prices was much more than the growth in bullion prices and exchange rates during the period under study. All these markets are found more stable in the era of economic reforms.

Methodology

Exchange rate exposure, defined as the effect of exchange rate changes on the values of a firm, does not employ any casual relationship between exchange rate fluctuations and changes in firm values. Both stock prices and firm values are assumed to be endogenously determined. This means that stock prices and exchange rates depends on the nature of the shocks affecting the economy (Jorion 1990). But for the purpose of the analysis, as in earlier studies, it is assumed that the exchange rates are exogenous to the value of the firm.

The exchange rate exposure of sample is measured using a two-factor model of stock return as dependent on the market return and exchange rate changes

$$R_{it} = \alpha + \beta_{im} R_{mt} + \beta_{ie} E_t u_{it} \quad (1)$$

Where R_{it} is the return on the stock of firm 'i' during period 't'. R_{mt} is the market return and E_t is the exchange rate factor. b_{im} and b_{ie} denotes the sensitivities of the stock returns to the market and exchange rate factors respectively. In order to overcome the problem of inter-correlation between market returns and exchange rates, the later is orthogonalised by running an auxiliary regression of changes in exchange rates as dependent on returns and the residuals of such regression to proxy E_t. (Results of auxiliary Regression is given in Table 3)

Data Sources

The study has used 225 weekly stock prices pertaining to BSE 100 companies and Rupee value against four major currencies, viz., Dollar, Euro, Pound and Yen to establish the above said relationship between the stock price and exchange rates. The main source of data is the CMIE Corporate Data Base which has provided data on prices of individual stocks as well as the Market Index value. It also contained summaries of Income Statement and Balance Sheet from which data on Export, Imports, Exports to sales ratio and the ratio of value of imported raw materials to total raw material consumed were obtained. However, data on exchange rates are collected from the website of RBI. (Rbi.org)

Sixty Two companies were selected out of BSE 100 companies. In order to get included into sample a company should fulfill anyone of the following conditions, viz., (a). Imports should exceed 20 per cent of total raw material; (b). Exports to sales ratio to exceed 20 percent of total sales; (c). Size of total imports exceeding 100 crores; (d). Annual size of Export sales exceeding 100 crores.

Results and Discussion

Exchange rate fluctuations are likely to influence the bottom lines of those companies whose operations involve either exports or imports on a large scale. In addition, the exchange rate fluctuations or their stability is likely to influence the capital flows of portfolio investment by Foreign Institutional Investors(FIIs). While the later phenomenon is of short-term nature the influence on firm level performance and its consequence on stock market prices is likely to have a long term implications in an economy.

The result of the study has been arranged here under two broad categories. At first , the distribution of market beta across sample firms and its statistical significance has been explored into. While market beta is an indicator of systematic risk that the given stock exhibits during a specific period of study, a comparison of sizes of beta reveal the interfirm /inter-sectoral differences in their risk profiles. The said market beta have estimated through the traditional characteristic line methodology, where in the market responsiveness of stock is estimated by regressing a time series of market return on the return of a individual stock

As it is proposed to consider only that part of exchange rate changes which could not be explained by changes in market factor, the values of exchange rate variable has been dglated as only unexplained component is included in the above equation.

In the second stage, the relationship contemplated in traditional CAPM has been tried. The traditional CAPM explain the cross sectional between the risk-return relationships in equity market, the present tried to examine such risk-return relationship with two risk variable, viz. market beta and exchange risk. This has been achieved by running a regressing equation with two independent variable ie market beta and exchange beta. Then the two factor CAPM tried the following the relationship across firms

The above said exchange of estimating market beta exchange beta and two-factor CAPM framework has been carried out severalty for two-factor CAPM framework has been carried in the present study.

The estimated results for each company based on a time series database of 225 weeks have been analysed separately for 'market beta' and 'exchange beta'. The tables have been prepared taking into account distribution of beta across companies. The results of two factor model against four currencies indicates that explanation (R^2 value) put forth by two risk variables on stock returns found to range in-between from 0.02 to as much as 0.35 indicating that Indian stock market's response to two systematic variables is to the extent of 15 to 20 percent, on an average. The company wise market 'beta' found more or less same for all the sets of results and thus giving stability to the estimated coefficients. It may be due to the fact that running of auxiliary regression has delimited the market index and exchange rates not to inter-relate and result in a multicollinearity problem

Distribution of Market Beta

The results indicate that market beta is statistically significant across the board in all the equations. For better understanding, the calculated market betas across the sample of 62 companies are tabulated against different ranges. Theoretically, these betas represent the responsiveness of individual scrip to the market index. Empirical results show that the size of the beta largely revolve around a range of 0.20 to 0.50 only. Seven companies out of 62 sample units possesses beta higher than 0.50. The prime reason for low beta values in case of majority of sample units is due to peculiar condition prevailing in the market during the period of study. Further, the weekly changes in stock prices report low beta value compared to monthly or quarterly changes.During April 1999 to March 2003, the market is very volatile for different external shocks like September 11 incidence, Gulf War II, and internal factors like Ketan Parak scam, introduction of derivatives and prolonged bearishness in stock browses.

Out of the few sample units who have reported a beta larger than 'one' include 'Iflex Solutions' with beta of 1.08 and 'Wipro Limited' with a beta of 1.12 are prominent. A beta of more than one for both the software companies indicate the tech stock boom during the period of study. On similar lines, Satyam Computers (beta = 0.70), Polaris Software Ltd (0.87), Infosys technology (beta=0.59), and Digital Global Soft (beta=0.63) report good value of beta and thus follows the bandwagon. The technology boom may be the one of the reason for many Old economy stocks to report a beta ranging before 0.30 to 0.40 during the study period. For example, Century

Textiles report a beta of 0.45, Mahindra & Mahindra 0.45, ABB 0.32, and Bharat Forge 0.40, Grasim industries 0.31, SAIL 0.54 and so on.

Exchange Beta-A Measure of Exposure

Distribution of exchange rate exposure of select sample units for four currencies have been tabulated and presented in Table 2. The exposure co-efficient has been called as 'Exchange Beta' in the present study. A negative sign of the coefficient for the exchange beta indicate that any depreciation in the value of the currencies likely to bring added advantage to the market value of the stock

It can be observed that very surprisingly that most of the (41) sample units report a negative beta against US Dollar. The said beta is more or less equally distributed against àll other ranges. In case of Pound Sterling the beta found concentrating a initial ranges of 0 to 0.30 in about 42 companies, similar trend is observed in case of Euro and Yen as well.

If one goes by company wise results, only six out of 62 companies exhibit significance that too at 10 per cent or 20 per cent levels. The story is more or less same across different currencies. However, if one considers the logarithmic results of exchange beta, it works out to be very significant in case of Dr. Reddy's Lab (1.99) Glaxco Smith (2.40) Hero Honda, Nestle, Workhard followed by Zee telefilms, Hai man, MRF.

Thus, the existence of exchange beta at least notionally observable when one considers the logarithmic result. The logarithmic regression co-efficient naturally works out to the elasticity of exposure co-efficient.

Two Factor CAPM

In the second pass, CAPM logic has been estimated to examine the impact of "Excchange Beta" in a given risk-return framework. The CAPM, time honored and much celebrated asset pricing framework, provides a logic that equity returns entirely depend upon the systematic risk which is alone to be compensated if the security markets are efficient. The firm specific exposure due to fluctuations in exchange rates are expected to be wiped out, if one construct efficient portfolios. However the present study aim at exploring the impact of exchange beta as an additional factor in CAPM frame work.

The present study has estimated a two-factor a CAPM using the following model

The cross sectional CAPM results for each currency indicate that the two factor CAPM has slightly higher explanatory power R^2 when compared to single factor CAPM. Further, the market beta is found positive although the exchange 'beta' showed mixed results. While the co-efficient is negative on US dollar regression the same is positive in other currencies. However, the insignificance of the coefficient of 'exchange beta' do not lend any clear support for any further argument for possible inclusion of it in asset pricing models in Indian context. Almost similar trend is observable when the data is reworked with logarithmic values.

Conclusions

The objective of this paper is to examine whether there exists any relationship between stock returns and fluctuations in the exchange rates among firms who are exposed to International operations Viz., Exports and Imports. In most of the companies exchange beta is not found significant implying that there is no significant exchange rate exposure. When the results are re-worked in logarithmic form, it is observed that a hand full of companies show significant exchange rate exposure. Literature suggests that if a firm undertakes sufficient hedging policies to minimize the effect of exchange rate risk ,a weak relationship is bound to found between foreign exchange exposure and firm's value (Collier,Davis,Coats and Longden(1990))

However, in the era of floating exchange rate regime and the integration of Indian stock market with the rest of the World, an investor is made to consider an additional risk factors viz., foreign exchange risk, apart from market risk in his investment decisions.

Table 12.1: Distribution of Market Beta

Range	*USD*		*GBP*		*EURO*		*YEN*	
	Abo	*Log*	*Abo*	*Log*	*Abo*	*Log*	*Abo*	*Log*
1	*2*	*3*	*4*	*5*	*6*	*7*	*8*	*9*
Below .10	2	5	2	5	2	5	2	5
0.10 - .20	10	5	10	5	10	5	10	5
0.20 - .30	21	20	21	20	21	20	21	20

(Contd...)

1	*2*	*3*	*4*	*5*	*6*	*7*	*8*	*9*
0.30 - .40	16	15	16	15	16	15	16	15
0.40 - .50	4	5	4	5	4	5	4	5
0.50 - .60	2	4	2	4	2	4	2	4
0.60 - .70	3	3	3	3	3	3	3	3
0.70 & Above	4	5	4	5	4	5	4	5

Table 12.2: Distribution of Exchange Beta

Range	*USD*		*GBP*		*EURO*		*YEN*	
	Abo	*Log*	*Abo*	*Log*	*Abo*	*Log*	*Abo*	*Log*
Below-0.5	27	37	3	6	0	1	0	4
-0.5 to -0.4	2	1	5	2	0	0	0	4
-0.4 to -0.3	4	2	1	2	0	0	0	4
-0.3 to -0.2	2	3	3	3	1	2	0	4
-0.2 to -0.1	3	2	9	4	2	2	0	8
-0.1 to 0	3	0	7	6	12	5	0	9
0 to.10	4	2	6	4	10	3	0	5
.10 to .20	1	1	8	10	21	7	8	7
.20 to .30	1	3	3	6	11	8	35	6
.30 to .40	0	1	8	2	4	9	16	4
.40 to .50	1	0	4	6	0	13	2	0
.50& above	15	10	5	11	1	21	1	6

Table 12.3: Coefficients for Regression of Exchange as dependent on Stock Market Index (Axillary Regression)

Model	*λ*	B_m	R^2
$\hat{R}_{\$} = f(R_m)$	0.00053 (3.20)	-0.0059 (2.21)	0.0219
$\hat{R}_{£} = f(R_m)$	0.00032 (0.44)	0.0032 (0.27)	0.0034
$\hat{R}_E = f(R_m)$	0.00018 (0.18)	0.0075 (0.48)	0.0010
$\hat{R}_Y = f(R_m)$	0.00032 (0.32)	-0.0146 (0.92)	0.0039
In $\hat{R}_{\$} = f(R_m)$	0.00052 (3.13)	-0.0061 (2.17)	0.0211
In $\hat{R}_{£} = f(R_m)$	0.00027 (0.38)	0.0036 (0.29)	0.0004
In $\hat{R}_E = f(R_m)$	0.00009 (0.10)	0.0069 (0.42)	0.0008
In $\hat{R}_Y = f(R_m)$	0.00019 (0.19)	-0.011 (0.68)	0.0021

Table 12.4: Two factor Capm results

Particulars	N	λ0		λ1		λ2		R^2	
		Abo	Log	Abo	Log	Abo	Log	Abo	Log
Pooled	60	0.0003 (0.33)	0.0003 (0.39)	0.0085 (3.70)	-0.0057' (3.18)			0.18	0.14
USD	59	0.0003 (0.33)	0.0003 (0.26)	0.0082 (3.57)	0.0057 (3.13)	0.0001 (0.30)	8.48E- (0.48)	0.18	0.14
GBP	59	0.0003 (0.38)	0.0003 (0.42)	0.0084 (3.68)	0.0057 (3.10)	0.0004 (0.29)	-0.0002 (0.21)	0.18	0.14
EURO	59	0.0007 (0.77)	0.0003- (0.25)	0.0082 (3.68)	0.0060 (3.29)	*0.0042* (1.35)	0.0016 (1.13)	0.21	0.16
YEN	59	0.0002- (0.29)	0.0003 (0.27)	0.0082 (3.55)	0.0060 (3.25)	0.0007 (0.36)	-0.0010 (0.7)	0.18	0.15

REFERENCES

1. Jorion, P,(1990) "The exchange rate exposure of US Multinationals", *Journal of Business*, Vol.63,No3, pp. 331-343.
2. Jorion, P, (1991)"The pricing of exchange rate risk in the Stock Market", *Journal of Financial and Quantitative Analysis,* Vol.26,pp,363-376.
3. Bodnar, G. and WM Gentry,(1993) "Exchange rate exposure and industry characteristics: Evidence from Canada, Japan and USA," *Journal of International Money and Finance*, Vol.12, pp.29-45.
4. Bartov, E and G.M. Bodnar,(1994) "Firm valuation, Earnings Expectation and the exchange rate exposure effect" *Journal of Finance*, Vol.XLIX,No5, pp.1755-1785.
5. Bany Arifin, Amain, Law Siong Hook, The relationship between stock price and Exchange Rate: Empirical Evidence based on KLSE market, *Asian Economic Review* (2000)
6. Gordon. M. Bodnar and M.H.Franco Wong, (2003)"Estimating exchange Rate exposures: issues in Model structure," *Financial Management*, page 35-67
7. Apte, P. G, "Currency Exposure and Stock Prices"(1997), *Journal of Foreign Exchange and International Finance*,Vol. XII, No. 2, , pp.135-143.
8. Apte, P G, (2001) "The Inter-relationship Between Stock Markets and the Foreign Exchange Market", *Journal of Social and Management Sciences*, VolXXX, No.1, pp.17-30.

9. Yamini Karmarkar and G. Kawadia, (2002)"The Relationship between Stock Index and Exchange Rate Empirical Evidence Based on Indian Stock Market", *Applied Finance*, Vol.VIII ,No.2, pp.51-56.

10. Nath, Golak C. and G. P. Samanta (2003), "Dynamic Relation Between Exchange Rate and Stock Prices – A Case for India", NSE News, *National Stock Exchange of India Limited* (NSEIL), pp.15-18.

11. Nath, Golak C and G P Samanta (2003), "Integration Between Foreign Exchange and Capital Markets in India: An Empirical Exploration", *Applied Finance*,Vol IX, No.6, 2003, pp.29-40.

12. S.V. Seshiaiah, Ganesh S. Mani and Srivyal Vuyyuri,(2003) "Effect of Exchange Rates and Inflation on Stock Returns", *Applied Finance*,Vol. IX, No.4, pp.51-61.

13. Manjri. D., Yamini Karmarkar and G.Kawadia(2002), "A Study of Market Integration Based on Indian Stock Market", *Applied Finance*,Vol.VIII, No.5, pp.40-49.

13

CORPORATE GOVERNANCE
AN OVERVIEW

P. Sriram* and **Dr. Talluru Sreenivas****

The primary objective of corporation is to maximise the shareholders' wealth in a legal and ethical manner. There are three players involved in this game – firstly, the share holders who have trusted the company and, consequently, invested their capital either through an initial public offering or through the secondary market. Secondly, the management that runs the company, which is accountable to the directors, and thirdly, the directors, who, in turn, are answerable only to the shareholders. They are not responsible to the so called owner influences or to the management. Together, these three are expected to govern the corporation ethically and legally.

We have to ensure that there is fairness to transparency in transactions with all the stakeholders, which include customers, employees, investors, vendors, the government, and the society at large. Corporate Governance is about building confidence and increasing the trust of the stakeholders in the way the company manages its affairs. It is about bringing efficiency and effectiveness through the use of fair and transparent means. In India, today, a good man is one who is nice to his friends and who is very nice to his relatives. A pious man who builds a temple is respected by society. We need to change this definition respected by society. We need to change is definition to say that unless one is nice to the large body of

* Lecturer, Dept. of Business Administration, P.B. Siddhartha College of Arts and Science, Vijayawada - 520 010.

** Reader, Dept. of Management Sciences, RVR&JC College of Engg., Guntur, A.P.

the unseen people, the large body that makes up this society, he is not a good person. In other words, we have to equate being a good person to being a good citizen. It is unlikely that we will have much respect towards the society or follow laws of the society unless this change in the mindset comes in.

Introduction

Why did so many corporate scandals happen? This is one of the key issues to be considered in formulating corporate governance courts. When we observe causes of unreasonable profit offering and other scandals on the part of banks and securities companies, it is recognized that such deplorable events were caused, not on a time basis, but due to fundamental, structural causes.

Why is it that the Board of Directors could not stop it? What accounts for the fact that the Auditors team could not check it? How did the function and structure of Management decision-making work? For whom and how were such companies being managed.

Corporate Governance is still a new concept in the World, even in the US and European countries just around ten years ago. However, it has been rapidly getting popular in Japan the past several years for the reason that conventional framework of management, cannot cope with the changes in today's active business environment, a new management system model and framework is being sought after. Corporate Governance is explained as a kind of code developed by stakeholders when direction and activities are to be decided. As conventional business customs become unable to cope with changing times once a company's business scenario changes Corporate Governance also has to change in its concept.

What is Corporate Governance?

For establishing effective functional Corporate Governance, a company is required to clarify its strategy to show the fundamental direction of its Corporate Governance, secure transparency through active management information disclosure and also to realize the company's innovativeness by establishing a social orientation. Hence, a Corporate Governance can be said to be a structural framework to make a healthy and competitive company which realizes self-cleaning and competitive-ness under such strategies, transparency, social orientation and innovativeness.

Corporate Governance focussing on relations between management and shareholders provides us with a key point of Corporate Governance theory on "How stakeholders monitor and control the activities of management in relation to the company's economic performance?" Corporate Governance theory addresses the issue of how and by which mechanism to provide operational responsibility to the management in order to bridge the gap between ownership and control.

Historical evolution of Corporate Governance–World Scenario

Any discussion on Corporate Governance must necessarily begin with the Cadbury Committee report in UK in early 1990s. Circumstances in which the Cadbury Committee was set-up deserve a special mention, as they are as relevant, or even more relevant, to the conditions today. First, there was a concern at the low level of financial reporting and the inability of auditors to provide safeguards that the users of financial information expected. The underlying factors were seen as the looseness of accounting standards which provided too many options, the absence of a clear frame work for ensuring that the directors kept the controls in their business under review and the competitive pressures both on companies and auditors which made it difficult for the auditors to stand up to the demanding boards. Second, there had been unexpected failures of major companies in the UK. There was a feeling that annual reports had failed to provide forewarning of companies which subsequently failed. Third, there were criticisms as far as boards were concerned that the directors of the board were being paid excessive salaries or remuneration that was unlinked to their actual corporate performance. It was for the first time that this committee gave Corporate Governance a definition by stating that it was a system by which companies were directed and controlled.

Other efforts in this regard include, among others, Corporate Governance principles adopted by the Organization for Economic Cooperation and Development (OECD), in the US, UK and Europe and other countries. The latest in the series is the set of reforms proposed by the New York Stock Exchange in May, 2002.

In Indian Context

The studies on this subject in India are comparatively of recent origin and include the reports of the taskforce of the confederation of Indian Industry (CIA) in April,1997, a committee of the Securities Exchange Board of India (SEBI) in 1999, advisory group of RBI in March,2001, and the RBI consultative group of directors of Banks, Financial Institutions in April, 2002.

The areas covered include, among others, size composition, charter, responsibilities and maintenance of the Board of Directors; Tenure of Directors, Age limit for appointment as Directors, Liabilities of Directors, Accountability to Shareholders and Stakeholders; access to information, nominee directors and their remuneration, committee on grievances of shareholders, executive vs non-executive Chairman of the Board, Audit Committee, Remuneration Committee, Nomination Committee, Board Procedures, Accounting Standards and financial reporting, disclosure and transparency, auditor independence, responsibilities of individual and institutional shareholders and matters relating to implementation of the canons of Corporate Governance.

Need of the Corporate Governance–World Scenario

First, it was Enron, then Tyco, Adelphia, Qwest, Global crossing and now the Worldcom and Aol Time Warner. Corporate America is today littered with cases accounting frauds and executive irresponsibility. In 1998, Comroad, a navigation technology company in Germany, invested 2/3 its revenue in the name of non-existent claimant in Hong Kong. Factors behind the current crisis in corporate sector, almost bear a striking resemblance to the ones which led to the Great Stock Market Crash of 1929 – Sky rocketing valuation of stocks on account of unprecedented rise in speculative activities insider-trading by company executives, ballooning of corporate debt and accounting maneuverings, given the scale and audacity of the current crisis which has it corporate America at its core, the task for the US Government is enormous. The objective before the Government is two fold. First, sending a strong signal to corporate wrong-doers and secondly, restoring the confidence of the average investor. Therefore, the above situation forces to study corporate responsibility and redefine a Corporate Governance to protect shareholders in corporate sector.

Some important crook downs in corporate sector of America due to the malpractice of the Board of Directors.

The Rogues' Gallery

Company	*Charges*	*Response of the Company*
WorldCom	Improper accounting of $3.9 billion dollars in expenses leading to bankruptcy.	Admits its accounting was bad.
Adelphia	Allegedly gave Rigas family $ 1 billion in hidden loans; fudged number of subscribers.	Adelphia has sued the Rigases for looting the company
Imclone system	Charges of insider trading on ex-CEO Samuel Waksal and others.	ImClone Systems has replaced Waksal as CEO.
Tyco Int'l	Alleged misuse of company money by CEO Kozlowski to buy art and other things.	New CEO appointed. Tyco says it's on sound footing.
Enron	Off-balance-sheet deals used to hide debt and inflate earnings.	Admitted it hid losses and loans with limited partnerships.
AOL Warner	AOL division accused of improperly accounting for some advertising revenue.	Defends its accounting as both appropriate and legal.

The Auditor's Hall of Shame

Auditor	*Companies*
Arthur Anderson	Enron, WorldCom, Qwest, Global Crossing, Dynegy, CMS Enegy, Halliburton, Peregrine, Merck
PricewaterhouseCoopers	Tyco
KPMG	Xerox
Deloittee & Touche	El Paso Corp., Adelphia
Ernst & Young	AOL, Williams Cos.

Americans are not alone in the fight against their former corporate heroes. Europe is at it too as can be seen from the case of Jeen-Marie measures of Vivendi Universal who has seen the investors turning against him due to lousy results, much publicized infighting and a 40% fall in the share price in 2002.

These cases have raised some important questions for training to Corporate Governance and institutional arrangements for its regulations.

Indian Context

Indian Corporate Sector chants the new mantra of economic liberalization and globalization incessantly and is not averse to teaching the Government and for that matter all other sections of society to set their houses in order to meet these new challenges. A reference may be invited in this context to only two of the recommendations of the report of the working group on Companies Act 1956. These are difficult to fathom, particularly with all talk of good governance which is heard at the five star hotel seminars organized by the CII and the other apex chambers of commerce and industry. The working group had recommended that at this juncture the requirement for audit committees and nomination or remuneration committees should not be mandated by the Companies Act. Instead, it should be voluntary with three apex industry associations – CII, FICCI and ASSOCHAM – playing a catabolic role. In other recommendations the working group has proposed that the provisions under section 233B concerning mandatory cost audit at the directive of the Department of Company Affairs should be removed. Both these are retrograde recommendations. Their significance and importance in the Indian context cannot be over-emphasized if Corporate Governance is to have any meaning

A few other issues have come to the fore in the Indian context. The first relates to the need for credible and strong regulatory mechanisms. Unfortunately, the record in this behalf is far from satisfactory. The powers given to SEBI are insignificant as compared to its counterpart, Securities Exchange Commission (SEC) in the US. With its limited investigative and penal powers, SEBI has been ineffective as a market regulator. Currently it does not have even the powers of search and seizure. The maximum penalty that the SEBI can impose on a market manipulator is paltry sumeof Rs.5.00 lakhs. Corporates have even offered to make this payment up front.

The travails of the Telecommunication Regulatory of India (TROI) have been equally distressing with the Government abolishing the erstwhile authority altogether when it found that it was too independent and enacting a new law for its reconstitution. In the process, TROI's powers were also whittled down. Acquisition of Indian Petro Chemical Corporation (IPCL) by Reliance Industries Ltd. (RIL) has raised major fears about the monopoly in petrochemical sector. RIL now has a strangle hold with share of about 67% of the market for most such products. Particularly worrisome is the fact that though import duties on most other products have been reduced substantially with the political growth of RIL, the average protection level on most petrochemical products is absurdly high. This shows the absence of concern of the Government for the common consumer. It is a travesty that now the demand for a level playing field has to be made for the public sector in the country. A specious and ingenious argument is being put forth by the Government that monopoly by itself is not bad. But at present, there is no law to protect the consumer against such abuse. It has referred earlier to the major issues which have come into prominence in respect of the audit of companies. Equally relevant are the matters pertaining to the credit rating agencies, their accountability and the transparency of their operations.

CRISIL has downgraded BPLs non-convertible debentures issue by full 12 stages from A to D as default category in one shot. As in the case of statutory auditors the management of the company, getting itself credit- rated, pays the credit-rating agency, whereas the rating is for the benefit of the investors. This often effects the independence and judgement of the agency. It is necessary that proper regulatory mechanisms are evolved by the RBI and SEBI to ensure that credit rating agencies do not let down the investors.

The issue of excessive salaries in the corporate sector is becoming as relevant in India as in some other countries. Dhirubhai Ambani of RIL, drew a salary of Rs.8.85 crores per annum in 2000-2001 (73.87%) increment over the previous year), followed by his two sons Mukhesh and Anil with Rs.7.13 crores each. Wipro's Ajay Premji's salary of Rs.4.28 crores was 130.8% higher than what he took home over the previous year. India now funds it millionaires and billionaires as proudly as US. The only difference is that India is poor country inhabited by rich people.

Measures–World Scenario

In order to improve the quality of Corporate Governance in publicly held companies, the following measures place a great deal of accountability squarely on the shoulders of CEOs of these companies in the global corporate sector.

1. Establishment of a Board of Accounting – Establishes the public company accounting oversight board to oversee the audit of public companies that are subject to the securities loss and to see audit report standards and rules and inspect, investigate and enforce compliance on the part of registered public accounting firms, their associated persons, and certified public accountants.
2. *Auditor Independence*– To prohibit an auditor for performing specified non-audit services contemporaneously with an audit (Auditor independence) requires pre-approval by the audit committee of the issuer for those non-audit services that are not expressly forbidden.
3. *Corporate responsibility*– confers responsibility upon audit committees of public companies for the appointment, compensation and oversight of any registered public accounting firm employed to perform audit services. Requires an audit committee member to be a member of the Board of Directors of the issuer and to be otherwise independent.
4. *Enhanced financial disclosures*– requires financial reports to reflect all material correcting adjustment that have been identified by a registered public accounting firm in accordance with rules and generally accepted accounting principles.
5. *Analyst conflicts of interests*– It requires to adopt rules governing securities analyst potential conflicts of interests including (i) restricting the pre-publication clearance on approval of research reports by persons either engage in investment banking activities or not directly responsible for investment research. (ii) limiting the supervision and compensatory evaluation of securities analyst to officials who are not engaged in investment banking activities. (iii) Prohibiting a broker and dealer involved with investment banking activities from retaliating against a securities analyst, as a result of unfavourable research report that

may adversely effect investment banking relationship of the broker or dealer with the subject of the research report.

6. *Corporate and criminal fraud accountability*– To impose criminal penalties for (i) knowingly destroying, altering, cancelling or falsifying records with intent to obstruct or influence either a federal investigation or a matter in bankruptcy (ii) auditor failure to maintain for a 5 year period all audit or review work papers pertaining to issuer of securities.

Indian Scenario

Major recommendations of Kumar Mangalam Birla Committee include composition of Board of Directors representations of financial institutions in the Board composition and functions of audit committee, composition of remuneration committee and disclosure of remuneration package, accounting standard and financial reporting of which are detailed as follows :

(a) *Board Committee:* This Committee has recommended a Board with at least 50% independent directors if Chairman is an executive, and alternatively a board with at least 1/3 independent directors if the Chairman is non-executive. For constituting the balance board it is important to constitute a nomination committee which advises the shareholders in the matter of nomination of independent directors. Independent directors or any of their relatives should not have any interest of the company.

(b) Remuneration Committee on the base of Executive compensation. Schedule 12 to the Companies Act suggests maximum ceiling of managerial remuneration with reference to the effective capital in case of companies having no profits or inadequate profits, and as a percent of profit in case of companies having profits. Its main objective is to establish a pay-performance relationship. Accordingly, it is necessary to have a remuneration committee that also has a representation of major lenders. Suggestible compensation norms as follows:

Executive Compensation

Return on shareholders funds	*Managerial remuneration*
Below 15%	Only sustenance salaries commensurate with the salary which is paid to a rank immediately below the position the Executive Directors.
15% – 20%	7.5% of profit after tax.
20% – 25%	10% of PAT
25% - 30%	12.5% of PAT
Above 30%	15% of PAT

(c) *Audit Committee and its role*: This committee has suggested certain other measures for improving efficacy of audit which include–

(i) adoption of a written charter of activities approved by a full board specifying responsibilities of the audit committee.

(ii) Annually public disclosure of activities carried out by the audit committee.

(iii) Authority for audit committee to represent to the shareholders, to propose appointment and replacement of outside auditors. Full authority for audit committee to carry out discussions with auditors with the board ensuring complete independence of outside auditors.

However, this committee has also suggested certain regulations on auditors functions. Such as

(a) The auditors should be appointed by the shareholders in the general meeting on the recommendations of the audit committee.

(b) Time frame for statutory audit to be conducted by the external auditors to be set out while entering into an audit contract i.e. the maximum of 3 years.

(c) There is a need for establishing an independent audit oversight board at the national level to review the quality of audit in the listed companies.

(d) *Accounting Standards* : There is a need for working towards global harmonization of accounting policies. The Kumar Mangalam Birla Committee has talked about the introduction of four accounting standards viz. Consolidated reporting by holding companies, Segmental reporting, Disclosure of related party transactions, and tax effect accounting. Major issues missing from the list of Indian Accounting Standards are–

- Related party disclosures
- Segmental reporting
- Accounting for investment in associates
- Accounting for joint ventures
- Impairment of assets
- Accounting for intangibles
- Financial instruments
- Earnings per share
- Provisions, contingent liabilities and contingent assets
- Tax effect accounting

The classificatory statement must include

Observation of the committee.

Management approach as regards the discussions held by audit committee.

Its observation as regards internal audit.

(e) *Share holders right*: The corporate governance stress on protection of shareholders rights as international capital flow bears a direct relationship with the degree of good corporate governance. Major issues covered are :

- Basic shareholder rights include, the right to secure methods of ownership registration, convey or transfer shares, participate and vote in general shareholder meeting, election of board members, share in the profits of organization.

- They have the right to be sufficiently informed of decisions concerning corporate changes; the authorization of additional shares and extraordinary transactions.
- They are given the opportunity to vote and should be informed of voting procedure, rules etc.
- Markets for corporate control should be allowed to function in an efficient & transparent manner.
- All shareholders of the same class should be treated equally.
- In side training & abusive self-dealing is prohibited.
- Members of the board & managers should be required to disclose any material interests in transactions or matters affecting the corporation.

Board Committee: 'Independent director' is defined as director who apart from receiving director's remuneration does not have any material pecuniary relationship or transactions with the company, its promoters, its management which in the judgement of the board may affect his independence.

Nomination Committee : Advises the shareholders in the matter of electing independent directors. The report of the nomination should be placed in the meeting of the committee.

Remuneration Committee : To establish a pay-performance relationship. Increasingly the formula for executive compensation on plan takes the synthesis of a fixed element linked to turnover, assets, capital or profit and stock option schemes.

(f) *Disclosure & Transparency:* Corporate governance frame work should ensure that timely and accurate disclosure is made on all material matters regarding the corporation and governance of the company. Important disclosures should include–

- Financial and operating results of the company
- Company objectives
- Major share ownership & voting rights
- Members of board, key executives & their remuneration

- Materials issues regarding employees & other stakeholders
- Governance structures.

In a developing country like India, an important objective of corporate governance should be to ensure proper utilization of the scarce capital and thus deployment of capital should never be a basis of executive compensation corporate governance encompasses the entire mechanics of functioning of a company and attempts to put in place a system of checks and balances between shareholders, directors, auditors and management.

Since companies raise billions of rupees from the public in the form of equity and debenture capital, the department should establish a vigilance wing to exclusively book the corporate culprits of the vanishing companies and make them severely penalized. If the above step is not viable, at the stock exchanges should be empowered to prosecute the erring issuers. SEBIs regulation of accounting standard with a comparison to international accounting standard would bring transparency in financial reporting. SEBI can tighten the norms on disclosure practices and adopt more transparency in offer documents. The information provided in the offer document should be fair and true and should facilitate the potential investors to take decisions with rationale on their investment. The consumer courts help in saving the investors in certain matters from the cruel hands of miscreants who mismanage their funds. After the Supreme Court's decision in Morgan Stanley case, they have stopped accepting complaints from affected investors. The end purpose of corporate governance must be to maximize a company's value. It has now been realized that the financial value depicts merely a small percentage of the total value. The value of human capital and natural capital is infinitely more than the value of finance capital. The true purpose of corporate governance is to maximize creation of company's total value.

Conclusion

Corporate Governance is essential for corporate success. Specific issues, which are significant, are, building accountability within the organization, service management, performance appraisal, sanctions and incentives removing constraints for reforms etc.

14

CORPORATE FRAUDS
A MODEL FOR GOOD GOVERNANCE

Ch. H.K.S. Kumar* and **Dr. Talluru Sreenivas****

The concern for effective governance of the corporate world has been intensified because of the types of impact that corporate (or financial) frauds create on all the concerned segments of the society, more directly in the form of capital invested, loss of employment to thousands of people right from the CEOs to the last rung worker, reduction in the confidence levels of the investing public in corporate enterprise, restatement of corporate profit figures for the last few years by the companies involved, all resulting in low levels of economic activity at the macro level, throwing nations into some type of a recession. As a consequence of the financial frauds in the Corporate World, in which accounting firms of international repute have played a prominent role, the credibility of the accounting profession all over the world is at stake now. The professional institutes of Accountants in various countries have started addressing themselves as to how best to restore the respect, trust and confidence of the investing public in the accounting and auditing profession. Against this background, the paper aims to discuss the role of different parties who are having direct or indirect relationship with Corporate Governance along with the influencing factors and tries to develop a model for good Governance.

* Lecturer in Management, Al Habeeb College of Engineering & Technology, Chevella, Hyderabad.

** Reader, Department of Management Sciences, R.V.R.& J.C.College of Engineering, Guntur-522 019, A.P.

Introduction

The type of corporate frauds that have been unearthed from out of the Boardrooms of the Corporate World and have been reported of late in the Financial Press, involving such giants as the Enron Corporation, the biggest private sector energy company in the World and the one once ranked 7th in the Fortune 500 companies, World Com Inc., the second largest long distance telecom major in the United States, which has to file bankruptcy petitions, Xerox Corporation, Merck & Co., Global Crossing Ltd., Quest Communications International Inc., among others, have once again brought the need for good Corporate Governance to the centre court for discussion among all the concerned – the academia, National Governments, the Regulatory Bodies of the corporate world, the Professional Accounting Institutions and the investing public at large.

Such scandals are no longer the sole prerogative of a country like the USA. Economic liberalization and globalization which facilitate easy and quick transmission of market intelligence and information across the geographical boarders of the nation states, has caused American Business Practices, both good and bad, to spread across the world, including our own country at the speed of thought. The temptations for financial frauds in developing countries like India with imperfect capital markets and inadequate Corporate Governance are perhaps much greater. The unauthorized payments allegedly to have been paid to Indian Government officials by Xerox Mode Corporation is one recent example that bears enough testimony in this regard. There are also clear instances from the Indian Corporate Sector, where Corporate CEOs draw huge emoluments mostly in the form of commission earned on the earnings made which is many more times higher than their annual salary. For example, out of Rs.9.85 crores drawn by the Chairman of Dr.Reddy's Labs for the year 2001-2002, Rs.9.64 crores is in the form of commission alone, leaving the remaining Rs.21.00 lakhs drawn towards annual salary and perquisites. The Chairman of the Hero Honda Motors earned Rs.7.57 crores during 2001-02 inclusive of commission of Rs.7.24 crores from net profits of the company.

In 2000-01, the late Dhirubhai Ambani of the Reliance fame, earned Rs.8.85 crores, while his two sons, Mr.Mukhesh and Mr.Anil were paid Rs.7.13 crores each inclusive mostly of commission on profits made and perks. A number of similar cases exist in the corporate history of our country. No doubt these huge emoluments made to the CEOs referred to here do not certainly suggest fraudulent methods followed by them. They only suggest that there might be a remote possibility of inflating profits of the companies managed by unscrupulous top managements to maximize the personal benefits in the form of huge commissions earned.

One of the primary motives of the past of the corporate managements for indulging in fraudulent methods is their strong laser-focus on current Earnings Per Share (EPS) and persistent desire to maintain the same earnings performance on quarter-to-quarter basis and also high prices on the Stock Market. Issue of Stock Options by companies based on high profits that form major component of pay packages of managers and employees in the corporate world has become a temptation for financial frauds. Further, since bonuses awarded to top corporate executives are directly linked to stock prices, there is an added attraction on the part of company managements to jack up stock prices, by hook or crook, through such fraudulent accounting methodologies as off-the Balance Sheet dealings, capitalizing revenue expenditure, non-expensing the stock options issued towards employee compensation, among other strategies. Obviously all this is done by company management with the help of or connivance of the accounting firms (such as Arthur Andersen) for the purpose of artificially boosting up the stock prices for making personal gain, even while suppressing the impending financial crises in the companies leading to a fall in stock prices later.

The corporate regulatory bodies like the Securities Exchange Commission in the US (SEC), the Securities Exchange Board of India (SEBI), the Department of Company Affairs in our country (DCA) and similar bodies across the world have also started looking for proper and more significant measures for effective governance of the corporate sector.

Corporate Governance

Corporate Governance is said to be a system by which companies are directed and properly controlled, making managements accountable to the shareholders of the companies with adequate concern for ethics and values. Good Corporate Governance involves transparency, accountability, investor protection, better compliance with statutory laws and regulations, value creation for shareholders. It helps in establishing a climate of trust and confidence among the stakeholders of the corporations.

Strictly speaking, Good Corporate Governance practices are much wider than mere transparency, disclosure and compliance. It calls for a paradigm shift in the role of the Board and Corporate Directors.

Thus, Corporate Governance is the overall control of activities in a corporation. It is concerned with the formulation of long-term objectives and plans and the proper management structure (organization, systems and people) to achieve them. At the same time, it entails making sure that the structure functions to maintain the corporation's integrity and responsibility to its various constituencies. The structure to ensure Corporate Governance, for our purpose, includes the Board of Directors, top management, shareholders, creditors and others. Role of each of these stakeholders is crucial in guaranteeing responsible corporate performance.

Scope of Corporate Governance

Corporate Governance is generally viewed from the standpoint of shareholders interests. Though this perspective is legitimate and important, another perspective that deserves attention is that of Economic Development, especially in the context of the East Asian Economic Crisis. From the development perspective, good governance is key to effective management of scarce capital resources, more so in developing countries. In the Indian context, the levels of transparency and standard of disclosure observed by the corporate sector leave much to be desired. The absence of transparent and accountable Corporate Governance shields the management against the discipline of market forces. Corporate Governance is a means of overcoming this problem as it seeks to minimize the malpractices by companies by establishing a system where more information about the transactions of the companies or decisions taken by the management are available to shareholders and public. In response to the Asian crisis, the World Bank is assisting countries in strengthening Corporate Governance. The World Bank, as a member of the OECD's task force on Corporate Governance, is bringing out voluntary guidelines and principles for improving Corporate Governance. The preliminary draft report comprises five principles on which Corporate Governance should be based. They are :

- Protect shareholders rights;
- Equitable treatment of all shareholders;
- Recognition of rights of stakeholders in creating wealth and jobs;
- Disclosure of timely and accurate information on matters regarding the financial situation and performance; and
- Strategic guidance and effective monitoring of the company by the Board, and Board's accountability to the company and shareholders.

Influencing Elements

Four factors influence Corporate Governance, namely (i) the ownership structure of a corporate, (ii) its financial structure, (iii) the structure and functioning of the company boards, and (iv) the legal, political and regulatory environment within which the company operates.

(a) *The Ownership Structure:* The structure of ownership of a company determines, to a considerable extent, how a corporation is managed and controlled. The ownership structure can be either dispersed among individuals and institutional shareholders as in the US and UK or can be concentrated in the hands of a large number of shareholders as in Germany and Japan. But the pattern varies across the globe. Our corporate sector is characterized by the coexistence of state owned, private and multinational enterprises. The shares of these enterprises (except those belonging to the public sector) are held by institutional as well as small investors. Specifically, shares are held by (1) the term lending institutions; (2) institutional investors, comprising government owned mutual funds, Unit Trust of India and the government owned insurance corporations; (3) corporate bodies; (4) Directors and their relatives; and (5) foreign investors. Apart from these block-holdings, there is a sizeable equity holding by small investors.

(b) *The Structure of Company Boards:* The Board of Directors is responsible for establishing corporate objectives, developing Board policies and selecting top level executives to carry out those objectives and policies. The Board reviews management's performance to ensure that the company is run well and shareholders are protected. Company Boards are permitted to vary in size, composition and structure so as to best serve the interests of the corporation and the shareholders.

(c) *The Financial Structure:* Proportion between debt and equity, has implications for the quality of governance. Contrary to the Modigliani-Miller hypothesis that the financial structure of the firm has no relationship to the value of a firm, recent research has shown that the financial structure does matter. It is no secret that the lenders exercise significant influence on the way a company is managed and controlled. Bank as creditors, for example, can perform the important function of screening and monitoring companies as they (banks) are better informed than other investors. Further, banks can diminish short-term biases in managerial decision making by favouring investments that would generate higher benefits in the long run.

(d) *The Institutional Environment:* The legal, regulatory, and political environment within which a company operates determines in large measure the quality of Corporate Governance. For example, the extent to which shareholders can control the management depends on their voting rights as defined in company law, the extent to which creditors will be able to exercise financial claims on a bankrupt unit will depend on bankruptcy laws and procedures; and the extent to which the market for corporate efficiency operates to discipline underperforming management will depend on takeover regulations.

A Model for Good Corporate Governance

The task of improving Corporate Governance does not fall on companies alone. New standards must also be supported by legal and regulatory frameworks and administrative systems. A beginning in this direction has been made by the Government of India through legislative framework by introducing in December 1999 the Companies (Second Amendment) Bill, 1999.

The Government has also hiked the penalties for various defaults ten times. Also, to ensure better Corporate Governance, the number of companies in which a person could be a Director has been brought down to Fifteen from Twenty.

Regulatory controls can play an important role in ensuring good governance in companies. The effectiveness of these controls depends on the extent to which the companies can depend upon the advice and guidance of qualified professional secretaries who have extensive knowledge of law, finance, administration and management and who operate under strict codes of professional ethics. There seems to be a dichotomy between regulatory controls and professional ethics that needs to be removed. Effective Corporate Governance is possible only if it is realized that it is not regulatory control versus professional ethics, rather it is regulatory control supported by professional ethics.

Some of the key elements for improved Corporate Governance are:

- Distinction between powers of the full Board and those of the CEO;
- Well-defined role of Non-Executive Directors;
- Access of information about the company to Directors;
- Board's active involvement in important matters.
- Ensuring proper match of resources to needs; and
- Proper system of accountability and control

As mentioned earlier, Corporate Governance depends on the contributions of the Board of Directors, Non-Executive Directors, institutional investors and the Audit Committee. Each of these has been explained below.

Role of Board of Directors : One of the most critical functions of the Board is to provide a framework of values in which the activities of the company can be carried out. Thus, the Board is required to provide the direction to the company. The next important function is to develop and monitor plans for the company. The Board should be able to guide the management team on how to develop a strategic plan and also take the responsibility of monitoring and evaluating the outcomes of these plans. Since the Board is a policy making body, it should be a balanced Board, i.e., a Board having a proper proportion of different categories of Directors. It should be an expert body capable of not only guiding the management but also overseeing the operations so as to sub-serve larger interests of those connected with the company. The type of guidance to be provided by the Board will depend on the state of financial health of the company. In the case of the companies that are doing well the Board could provide guidance for consolidation and further growth, whereas in the case of companies that are not doing well it could be in the nature of policies towards corrective action. The role of the Board should support the CEO as long as he is working in the interest of the company and its shareholders. In case this is not so, the Board should intervene. To bring about better Corporate Governance the Board should be the conscience keeper of the company's vision and mission. It should focus more on ethical conduct of business and upholding corporate values. Another important function of the Board is to safeguard the company's assets – financial, physical and intellectual. Thus, the role of the Board and top management in the future will predominantly be that of providing intellectual leadership. Boards have duel responsibility. They need to educate and empower the management, at the same time they also have to be active in their monitoring role. The major function of the Board is, therefore, to provide direction and long-term strategy, evaluate management performance, evaluate current performance and follow ethical and legal practices. To be able to contribute towards the Board activity Directors are required to have knowledge about contemporary issues of the business environment, specific company related knowledge and company specific knowledge.

The size, nature and composition of the Board would depend on the size of the company and the complexity of the business the company is in. With regard to the size of the Board, Lipton and Loesch have done an analysis of the functioning of Boards and they are of the view that as the size of the Board increases, it becomes less effective because the advantages of wider participation get marginalized by the problems of coordination. Hence, they have suggested that the size of the Board be limited to seven. In the Indian context, this seems to be particularly relevant because of the large number of companies and the dearth of competent and qualified Directors.

The challenges for the future Boards will be to focus less on monitoring internal procedures and more on supporting, enabling and building external relationships and ensuring that the organization adapts well to changes. With the emergence of network and virtual corporations, the new Boards will have to adopt different mechanisms of governance. The Board should be responsible for ensuring the Four Ps (Purpose, Principles, Practices and Performance Measurement) in the functioning of companies.

The Role of Non-Executive Directors: Non-Executive Directors can provide an independent judgement on the issues of strategy and performance including key appointments and standards of conduct. The Non-Executive Directors need to play a very crucial role in terms of evolving appropriate performance criteria. The Non-Executive Directors are expected to possess the qualities of independence of mind and thinking and the ability to communicate objectively the alternate points of view.

Non-Executive Directors can provide a constructive and critical supervision of executive management. They should not only react to issues placed before the Board but also take an enlightened interest in strategic business issues. In many companies world over, including a few in India, Non-Executive Directors functioning as members of audit committees are providing constructive advice in improving the standards of Corporate Governance.

For the Non-Executive Directors to be able to improve their contribution towards Corporate Governance in their companies they should have access to all important and relevant information about the company. This information should include comprehensive monthly performance reviews, annual (and monthly) operating plans, and long range plans relating to capital expenditure, manpower, product composition, future expansions and diversifications, etc.

Role of Institutional Investors: Until recently financial institutions were passive investors and lenders. But this is changing. As more of these institutions are increasingly relying on stock and debt markets for funds they are becoming more concerned about the companies, mainly to protect their own interests. In addition to safeguarding their own interests institutional investors can play a significant role in proactive manner and thus contribute towards Corporate Governance by appointing nominee Directors taking advantage of the large reservoir of professionals like Company Secretaries and others available in the country. These Company Secretaries would be in a better position to function as independent professional Directors on behalf of the Financial Institutions and serve as experts in the decision making process. Secondly, institutional investors with their increasing equity ownership as against individual shareholders can contribute towards Corporate Governance in the following ways:

- The financial institutions through their representatives on the Board of companies can act as intermediaries to resolve the disputes between management and dominant shareholders group and help to minimize the differences in opinion by clarifying issues and hidden agenda.
- They can also act as the 'watch dog' and 'whistle blower' to ensure that investments proposed by the management are critically examined at the planning stage itself.

Financial institutions need to act as the real owners of corporations rather than as lenders and take a long-term perspective. Towards this end, financial institutions should encourage competition between Indian and foreign companies. Promoters who have a good track record should be supported by financial institutions. They should be willing to lend to companies to help them raise finance to buyback their shares.

Role of Audit Committees : Auditors of the companies play an important role in Corporate Governance. They provide an objective check on the reliability and fairness of the financial statements prepared by the companies. The effectiveness of the Audit Committee will depend on the competence, commitment and independence of its members as also on its terms of reference, access of information and availability of resources.

Conclusion

The financial frauds in developing countries like India are becoming so common because of imperfect capital markets, and inadequate Corporate Governance. As a consequence of these financial frauds, accounting firms of international repute have started addressing themselves as to how best to restore the respect, trust and confidence of the investing public. Obviously, the concern for Corporate Governance has been intensified. The Indian model of Corporate Governance should be based on how capital is raised here. Good Corporate Governance can be ensured only through self management based on core values of being responsible corporate citizens. Structures and systems can only serve the purpose of providing guidelines and regulatory authorities can provide supervision within this broad framework.

SECTION–II
HUMAN RESOURCE MANAGEMENT

15

DEVELOPMENT OF TECHNICAL ENTREPRENEURSHIP

Dr. D. Nagayya*

The paper reviews (a) the major findings and recommendations of select research studies covering technical entrepreneurship, (b) the activities of the National Science and Technology Entrepreneurship Development Board (NSTEDB) of the Department of Science and Technology (DST), (c) progress of Science and Technology Entrepreneurs Parks (STEPs), and (d) strategic alliance of National Small Industries Corporation (NSIC), Council of Scientific and Industrial Research (CSIR), and Asia – Pacific Centre for Transfer of Technology (APCTT) for technology transfer and technological upgradation. In the concluding part, it presents the challenges of the present and future scenarios of the small scale sector in the context of liberalisation, privatisation and globalisation, and the role of various agencies associated with the promotion of small enterprises, including technology-intensive firms.

Introduction

When we refer to science and technology (S&T) persons in the context of entrepreneurship development for small enterprises, we are referring to the entire institutional frame available for the small scale sector at national and state levels. Organisations under the Ministry of Industry at the national level and those created at the state level cater to all categories of entrepreneurs interested in setting

---

* Consultant on Small Enterprises at Guntur; and former Director(Industrial Development), National Institute of Small Industry Extension Training (NISIET), Hyderabad.

up of small enterprises. These include S&T entrepreneurs as well. Under the Ministry of Industry, National Entrepreneurship Development Board (NEDB) is overseeing the programmes of entrepreneurship development under the overall guidance of Development Commissioner (Small Scale Industries). There are organisations under the Ministry of Human Resource Development (HRD) and other ministries involved in encouraging entrepreneurship development efforts. A whole range of support services created at the state level for helping existing and prospective entrepreneurs are functioning all over the country. Involvement of banks and other financial institutions at the apex and field level in supporting entrepreneurship among existing and prospective entrepreneurs is of a high order. For providing special thrust and encouragement to the first generation S&T background entrepreneurs, the DST at the national level has taken the initiative in creating National Science and Technology Entrepreneurship Development Board (NSTEDB) in 1982, and through it launched a number of programmes all over the country. Role and responsibility of technical education institutes in innovation and entrepreneurship for creating a techno- entrepreneurial society has been the main direction of efforts of DST and Ministry of HRD.

Findings and Recommendations of Select Research Studies

Researches point out that firms set up by technical entrepreneurs have a high level of multiplier effect on other industries and activities, in terms of jobs created, incomes generated, technical advancement made, in promoting a new work culture, and quality and sophistication of the products.

A number of studies have been carried out in the country on the profiles of S&T entrepreneurs and strategies for promoting these entrepreneurs. At Shri Guru Gobind Singhji College of Engineering and Technology, Nanded (Maharashtra), S.P. Kallurkar submitted his doctoral dissertation to the National Institute for Training in Industrial Engineering (NITIE), Mumbai in 1993 on Underlying Factors for the Success of S&T Entrepreneurs in Marathwada Region of Maharashtra. This is being followed up at the College by a project – Utilisation of Oriental Techniques for the Development of Enterprising Pesonalities – under the sponsorship of the Ministry of Human Resource

Development. As per Kallurkar's study, the characteristics and attributes of technical entrepreneurs as revealed in the study of Marathwada region brought out through factor analysis of 52 variables based on responses gathered from S&T entrepreneurs and support organisation personnel, are as follows:

(i) Well rounded professional core

(ii) Nerve power (strong focus)

(iii) Entra-managerial qualities

(iv) Outward looking (open minded to change)

(v) Need for autonomy

(vi) Tenacity

(vii) Scientific vision

(viii) Leadership quality

(ix) Innovativeness

(x) Positive thinking

(xi) Risk taking ability

(xii) Legitimate action oriented.

The present study on oriental techniques focuses on the following issues and plans to evolve a training module for adoption in entrepreneurship development programmes utilising the oriental philosophy.

(i) How to inculcate ethical approach amongst prospective and existing entrepreneurs?

(ii) How to develop qualities like nerve power in its true sense so as to reduce the infant mortality rate among small scale entrepreneurs?

(iii) How to develop qualities like innovativeness?

(iv) How to bring in the transformation in one's personality and character so as to suit the demand of the profession and in the interest of the society at large?

(v) How to reduce one's perplexity?

For developing enterprising personalities, the methods based on oriental approach covering a combination of knowledge and duty paths are planned to be developed and tested with different sets of prospective and existing entrepreneurs.

D. Nagayya in the study of S&T entrepreneurs in Marathwada region as part of his doctoral dissertation on Effectiveness of Industrial Estates – a locational comparison submitted to the University of Rajasthan in 1984, delineated the attributes and choices of S&T entrepreneurs as follows:

(i) S &T entrepreneurs select products based on inter-firm relationship including industrial services, parts, components and sub-assemblies, involving specialised skills.

(ii) They adopt flexible specialisation strategies when the market position undergoes change, i.e., ability to adapt to changing environment by manufacturing allied products for which the machinery is found suitable with certain modifications.

(iii) Capital intensity of the firm is high; however, capacity utilisation of the plant tends to be low.

(iv) They are mobile; are keen on moving to places which offer greater opportunities; and are not tied down to places of nativity or nearby centres alone.

(v) They are progressive in the selection of the product line – very often high value added, high risk, innovative products/ processes are selected.

(vi) They move to industrial areas where opportunities for growth are likely to be high because of cluster development of small and large firms, and availability of more space for the expansion of the firms.

(vii) They are venturesome to obtain raw material from distant places; sell their products at distant markets, and locate the plants at places which offer potential for further development.

(viii) Their reliance on technical and managerial counseling services is high and dependency on high level of financial support is also noticed. Need is felt for mobilising resources for equity and venture capital support. Escort services need to be of a high order to encourage a technocrat entrepreneur to move forward briskly with his plans for starting an innovative enterprise.

D. Nagayya et al. of the National Institute of Small Industry Extension Training (NISIET), Hyderabad in their study on *Industrial Development of Madhya Pradesh : Status and Opportunities*, with focus on technology transfer from R&D institutions to the small scale sector in Madhya Pradesh, covered a number of S&T entrepreneurs who received know-how from national R&D organisations, in particular CSIR laboratories. For the study published by NISIET in 1990, field survey was carried out in 1987. The project and the publication were funded by DST. The study brought out experiences of entrepreneurs who received know-how from national laboratories, and suggested an action strategy for transfer of technologies from R&D institutions. Out of 130 small scale entrepreneurs from Madhya Pradesh who received 74 NRDC processes from 15 CSIR laboratories during 1972 to early 1987, only 40 units were in production, 17 were at various stages of implementation, 11 were not working, 12 were not traceable, 36 received know-how only less than a year ago, and 14 abandoned the envisaged lines of manufacture and switched over to other products. Thus only 31 per cent of the units went into production in a span of nearly 15 years. Major part of the technology transfer was effected during 1985 and 1986 through the special efforts of the CSIR Polytechnology Transfer Centre (PTC) at Bhopal and the Madhya Pradesh Consultancy Organisation in releasing processes particularly in Mandideep industrial area (Raisen district) close to Bhopal. This speaks of the strong need for backup support and provision of escort services to entrepreneurs in a sustained manner.

Some of the problems faced by entrepreneurs who effected technology transfer are as follows:

(i) Inadequate technical support from the laboratory and non-involvement of the laboratory over a substantial period when the support was actually felt

(ii) Delay on the part of National Research Development Corporation (NRDC) in completing the preparatory steps for releasing the processes

(iii) Lack of marketing guidance and support

(iv) Delay in sanction of loans by the State Financial Corporation

(v) Need for providing managerial guidance and entrepreneurial training

(vi) Non-involvement of agencies at the state level as a package deal for providing support and escort services when processes were released, in the absence of a formal institutional arrangement with the national laboratories

(vii) Inadequacy of raw materials supplied through controlled or institutional sources

(viii) Disputes among partners

(ix) Lack of seriousness among entrepreneurs right from the stage of product selection, and while carrying out preparatory work to ask for necessary assistance from various agencies.

In the action strategy suggested, key aspects covered are as follows:

(i) Role of R&D organisations and tie-up with state level agencies: Up-to-date account of the state of exploitation of the processes and firms which commercialised the know-how earlier, will facilitate entrepreneurs visiting a few of the existing units on product lines of their interest. After the release of the know-how, the laboratory concerned may consider providing project consultancy, engineering design and managerial consultancy services to the extent practicable and these need to be supplemented, wherever necessary, by a reputed consultancy organisation. For managerial counseling and escort services, the laboratory should enter into a tie-up arrangement with a state level institution. It is important to ensure continuity of these services at the project formulation and implementation stages, and for a few years after the unit goes into production.

A technology task force may be created at the state level to oversee technology transfer and provide guidance to entrepreneurs. Polytechnology Transfer Centre, Small Industries Service Institute and Technical Consultancy Organisation should take the lead in this direction and involve technical institutions such as engineering colleges, polytechnics and R&D organisations located nearby.

(ii) Incentives : Venture capital scheme and equity participation : Liberal venture capital scheme provisions need to be evolved for meeting the risks of projects promoted by entrepreneurs with professional background and experience who take up unproven innovative projects. Equity participation and provision of seed capital is another direction of support needed by S&T entrepreneurs.

(iii) Promotional efforts, infrastructural support and comprehensive package of entrepreneurship development programmes.

Vinayshil Gautam of the Department of Management Studies of the Indian Institute of Technology, New Delhi, in his study of *Design and Development of a Science and Technology-based Entrepreneurial Index* (1992) brought out a variety of aspects covering S&T entrepreneurs. The project was supported by DST. A few of the salient findings are recalled here.

(i) Perseverance and hard work is considered as the most important factor contributing to success.

(ii) Good education and academic background are considered a prerequisite to launch on technology-intensive firms.

(iii) Good contacts and good marketing skills are seen as extremely relevant for success.

(iv) The importance of sound financial planning, high level of supervision and adequacy of funds is also stressed.

(v) A successful entrepreneur is a very socially conscious person, who desires to contribute to the society at large. A strong social orientation is an important aspect of the entrepreneurial personality.

(vi) Relevant work experience provides the entrepreneur with sufficient confidence on his technological capabilities to be able to go ahead with the project on his own.

(vii) Most entrepreneurs had to develop their own technologies or adapt to their needs on the basis of their technical knowledge.

(viii) The average start-up time is over a year, about 16 months.

(ix) Marketing of products was seen as a major problem. Major obstacles to starting a venture were noticed to be bureaucracy and red tapism.

Involvement of DST in promoting S&T Entrepreneurship

Among the numerous initiatives taken by the Department of Science and Technology, Government of India, a few prominent ones are reviewed in this section. With the establishment of National Science and Technology Entrepreneurship Development Board (NSTEDB) in 1982 for fostering entrepreneurship among persons with S&T background, employment generation through entrepreneurship development has been an important direction for the application of science and technology by encouraging innovative methods, techniques and equipment, and support through information and trained S&T manpower.

NSTEDB has been sponsoring Entrepreneurship Awareness camps, Entrepreneurship Development Programmes (EDPs) of 6 to 8 weeks duration, supporting ED cells in engineering colleges, and organising faculty development programmes of 2 to 3 weeks duration, promotion of Science and Technology Entrepreneurs Parks (STEPs) from 1984, and Science and Technology Entrepreneurship Development (STED) project at district level in 12 backward districts from 1985. For all these activities, at the state level, State Council / Committee on Science and Technology is given the stimulatory and monitoring role.

Under STED project, activities initiated at the district level include preparation of resource inventories for identifying and documenting specific entrepreneurial opportunities based on local resources, skills, demand and location-specific, and matching them with prospective entrepreneurs, preparation of thematic resource maps, generation of entrepreneurial opportunities, identifying prospective entrepreneurs, dissemination of information, organisation of skill development programmes, and EDPs.

To take up the needs of persons with S&T background, open learning programme in entrepreneurship (OLPE) was initiated in 1995 as a joint programme of NSTEDB and Entrepreneurship Development Institute of India (EDI I), Ahmedabad. The programme aims at spreading awareness about entrepreneurship at a faster pace and covers a large number of beneficiaries in a short span of time. The programme consisting of two modules, namely (i) knowledge development & (ii) skill development, is spread over a period of 11 months. While the methodology followed in knowledge development is that of distance education, the skill development is achieved through contact programme by identified counselors from the respective regions. Gujarat, Maharashtra and Karnataka have been covered initially. Madhya Pradesh and Uttar Pradesh are planned to be covered next. It is proposed to extend this programme to other regions in a phased manner. Efforts are underway to use local languages as the medium of instruction.

Another important direction in distance learning education in entrepreneurship development is the lead taken by Development Education (International) Society in Pune, established in 1987. The Pune institute has been popularising entrepreneurship training through mass media such as radio / television / video / audio programmes. Madhya Pradesh, Maharashtra, Orissa and Uttar Pradesh have been covered so far. SIDBI has supported this Society in conducting the programmes in local languages in a few states, and also in producing video cassettes on various aspects of entrepreneurship development. Another direction in which SIDBI supported this society is on 'Poverty Alleviation and Prevention through Enterprise Development in India'. The project which started in 2002-03, would cover the states of Uttar Pradesh, Madhya Pradesh, Maharashtra, Orissa and Assam. Under the project, non-credit, media & field programme-based training inputs would be provided to target groups such as people below the poverty line, underprivileged and disadvantaged women, and school going children.

Response from the listeners has indeed been quite positive. It is catching up fast.

Science & Technology Entrepreneurs Parks (STEPs)

The main objective of STEP is to provide the missing links between University, Research and Industry on the one hand, and promotion of innovation-based entrepreneurship on the other. The programme jointly launched by the NSTEDB and the all-India financial institutions, envisages the establishment of STEPs in and around academic institutions of excellence. Thirteen STEPs are functioning in eight states, and they are at various stages of development. These are at Ranchi in Jharkhand; Mysore and Suratkal in Karnataka; Bhopal in Madhya Pradesh; Mumbai and Pune in Maharashtra; Ludhiana and Patiala in Punjab; Coimbatore and Tiruchirapalli in Tamil Nadu; Kanpur and Roorkee in Uttar Pradesh; and Kharagpur in West Bengal. STEPs at Coimbatore and Patiala have been recently established. The STEPs have formed themselves into an all India association of STEPs.

STEP envisages promotion of self-employment avenues for unemployed and under-employed scientists and technologists by fostering a research-industry culture, nurturing innovative ideas and inculcating an enterprising spirit among prospective entrepreneurs through industry-institution linkage. STEP creates a number of facilities for prospective as well as existing entrepreneurs. These include nursery sheds, testing and calibration facilities, precision tool room / workshop, prototype development, business facilitation, business incubation centre, computing, library and documentation, data bank / communication, seminar hall / conference room and other common facilities such as fax, telex, telephone, etc. The park will function as a nursery for entrepreneurs, who will under the guidance of experts, make feasible projects for setting up industries and gain confidence in managing industrial units.

STEP, promoted by an engineering / technology institute or one or more departments of a university, and constituted as an autonomous body, can cater to one group of industries or multiple product lines belonging to different industry groups. Activities envisaged are training of prospective entrepreneurs, nursing them, guiding them in the preparation of feasibility studies, liaisoning with various agencies including financial institutions, undertaking R&D work for development and upscaling of new products and processes, and providing facilities for quality control and certification. Nursing period visualised is 3 years by which time entrepreneurs are expected to move out to transplantation sheds. Subsequently when they set up industrial units, they are encouraged to avail of the facilities and consultancy services available at STEP. Industrial houses located in the state are invited to establish their R&D wings in STEP, apart from national laboratories putting up upscaling and demonstration plants in STEP, for popularising the commercial viability of processes developed by the laboratories.

13 STEPs have formed themselves into an association - Indian Association of Science and Technology Entrepreneurs Parks (ISTEPA) - with headquarters at STEP, Roorkee. Annual / biennial conferences have been taking place. Expert advisory committee on STEPs chaired by R. Rajamani submitted its report to the DST in 1991. The Committee reinforced the view that STEPs have fulfilled the main objectives for which they have been established, and have been proved useful in promoting a new breed of entrepreneurship in the country. Progress in half of the STEPs has been quite encouraging, though in others progress has been slow. While recommending that the Government of India should continue to extend support for this programme, the Committee felt that the period for which support needs to be given in each location is based on the host institution which should get financial support from other promoters, namely, State Government and all-India Financial Institutions. The programme should be basically viewed as promotional, in the opinion of the Committee.

While STEPs in India are devoted to grooming, training, launching, supporting and encouraging small scale entrepreneurs belonging to the S&T spectrum, the Science Parks, Research Parks, etc. in advanced countries are engaged in providing facilities to existing entrepreneurs for launching enterprises, similar to the industrial estates programme of India. Some of the locations, where STEPs have performed well, have demonstrated that the success of STEP model is largely dependent upon the energy, enthusiasm, dynamism and tenacity of the STEP director, combined with the excellent support from the parent (host) institution. The success rate of EDPs conducted by STEPs has been much higher compared to those conducted by other organisations. Support provided by STEPs to entrepreneurs has been of a high order. However, entrepreneurs who have set up units in the nursery sheds have not shown the inclination to move out to regular industrial estates. STEPs have not been able to earn income in any significant manner through royalties, rentals, technology transfer and other avenues open to them. Performance of many STEPs in this direction has been moderate. Future efforts should be directed at making the less active STEPs become aggressive in their efforts and make more institutions take up models developed by the successful STEPs in other parts of the country.

Some of the questions to be researched on the role of STEPs in entrepreneurship development are listed here.

(i) Analysis of the impact of the systems approach adopted by STEPs for promoting entrepreneurship development.

(ii) Development of revenue earning centralised services and impact on new and existing industrial units. In what ways can the performance be improved?

(iii) If the existing entrepreneurs in the nursery sheds have not moved out, what can be the future alternatives? When more and more new entrepreneurs are entering the field under the umbrella of STEP, infrastructure facilities need to be created on a priority basis to STEP-promoted entrepreneurs in other locations.

(iv) Study of the linkages promoted by STEPs – in what directions can these be strengthened? Industrial houses and R&D institutions could be encouraged to utilise STEP premises for locating their establishments, and provide support to new entrepreneurs.

(v) Development of the profile of S&T entrepreneurs, and experiences of enterprises promoted by them, and the multiplier effects of these units on the region.

Strategic Alliance of NSIC, CSIR and APCTT for Technology Transfer and Technological Upgradation in the Small Scale Sector

National Small Industries Corporation (NSIC) has been active in the field of small industries in a variety of directions. It has helped small units in identification, adoption, adaptation, absorption and transfer of technology, entrepreneurial and technical training, common production facilities, marketing and financial support. NSIC has also in the recent years provided assistance in technology sourcing and acquisition to the small scale sector. It has set up a technology transfer centre (TTC) in July 1995 in its premises at New Delhl. TTC aims at assisting small units in strengthening their technological capabilities through dissemination of information on technologies available for transfer from national and international sources. TTC also acts as a facilitating institution and provides face to face contact between enterprises in India and the developed countries. Council of Scientific and Industrial Research (CSIR) is an important technology generating network in the country with a strong delivery system, and has a lot of S&T inputs to offer to the small scale sector. Processes developed by the CSIR laboratories are released for commercial exploitation by the National Research Development Corporation (NRDC), as well as by individual laboratories directly. Technology Utilisation division at CSIR headquarters in New Delhi is concerned with promoting the utilisation of CSIR results and expertise, and securing legal protection for CSIR research results. Asia-Pacific Centre for Transfer of Technology (APCTT) has a comprehensive data bank of information on appropriate technologies in diverse industrial fields with access in the region covered by the Economic and Social Commission for Asia and the Pacific (ESCAP) and elsewhere. It is also linked with the data information base on technologies of the UNIDO (United Nations Industrial Development Organisation). The alliance of these organisations aims at assisting the small scale sector through a single point contact for technology sourcing.

A four-pronged strategy adopted by the alliance in this context is as follows:

(i) Networking of enterprises and flow of information

(ii) Access to advanced technology and assistance in its adoption

(iii) Strong linkages of SSIs with R&D and other facilitating institutions

(iv) Access to finance and ventures capital.

The alliance organised eight technology workshops during July – October 1994 in different cities. The workshops were held at New Delhi, Bangalore, Chennai, Mumbai, Ahmedabad, Indore, Ludhiana and Kolkata to sensitise the small scale units to technology issues, and apprise them of the assistance available through the pooled resources of the three organisations. Some of the energy saving and environmental friendly clean technologies that can be adopted were highlighted. The workshops provided an opportunity for the R&D institutions, enterprises, consultants, technology promotion and transfer agencies to exchange details of transferable technologies as well as sought by SSIs in specific sectors. The technological and financial problems encounted by SSI units in upgradation and modernisation programmes were also discussed.

A number of initiatives are being taken by the consortium and related organisations for following up the recommendations of these workshops. Match making is being organised through Techmart India annually, as part of the India International Trade Fair at New Delhi. The technology offers and technology requests are being sent to relevant agencies within and outside the region to identify matching partners interested in technical cooperation and business collaboration. It is proposed to organise specific business meetings and technology missions to selected countries to facilitate technology transfer negotiations. Some of the problems are being referred to the national R&D organisations for possible assistance in the matter. Integrated approach to assist SSIs in technology-related issues is being evolved in cooperation with other relevant national agencies and financial institutions.

An urgent need is felt to upgrade technology in the small sector, especially in view of the liberalised economy. Large number of SSI units operate at low volume of production and low level of technology. Lack of information and adaptability to international trends is another problem area in this sector. Modernisation and technology upgradation has become critical for the growth and diversification of the sector. The essential ingredients for technology upgradation activities, namely, developing and sourcing of technology and other S&T inputs, rendering financial, infrastructural and physical inputs, and providing data base services from the pooled resources of the NSIC, CSIR and APCTT would be helpful to SSI sector. Industry associations and promotional agencies at the state and district levels should draw upon the new pool of resources for technology transfer and technology upgradation.

Initiatives taken by SIDBI

With a view to encouraging SSI units to modernise their production facilities by acquiring capital equipment embodying advanced technology and technical know-how, acquiring standard quality certification, upgrading the process technology and improvement in packaging so as to strengthen their export capabilities, *Technology Development and Modernisation Fund (TDMF)* has been launched by SIDBI (Small Industries Development Bank of India) in April 1995 by earmarking initially Rs.200 crore. The minimum need-based assistance under the scheme either by way of term loan in domestic and foreign currency, or equity or both, has been fixed at Rs.10 lakh per unit. Other provisions include promoters' contribution at 20 per cent of project outlay and exemption from levy of upfront fee. Apart from providing loans / equity assistance to individual projects, SIDBI also provides assistance to accredited agencies for undertaking a wide range of developmental activities.

To accord a focused attention to the marketing-related services, needed by SSI units, a new department, namely, Marketing Finance and Development Department has been set up by SIDBI at New Delhi which became operational in January 1996. Besides strengthening the existing marketing channels and infrastructure through financial assistance and other measures, the new department is also expected to adopt innovative approach in supporting high risk marketing activities like advertising, cataloguing, test marketing, sponsoring trade delegations to foreign countries, etc.

SIDBI has entered into MoU with 18 banks. While the banks fully meet the working capital requirement of the units, they have the option to share the term loan with SIDBI. SIDBI has signed MoU with CSIR. It envisages financial assistance packages including venture capital assistance by SIDBI to units using technologies developed by CSIR. SIDBI would also collaborate with CSIR in marketing technologies developed by the latter which are ready for commercial exploitation, including promotion of the technology internationally through Technology Bureau of Small Enterprises set up at the APCTT. SIDBI has also entered into MoU with the Small Industry Development Organisation (SIDO) headed by Development Commissioner (Small Scale Industries) for focusing attention on identified thrust areas for development such as development of clusters, promotion of ancillaries, technology transfer, technology upgradation and modernisation, export promotion, quality improvement, energy conservation, pollution control, etc.

Challenges Facing the SSI Sector, Tests in Growth and Survival of Enterprises, and Future Directions

Definition of small scale industries, ancillary industries and export-oriented units has been revised in December 1999. The present investment ceiling in plant and machinery goes up to Rs.one crore for these units, and for tiny sector units, ceiling is Rs.25 lakh. In 71 specified product lines, with focus on exports, investment ceiling for SSI units has been raised to Rs.5 crore. With these contours defined at the national level, many changes are taking place in the environment governing the SSI sector. The process is on for integrating the economy, particularly the industrial sector with developed and other developing countries through the process of globalisation.

Entrepreneurs in SSI sector have expressed appreciation for the opening up of the economy by creating a competitive, market-friendly environment, and facilitating the process of integration with global trends. They are aware of the new challenges, risks and opportunities that have been alien to them earlier. The emerging forces of globalisation, deregulation and technology transfer as well as increasing and shifting demands of consumers are changing the contours of the SSI sector. In days to come, there will be considerable shift in the way entrepreneurs can perceive business opportunities. Some of thern are as follows:

(i) Tie-ups for joint ventures within and outside the sector

(ii) Growth in demand for differentiated products

(iii) Access to new technology and process of manufacture based on flexible manufacturing system to serve the demand of differentiated products

(iv) Access to markets which are non-homogeneous and rapidly changing

(v) Expanding service sector.

While pursuing entrepreneurship development, it is not enough to think of promoting an enterprise. Growth and overcoming the problems faced from time to time are equally important. It is important to visualise the enterprise from a holistic viewpoint. Comprehensive theory of entrepreneurship encompassing all stages needs to be kept in view for formulating strategies, conducting training programmes, and devising monitoring, evaluation and escort services.

At the EDII, Ahmedabad in a publication released by them, crises stages of an enterprise in its life cycle are detailed here: The publication authored by V.G. Patel is *The Seven Business Crises – How to beat them*, published by Tata McGraw-Hill Publishing Company, New Delhi in 1995.

- The starting crisis
- The cash crisis
- The delegation crisis
- The leadership crisis
- The finance crisis
- The prosperity crisis
- The management – succession crisis
- Another stage is planning for survival and growth

All the eight stages have been portrayed with live examples in the EDII publication as well as released as video cassettes. These will be of great relevance for existing and prospective entrepreneurs.

Conclusion

Some of the important areas on which deliberations can be held for exchange of experiences to review the lessons learnt, and to evolve guidelines for the future can be listed as follows:

(i) Need for research to supplement training – identify researchable areas

(ii) Preparation of case studies and video documentaries of programmes, and profiles of S&T entrepreneurs

(iii) Critical look at the strategies adopted so far and modifications needed in the context of the changing economic environment

(iv) EDP training, and need for training for growth and survival of the enterprise at various stages

(v) Modifications needed in the curriculum of EDPs as organised at present

(vi) Thrust of the programme at state and district levels in the light of earlier experiences.

16

PERSPECTIVES OF ENTREPRENEURSHIP DEVELOPMENT

ROLE OF STEPs, AND INNOVATION AND BUSINESS INCUBATORS

Dr. D. Nagayya*

Entrepreneurship development in the context of the changing international economic environment in promoting small enterprises needs a slightly different focus compared to the strategies pursued in other contexts. Technology and specialised managerial input, as well as quality assurance and environmental impact assessment norms assume importance for bigger small enterprises and medium enterprises, in particular. It is neither technology alone nor management specialisation alone, that is relevant. Both have to be provided simultaneously in the required dosage to ensure the success of an enterprise. The article reviews two recent programmes dealing with technology absorption, adoption and adaptation for promoting small enterprises. These are Science and Technology Entrepreneurs Parks(STEPs) in Section 1, and Technology Business Incubators(TBIs)/ Innovation and Business Incubators (IBIs) in Section 2. Review is attempted of the approaches adopted by the concerned promoters of the programmes in different parts of the country for the benefit of young professionals/innovators to be groomed as entrepreneurs. Section 3 deals with the role of incubators, and Section 4 presents conclusions. Multi-faceted support by a wide variety of educational

---

* Consultant on Small Enterprises at Guntur, and former Director (Industrial Development), National Institute of Small Industry Extension Training (NISIET), Hyderabad.

institutions is advocated through business incubator services. It is hoped that the illustrations cited in the article will enthuse many educational institutions to follow the lead shown by premier organisations in the country such as IITs, IIMs, and Indian School of Business (ISB).

Introduction

In the changed context of the scenario of small enterprise development in the liberalisation era, expectations and strategies for promoting entrepreneurship development(ED) have undergone considerable change, particularly at higher investment levels and in the emerging technologies where commercialisation has not been done at all or attempted so far on a limited scale. Existing and prospective entrepreneurs have to be made conscious of the technological innovations, quality assurance, environmental safeguards in the international business scenario, apart from the complexities of management in small and medium enterprises(SMEs). The orientation and focus of the programme of ED to enthuse the young talent with basic technical or managerial skills, but hardly any industry exposure needs nurturing of a high order to provide the backup services in establishing and managing an enterprise successfully. Combination of multiple talents, and group approach combining different areas of specialisation need to be encouraged for promoting modern enterprises involving high level of technology and innovation. Entrepreneurship has to be more and more trade-specific or product/ process-specific based on its relevance in different regions.

From the generalist approach, ED institutions have to switch over to a more specialised role for training individual entrepreneurs or for developing/equipping a team of entrepreneurs to take up ventures in groups in specialised product lines. ED institutions need to work closely with R&D, and trade-specific specialised institutions in conducting ED programmes. The intensity of collaboration varies with the extent of technology absorption and adaptation needed for the enterprises.

While pursuing ED, it is not enough to think of only promoting an enterprise. Sustainability and growth over a period are equally important. Holistic view is to be taken regarding the promotion of an enterprise. Comprehensive theory of entrepreneurship encompassing all stages needs to be kept in view for formulating strategies, conducting training programmes, and devising monitoring, evaluation and escort services.

1. Science and Technology Entrepreneurs Parks (STEPs)

The National Science and Technology Entrepreneurship Development Board (NSTEDB) under the Union Department of Science and Technology (DST), initiated the Science and Technology Entrepreneurs Park (STEP) Programme in 1984 with the following objectives:

1. To forge close linkages between universities, academics, and Research& Development(R&D) institutions on the one hand, and industry on the other;
2. To promote entrepreneurship among Science and Technology (S&T) persons, many of whom were otherwise seeking jobs soon after their graduation;
3. To provide R&D support to small scale industries, mostly through interaction with research institutions.

STEP provides a reorientation in approach to innovation and entrepreneurship involving education, training, research, finance, management counselling, and governmental support. It creates the necessary climate for innovation, for sharing of ideas, experience and facilities, and opens up avenues for students, teachers, researchers and industrial managers to grow in a common trans-disciplinary culture; each understanding and depending on others' inputs for starting a successful business venture in manufacturing or service category.

The task, therefore, is to create an 'employer culture', where S&T persons will increasingly seek to become self employed. It also involves changing the mindset of seeking jobs; and looking for a career in small business through entrepreneurial pursuits. To create an impact on this situation requires reorientation in the educational curriculum, in the way in which occupational choice is developed, in the way in which career advice is given, and ultimately contributing to the role of small scale sector in wealth generation.

Promoters of STEPs and Criteria for Selection of Locations

The DST took the initiative on behalf of Government of India, and involved three leading all India financial institutions, namely, Industrial Development Bank of India(IDBI), Industrial Finance Corporation of India(IFCI), Industrial Credit and Investment Corporation of India(ICICI). In addition, the state government and the host institution promoting the STEP are all partners in this endeavour.

Among the reputed institutes of technology and universities, based on the presence of a strong S&T orientation and a nucleus of R & D activity in the host institution, and commitment to promote S&T entrepreneurs, location is selected for establishing the STEP. Other criteria kept in view while selecting locations are as follows:

1. Development of a comprehensive well thought out plan of action.
2. Compatibility amongst the industrial activities envisaged in the STEP.
3. Compatibility between STEP and the host institution activities.
4. Shared central services.
5. Easy access to the host institution facilities.
6. The existing relationship between the academic institution and industry.

The project cost of STEP generally ranges between Rs.1.5 to 2.0 crore. Developing linkages between R&D institutions, academic institutions and industry is one of the key objectives of STEP movement to develop entrepreneurship among S&T background persons through small enterprises.

Status of STEPs and Key Parameters for the Success of the Programme

In the second half of 1980s and early 1990s, fifteen locations were finalised for STEPs. Two more have been added recently. Four of the earlier ones have not become operational, even after a long time. Thirteen STEPs which are functioning in eight states at present are at Ranchi in Jharkhand, Mysore and Suratkal in Karnataka, Bhopal in Madhya Pradesh, Mumbai and Pune in Maharashtra, Ludhiana and Patiala in Punjab, Coimbatore and Tiruchirapalli in Tamil Nadu, Kanpur and Roorkee in Uttar Pradesh, and Kharagpur in West Bengal. Among them, STEPs at Coimbatore and Patiala have been recently established. The STEPs have formed themselves into an all India association of STEPs. This facilitates convening of annual gatherings, exchange of experiences and periodic review of the programme in different locations. In 1998, National Council of Applied Economic Research (NCEAR), New Delhi made a comprehensive evaluation of NSTEDB programme, including STEP, and its impact on entrepreneurship development, employment generation, and technology transfer.

Table 16.1: Status of STEPs (end – March 1999)

Sl. No.	*Location of STEP*	*No. of SSI Units Established*	*No. of Technologies Developed*	*Employment Generated*
1	Tiruchy	106	26	1100
2	Mysore	95	17	800
3	Ranchi	60	60	695
4	Mumbai	45	-	200
5	Roorkee	14	40	150
6	Kharagpur	31	59	313
7	Ludhiana	95	53	680
8	Kanpur	31	10	200
9	Bhopal	46	8	200
10	Pune	25	60	160
11	Suratkal	50	4	200
12	Coimbatore	6	3	18
13	Patiala	1	-	5
	Total	**605**	**340**	**4721**

Source: Government of India, Department of Science and Technology, New Delhi.

Box-1 Science and Technology Entrepreneurs Parks(STEPs), and their Thrust Areas

Host institution of the Science and Technology Entrepreneurs Park (STEP), location and year of establishment of the Park, and thrust areas identified for its activities are given below for each STEP. Thirteen STEPs are in operation at present in eight states. Among them, two, located at Coimbatore and Patiala have been established recently.

1. Tiruchirapalli National Institute of Technology, Tiruchirapalli (Tamil Nadu) (TNIT - Tiruchy, 1986) - *Mechanical and machine tool–based industries,* electronics, production engineering.
2. Sri Jaya Chamarajendra College of Engineering, Mysore (Karnataka) (SJCE - Mysore, 1985) – *Electronics and software development.*
3. Birla Institute of Technology (BIT), Mesra, Ranchi (Jharkhand) (BIT – Ranchi , 1985) - *Mechanical engineering,* mining equipment, electro mechanical engineering , electronics.
4. Jawaharlal Nehru Entrepreneurs Chemical Park, Mumbai (JNECP – Mumbai, 1985) - *Chemicals.*
5. Indian Institute of Technology, Roorkee (Uttaranchal) (IIT - Roorkee, 1987) (earlier known as University of Roorkee) – *Electronics and Computer related activities,* mechanical engineering, survey instruments, chemical industries, agro and horticulture-based industries.
6. Indian Institute of Technology, Kharagpur (West Bengal) (IIT – Kharagpur, 1986) – *Electrical and food–based industries,* electrical, metallurgy, mechanical, chemical, agro related, computer related industries.
7. Guru Nanak Engineering College, Ludhiana (Punjab) (GNEC - Ludhiana, 1986) – *Machine tools,* automation and controls, electronics and computer application-based industries, pollution control industries.
8. Harcourt Butler Technical Institute, Kanpur (Uttar Pradesh) (HBTI – Kanpur, 1986) – *Chemicals,* electronics and computer related activities.

9. Maulana Azad National Institute of Technology, Bhopal (Madhya Pradesh) (MANIT - Bhopal, 1989) – *Power engineering including development of equipment for using alternate energy sources,* electronics, materials science.
10. University of Pune, Pune (Maharashtra) (PU - Pune, 1990) –*Solar power generation,* computer related activity, multimedia software, instrumentation.
11. Karnataka National Institute of Technology, Suratkal, Mangalore (Karnataka) (KNIT –Suratkal, 1994) – *Informatics and software development,* pollution control equipment, biotechnology, engineering design and consultancy, environmental engineering.
12. P.S.G. College of Technology, Coimbatore (Tamil Nadu) (PSGCT – Coimbatore)
13. Engineering College , Patiala (Punjab) (EC – Patiala)

Source: Government of India, Department of Science and Technology, New Delhi.

Host institutions of STEPs and thrust areas identified by them are given in Box 1. Progress of start-up units, technologies developed and employment generated through small enterprises promoted in the 13 STEPs at the end of March 1999 is given in Table 1. Each STEP has been established as an autonomous registered society having an independent legal status, which is external to the administrative structure of the host educational institution. Each STEP also follows its own model depending on the local environment and needs. Thrust areas in technology development and commercialisation have been identified, based on the strength of the host institution, and the industrial milieu of the industry in the vicinity. In the 13 functioning STEPs, up to the end of March 1999, 605 small scale units were established, and 340 technologies were developed. Employment generated was 4,721 persons (Table 1). STEPs at Tiruchy, Mysore, Ranchi and Ludhiana have made a significant contribution to the progress of the movement. Some others have laid greater emphasis on development of technologies rather than on establishment of new enterprises. STEPs at Roorkee, Kharagpur and Pune are in this category. Facilities available at STEPs and services offered by STEPs to existing and prospective entrepreneurs are listed here.

Facilities available at STEPs: Incubation space/nursery shed, testing and calibration, central workshop, prototype development, computing facilities, data bank, library and documentation, conference hall, common facilities such as telephone, fax, e-mail, website, internet, reprography, etc., pollution control laboratory, pilot plant facility, and quality assurance centre.

Services offered by STEPs to entrepreneurs: Testing and calibration, consultancy, research, training, software development, product development, process development, human resources, technical support, business facilitation, common facilities, Bureau of Indian Standards extension, escorting to ISO, Patent Facilitation Centre.

Main activities of STEPs are envisaged as follows: training of entrepreneurs, nursing them, guiding them in product and process development through R&D work, and in the preparation of feasibility studies, liaisoning with various agencies including venture capital companies, banks and financial institutions, upscaling of new products and processes, and providing facilities for quality control and certification. Nursing period visualised is three years by which time entrepreneurs are expected to move out from nursery sheds to transplantation sheds. Simultaneously, industrial houses are being invited to establish their R&D wings in STEP with access to all facilities of the educational institution sponsoring it. Through problem-oriented research work, the R&D personnel of existing units and faculty of the educational institution can interact frequently for mutual benefit. Laboratories are being invited to set up testing facilities and pilot plants in STEP to enable entrepreneurs to work on them for gaining confidence about the commercial viability of the product lines chosen by them. Upscaling is a proposition being tried out under the guidance of laboratory scientists to enable entrepreneurs to set up their own units later. STEP, thus, offers opportunities for university-industry interaction of a high order.

STEP aims at developing a new breed of technology oriented and quality conscious entrepreneurs. It is visualised that a large number of them would have S&T background. An analysis of STEP entrepreneurs' educational background indicates that majority of them have degree in engineering (47%), followed by graduates in science

(21%), diploma holders in engineering (21%), and others (11%). The industry-wise distribution shows that a majority entered into engineering related businesses (42%), followed by electronics and information technology (18%), chemicals and pharmaceuticals (18%), services (10%), and others (12%). The progress of individual STEPs varied substantially from one location to another. It has been quite a slow process. Leadership role played by the STEP director, and the support extended by the host institution have played a key role in accelerating the pace of development of S&T entrepreneurship in each location.

Periodic reviews of the programme and evaluation study revealed the crucial role of the head of STEP in ensuring the success of the programme in a region. The selection of the agency head should be done with due regard to the facts that such institutions can be made effective and sustainable only if there is a mission oriented business-like approach. The bulk of the inputs and outputs are 'soft', and the result is critically dependent on the vision, business management capabilities, and ability to communicate effectively with all levels of government and industries. Similarly while selecting the agency for establishing the STEP, care has to be taken to fulfil the desired criteria as detailed earlier.

STEP facilities are particularly capital intensive. In view of the high investment involved, it is important to make effective use of the facilities and services offered by STEP for existing and prospective small scale entrepreneurs. The following conclusions are drawn from the experience of recent years.

1. There should be greater effort to reduce the chances of failure of these schemes, for which they should be implemented with more 'project oriented inputs'.
2. By the very nature of these schemes, there should be as much of market-based inputs as there are technology-based ones; for this reason, ways should be found to have closer interaction between industry and the host technical institutions in relation to the location of STEPs, their implementation and actual operation. A few key pointers noticed in the implementation of STEPs are as follows :

- Self sustainability should be a specific aim for which the centralised services created in STEP could make a beginning by providing services to the existing small and medium enterprises(SMEs) in the neighbourhood.
- Leadership skills are the key to success. The combination of technical and managerial skills, and vision will go a long way in accelerating the progress of the project.
- Commercialisation of activities should be encouraged in the liberalised environment.
- Importance of linkages with other institutions needs to be consciously pursued. Wherever possible, STEP units should be integrated with the proposed setting up of industrial and export promotion parks in different states, apart from industrial estates and industrial areas promoted earlier.

3. A notable feature of the STEP programmes' success is the importance attached to proper selection of candidates, product lines and linkages with R&D organisations. This is done by: (a) targeting prospective entrepreneurs from amongst working professionals in industry or government; (b) providing for an extended training period (up to two years) in an industry to fresh trainees coming out of the colleges/institutes before they are inducted as entrepreneurs.

4. Linkages with industry associations in a formal form is necessary at state and national levels, apart from local industrial, small industry and trade oriented associations, to develop a platform to assist young and enthusiastic professionals with sufficient technical and managerial background. NSTEDB is already sponsoring entrepreneurship awareness camps, and also encouraging inclusion of entrepreneurship as a subject in engineering colleges/institute of technology/polytechnics. Similarly All India Council for Technical Education(AICTE) is pursuing the same direction with institutes of management and other specialised institutions. All India Management Association

(AIMA) and Association of Indian Management Schools (AIMS) are popularising entrepreneurship movement through distance education programmes, and specialised publications on recent developments on management, enterprise development, and international business scenario. Training programmes, seminars, workshops and conferences sponsored/organised by these bodies strengthen the role of SME sector, and the role of specialised breed of entrepreneurs.

5. It may be worthwhile to promote a scheme to pay stipend to the final year students to do their project placement in a successful SME, to enable them to gain first hand exposure and insight. A suitable screening of units which offer such placement should be devised. Subsequently, a two-year placement in an industry will enable the young professionals to acquire experience, before they can consider joining STEP for promoting an industry. Combination of technical and managerial insight is crucial for becoming a successful entrepreneur.

2. Technology Business Incubators (TBIs) & Innovation and Business Incubators (IBIs)

TBIs Supported by DST

The Technology Business Incubator is another mechanism initiated by NSTEDB to provide advisory, training and information services, management counselling and marketing support, linkages to research faculty and facilities, and access to capital; thereby, enhancing the chances of success of the early stage technopreneur. It is a cost effective instrument for technology transfer and development of knowledge-based and hi-tech enterprises.

The main concern of TBIs is to bolster the technological development stage, and to complete the process of technological ideas for technologies currently under development in R&D institutions. However, technology incubators are commonly known to include the concept of technology business incubators, and innovation centres. The goal of technology incubator is also to promote technology-based firms, and to address regional and local developmental issues through S&T entrepreneurs. TBIs are located at or near reputed technical institutions, and are characterised by institutional links to knowledge sources including technology transfer agencies, research centres, national laboratories, and skilled R&D personnel. TBIs promote technology transfer and diffusion while encouraging entrepreneurship among researchers and academics. Incubators in the premises of universities and other academic institutions can act as a training ground for young professionals to be turned into technopreneurs, in particular. Creating awareness among academic institutions about the requirements of industry, and reorient their R&D programmes to suit the needs of industry is an important function of incubators. They can also act as a problem-solving agency not only in the areas of technology but also in other related areas of business development.

A TBI is a managed work space with low cost office facilities, and business and professional services necessary for nurturing and supporting early stage growth of technologies and technology-based enterprises. The services may include modern communication and information services, and access to R&D, testing, design and engineering, etc, for facilities and services. The objective is to cover some of the risk involved in the early stages of incubation of technologies and technopreneurs, particularly in the area of high-risk technologies, and advanced unproven technologies. In addition to work space, the services of incubators include various forms of business planning and managerial advice, office facilities, finance, accounting, access to business networks, and legal services.

One TBI project is planned to be located at NOIDA, close to New Delhi with the support of DST. Under UNDP support on technology management, it is proposed to set up two TBIs. In addition, several privately managed incubators are likely to come up in different parts of the country.

Incubation Centres Supported by SIDBI

Small Industries Development Bank of India(SIDBI) launched a National Programme on Innovation and Incubation for Small Industries in March 2000. Under this programme, the Bank entered into MoUs with two institutions in 2001 - Indian Institute of Technology(IIT), Kanpur(Uttar Pradesh) and Birla Institute of Technology(BIT), Mesra, Ranchi(Jharkhand) for setting up incubation centres. BIT, Ranchi is already associated with STEP. While the centre at IIT, Kanpur has become operational, the other at BIT, Ranchi is expected to commence operations in 2004. Through the incubation centres, SIDBI plans to catalyse the creation of world class R&D facilities for small scale industries to face the challenges of the new Intellectual Property Rights and liberalised trade regime. The thrust areas of IIT, Kanpur incubator would include information technology, bio-technology, pharmaceutical, food and agro processing industries.

SIDBI's commitment to the centre would be a grant of Rs.2.35 crore financing the capital cost, and meeting the working expenses of the incubator for the first two years, and Rs.2 crore initially by way of grant to the fund corpus of Rs.5 crore to be set up for meeting the working expenses of the incubator from the third year onwards.

The incubation centre will act as a nursery to help promote innovative ideas by providing a wide range of facilities to young professionals with science and technology background. The facilities include financial and infrastructure support during the incubation stage, assistance in determining the technological, marketing and financial viability of entrepreneurial ideas, and drawing up R&D plan, provide professional advice, expertise, and mentoring entrepreneurial projects. Other services include secretarial and administrative support, maintenance procurements, accounting and legal, financial and other related expert advice, assistance in raising capital, and preparing for project launch, organise seminars, conferences and workshops for exchanging ideas, and disseminating knowledge generated at the centre. Assistance in obtaining finance and requisite manpower including R&D team support would also be available.

The incubation centre would be managed by setting up an Apex Committee, an Advisory Committee, and an Evaluation Committee. The Apex Committee would be primarily concerned with overseeing and guiding the overall operations of the centre. The Advisory Committee would provide the policy framework for the centre, and monitor the projects periodically. The Evaluation Committee would examine every project proposal for its viability. All the committees would include experts from different fields.

Innovation and Business Incubation Centres (IBICs) at other Educational Institutions, Associations and in the Private Sector

All Indian Institutes of Technology(IITs), and Indian Institutes of Management(IIMs) are moving in the direction of supporting young professionals to become entrepreneurs in their chosen areas by setting up specific facilities, referred to as Centre for ED/Innovation and Incubation Centre/Business Incubator/Technology Business Incubator.

IIM Ahmedabad has set up a Centre for Innovation, Incubation and Entrepreneurship(CIIE). This Centre has a slightly different perspective for entrepreneurship promotion compared to what many incubators focus on developing entrepreneurship among different target groups. The centre focuses on entrepreneurial activities that revolve around innovation. Innovative and risky projects will be considered for promotion by young professionals with management background. A unique feature of the IIMA incubator is the active search of the innovators in public, private and informal sectors, including alumni of IIMA who have the capability to convert an innovation into a value added product/service, but might not have been able to do so because of certain limitations. IIM Bangalore has set up N.S. Raghavan Centre for Entrepreneurship Development (CED) in 2000, supported by N.S. Raghavan, co-founder of Infosys for promoting entrepreneurship among management professionals. Another prominent centre is Wadhwani Centre for Entrepreneurial Development (WCED) promoted by the Indian School of Business(ISB), Hyderabad, which started its operations in 2001. WCED has been funded by Ramesh Wadhwani, founder of Aspect Development, and now Vice Chairman of 12 Technologies. WCED is the first Centre of Excellence at ISB started with a mission to create entrepreneurs from among the student community with management background, and to promote entrepreneurship through a wide spectrum of activities, abbreviated as MATTER; standing for Mentoring, AIM-e, Teaching, Training, Enterprise-partnering, and Research. AIM-e stands for Academic Institutions Movement for Entrepreneurship.

To students, WCED provides entrepreneurial spirit, and expertise needed to succeed in an ever-changing business environment through Mentoring, Teaching, and Enterprise-partnering. It enables the sharing of entrepreneurial experiences, and provides opportunities for action learning, such as business plan competitions. Mentoring refers to the role of a mentor, an experienced entrepreneur or consultant who volunteers to support the process of grooming a prospective entrepreneur, which involves training, coaching, counselling and providing direction at periodic intervals to enable the prospective entrepreneur succeed in his maiden venture. The mentor counsels entrepreneurs to overcome hurdles faced by them at various stages of the growth of the enterprise. Mentors become great motivators, and often act as sounding boards for entrepreneurs. For the entrepreneurial community, the WCED offers training and networking opportunities to help build global competitiveness. It undertakes research focussing on challenges of entrepreneurship in developing countries. AIM-e supports a strong collaboration among various academic institutions, technology institutions, and development agencies for promoting entrepreneurship. The WCED organises a variety of programmes to help share, update and build knowledge by : (a) inviting high growth entrepreneurs to ISB-WCED Winners Club in recognition for innovation and wealth creation. These future industry leaders will be role models for aspiring entrepreneurs. Research programmes at WCED are based on application-oriented, multi-disciplinary approach to fostering entrepreneurship in developing countries.

AWAKE, Bangalore, a non-governmental organisation (NGO), Association of Women Entrepreneurs of Karnataka, is one of the earliest in the country to set up an incubation centre in Rajaji Nagar Industrial Estate, Bangalore, for promoting entrepreneurship among women through constant guidance, and R&D support for product lines of interest to them. IDBI and DST supported this institution in early 1990s.

Science & Technology Entrepreneurs Park (STEP) at Mysore (Karnataka) has promoted a technology incubator with focus on Net Telephony, embedded software and e-commerce. Known as SEED-Software Entrepreneurs and Employees Development-, it was started at Mysore in 1999. SEED of the opinion that connectivity alone cannot nurture the start ups in software development, and information technology enabled services. SEED is providing a wide range of services to entrepreneurs. This incubation centre with infrastructure support, R&D, and HRD centres, and access to venture capitalists and angel investors, apart from Union Department of Science & Technology is nurturing a number of start up companies in the field of IT in Karnataka, particularly around Mysore and Bangalore. The incubator offers communication and business infrastructure, access to finance, technical support, and R&D assistance. These facilities are fee-based, and fee charged is nominal, as the focus of SEED is on encouraging entrepreneurship in the software field in particular. The incubator does not look for an equity stake in the company. It provides all the support services to encourage largely first generation entrepreneurs. It is of the opinion that conducive environment and support services will go a long way in helping entrepreneurs in a sustained manner.

Among other management development academic institutions, mention may be made of the ICFAI Centre for Entrepreneurship Development(ICED) promoted by the Institute of Chartered Financial Analysts of India(ICFAI) at Hyderabad in 2002. It focuses on management professionals to be groomed as entrepreneurs highlighting innovation as the most useful practice for SMEs to stay ahead of competition, and realise the full potential of the business. Technology transfer from R&D institutions is also one of the objectives for commercialising new products and processes developed by national laboratories. The Centre is also termed as incubation centre or business incubator, an incubator to promote new business ventures by training, counselling and supporting young professionals who have completed MBA, MCA, CFA, engineering and other courses organised by ICFAI University. Efforts will be made in the Centre to encourage new and innovative businesses. The specialists drawn from industry and academics will screen the business plans, and provide guidance to those that are finally accepted for 'incubation'. Aspiring entrepreneurs will be encouraged through necessary guidance in the preparation of business plans, training, and escort services, apart from provision of seed capital through institutional sources. Short and long duration training programmes on entrepreneurship and management development will also be organised by ICED, apart from periodic seminars and workshops on innovative themes of current day interest. Typically an incubation centre promotes the spirit of entrepreneurship among people who have 'ideas and concepts' but not the means to turn them into an industrial and business venture. ICED will also be partnering with a few corporates to sponsor candidates for commercialising technologies of unproven nature.

GITAM Institute of Foreign Trade(GIFT), Visakhapatnam has started a Centre for Innovation and Entrepreneurship in 2003. The following are among the main activities of the Centre in the initial years: Faculty development in entrepreneurship training, entrepreneurship education through a two-year Masters Programme in International Business, human resource development for SMEs, community-based participative action research programme on self employment and livelihoods, organising trade fair events, international trade facilitation, cluster development under rural industrialisation programme, and organising a number of executive development programmes, seminars and workshops for personnel of SMEs apart from the personnel of organisations associated with SMEs. The range of activity, thus, covers teaching, research, training, organising awareness programmes, counselling, and provision of escort services to alumni of GIFT and other GITAM institutions which include College of Management Studies, engineering and science colleges, as well as entrepreneurs in the SME sector.

Pune has a very prominent private entrepreneur-promoted incubator in the country with 31 small enterprises with an aggregate investment of Rs.5 crore . Nearly 90 per cent of these enterprises are technology related, and are undergoing the process of enterprise development at the incubator. The incubator was started in 2001 with the active involvement of a consultancy organisation, Maharashtra Industrial and Technical Consultancy Organisation(MITCON), Pune. The person who floated this incubator hopes that even if after five years, there is a success rate of less than 10 per cent, he would be making around 50 times the investment he has incurred in this business incubator. Here, the business incubator becomes an enterprise in itself. Out of the 31 companies that are promoted by technocrats with the sole objective of developing new products, two companies have already started making profits within a span of about 18 months. All these companies have the technology and know-how. The support they need is that the incubator should provide all the support facilities including tie up on marketing aspects, and the entrepreneurs take care of the main business of developing the products, and converting them into sustainable commercial ventures.

In the light of the widespread use of entrepreneurship career curriculum and operational steps for supporting young professionals with the background of science and technology, management, information technology, and other professional courses, which offer scope for the young talent to be moulded into entrepreneurs, a number of institutions in the country are moving in that direction by promoting technology business incubation centres, innovation and incubation centres, and centres for innovation and entrepreneurship development. This is a very healthy trend in providing an environment conducive for developing entrepreneurship with focus on promotion of SMEs.

3. Innovation, Incubation and Role of Incubators

A few questions that need to be answered to conceptualise the role of an incubator for promoting entrepreneurship among the youth though small enterprises are as follows : 1. What is innovation, and what is incubation? 2.What is the process of incubation needed for commercialising an innovation or unproven or relatively new technology? 3. What role can incubators play in this context ?

What one would consider innovation relates not only to the question of doing new things, but also a question of doing things in a new or different manner. Even this approach of doing things differently, which involves risk, requires considerable amount of support in terms of incubation facilities. An innovative entrepreneur/ te..hnopreneur should adapt to the changing demand patterns of the market. The adaptation may be with regard to technology, marketing, business idea or business plan. The concept of incubation originated in the medical field. The incubator provides a simulated environment for a child born premature, to enable it to grow and withstand the normal environment after some time. The incubator monitors the life systems so that the child reaches a stage from where it can be nurtured and brought up like a normal child. The incubation stage, thus, refers to a limited period to enable the child to grow under normal conditions. In business development/new enterprise creation, the concept of incubators is applied more to project ideas which have a high degree of uncertainty. The aim of the incubator is to facilitate the survival of such companies, and also to nurture them for growth and success, by providing the inputs needed by the company at different stages. Incubators play the role of risk sharing, and providing credibility to an idea as it progresses from being an idea to some kind of a product. It minimises uncertainty and increases the success rate of an enterprise that is at a very nascent stage.

The difference between promotional efforts and hand-holding is that promotional effort is the assistance given for setting up a business whereas in an incubator, individual attention is paid at various stages through more of a hand-holding. The incubator facilitates single window services as in an assistance programme; and it goes beyond that stage with hand-holding by counselling and providing necessary inputs for reducing the impact of uncertainty. However, if the hand-holding operation continues for a period longer than required, the innovator becomes dependent. Shifting the innovator from the incubator to a normal environment as early as possible is important.

An innovator or a scientist may not be inclined to become an entrepreneur for developing a business enterprise. He prefers to concentrate on creation of more and more innovations. Hence the role of business application or commercialisation of innovations has to be played by an entrepreneur interested in a business venture. Incubators can feel the pulse of innovators, and provide linkage between innovators and those who can convert the innovation and develop it into a business proposition. The incubator not only supports innovation, but also encourages it to be converted into an enterprise, perhaps by a different person, if need be. Many innovation-based enterprises stagnate because they are not able to come up with another set of innovations as their enterprise develops. Innovator need not be burdened with enterprise building, if he does not have the inclination to pursue that direction. Managerial skills should supplement technical skills for ensuring the success of start-ups. The biggest benefit of being in an incubator is that the process insulates the entrepreneur from the outside environment, and he can concentrate on getting his idea fool-proof for the market. The incubator provides S&T input, good managerial expertise, and also linkages with venture capitalists, and others. All ventures do not need incubation; the need is particularly for high risk ventures. Incubators can also provide the network, linking innovators with the societal resources. The network is of two kinds - knowledge network and social network.

The role of angels and venture capitalists in supporting innovators and entrepreneurs at different stages by providing venture funds as start-up capital or seed capital, is an important facility for innovators/entrepreneurs in the nascent stage. Venture capitalists also provide a variety of services needed by the enterprise through networking; including managerial guidance, monitoring, and soliciting support from specialists. Venture capitalists consider proposals with high risk and high reward, and reject many proposals that do not fall in this category. Same is the case with business incubators.

Incubators can be of many types, depending on the type of support needed by an innovator : 1. Technology business incubators focus on commercialisation of emerging technologies as well as R&D work, apart from formulation of business plans. 2. Innovation and business incubators: They cater to the needs of single window support services needed by a wide range of professionals of first generation entrepreneurs. 3. Empowerment/micro enterprise incubators: They support low income vulnerable sections, minority and women-promoted enterprises, whose familiarity with enterprise development is quite inadequate. High technology or innovation content in these enterprises is generally not there. The enterprises are based on well established technologies; only the aspirants are new to enterprise building.

The incubators supported by government organisations, development financial institutions, and associations have a developmental role. Those promoted by corporates or private sector companies may be organised with profit motive. In both the cases, self sustainability of the incubator over a period is important. In the Indian context, the incubator concept is very recent. Educational and R&D organisations, as well as associations can play a leading role in promoting the incubator culture for supporting the young first generation professionals/ innovators/ entrepreneurs. Experiences of developed countries such as USA and UK, and developing countries like China, Taiwan and Israel, present a highly encouraging picture to be emulated by Indian organisations.

Conclusion

Among a number of approaches adopted for entrepreneurship development in the country, this article refers to two important experiments, which are very recent. STEP programme being practised in 13 locations of eight states, and Technology Business Incubators/ Innovation and Business Incubators being promoted in recent years in a number of educational institutions have made a good beginning. Initial results are quite encouraging, though the gestation period has been quite high. Leadership role in enterprise building, and in incubation centres and STEPs is very prominent to ensure the success of an enterprise in commercialising risky technologies. Providing new technologies/S&T inputs, along with managerial inputs and single window services of a wide variety needed for enterprise building in the fast changing business environment is crucial for supporting innovators to be transformed into entrepreneurs. Novel approaches to finance innovative or high risk ventures through venture capital funds, and certain new patterns in conventional and developmental loans are becoming popular in the country with the initiative of the concerned organisations and industry associations. A good blend of technical and managerial specialisations is the key for the success of an enterprise. These can be in the same person or in a group of persons associated with the enterprise. It is hoped that the experiences presented here will set the tone for many educational institutions and industry associations to play the innovation and incubation role in various contexts.

REFERENCES

1. Bhagwan Prasad, 2003. *Developing Entrepreneurial Skills among Management and Engineering Graduates.* Hyderabad, Osmania University (AICTE-sponsored Project).

2. Kondaiah, C., 2002. *Entrepreneurship in the New Millennium – Challenges and Prospects*. New Delhi, Tata McGraw Hill Publishing Company.

3. National Council of Applied Economic Research (NCAER), 1998. *Evaluation of NSTEDB Programme and its Impact on Entrepreneurship Development, Employment Generation and Technology Transfer.* New Delhi (Union Department of Science and Technology– sponsored Study)

17

MANAGEMENT OF HUMAN RESOURCE

Dr. V.K. Bhaskara Rao*

Human Resource Development (HRD) is an important factor that has come into increasing realization in recent times. It is a part of human resource management which includes the study of industrial relations, organizational development, training and motivation of the employees. People are the greatest assets of an organization. HRD mainly aims at improving constantly employee efficiency and competence levels. Industries and organizations in advanced countries have given long back greater attention to human resource as a means to increase productivity, efficiency and gain competitive advantage. However, it was only since two decades or so that the Indian Industries have realized the imminent use and applicability of human resource concept for their growth.

Employees of the company are its greatest and most valuable resources. In fact, they are more than mere resource and it will be the company's sincere endeavour to treat people with all respect and sensitivity than warranted when employees are seen as more than mere instrumentalities. While, on the one hand H.R.D. should appropriately harness employee potential for the attainment of company objectives, on the other, the company, as its corporate responsibility, should create an enabling climate where in human talent gets the best opportunity for self expression, all round development and fulfillment. H.R.D. should eventually be a core philosophy of all management actions. It is imperative that all functional and divisional

* Reader, P.G. Dept. of Commerce & Management Studies, VRS & YRN College, Chirala.

heads responsible for various activities of the company should imbibe the H.R.D. spirit, and suitably integrate H.R.D. into their plans, decisions and actions.

Introduction

Employees of the company are its greatest and most valuable resources. In fact, they are more than resource and it should be the company's sincere endeavour to treat people with all respect and sensitivity that is warranted when employees are considered more than mere instrumentalities. While, on the one band H.R.D. should appropriately harness employee potential for the attainment of company objectives, on the other, the company, as its corporate responsibility, should create an enabling climate where in human talent gets the best opportunity for self expression, all round development and fulfillment. H.R.D. should eventually be a core philosophy of all management actions. It is imperative that all functional and divisional heads responsible for various activities of the company should imbibe the H.R.D. spirit and suitably integrate H.R.D. into their plans, decisions and actions.

Significance of H.R.D.

The concept of H.R.D. encompasses a broader framework of personnel Management. H.R.D. is the process of improving, changing and developing skills, knowledge, aptitudes, values and abilities of the employees based on present and future work and organizational requirements. It comprises a set of components like recruitment, selection, placement, training, transfer, promotion, deputation, motivation, reward, punishment and retirement of workforce etc. It also attaches importance for the utilization of human resource effectively and maintaining a healthy productive work culture in an organization. H.R.D. is also otherwise called manpower management or employee management. It establishes interconnected working relationships among the employees to attain maximum individual development and thereby, their talents and skills are increased. It is, in fact, the vital component of any organization in deciding its fate of success or failure. Hence, H.R.D. is undoubtedly a means for improving effectiveness of an organization.

Some years back, the H.R.D. had remained confining to managerial class of people in relation to workers who were in large number in organizations. However, the situation has now under gone a sea change while the concept of H.R.D. is largely being used from the level of Chief Executive at the top, down to the lowest rung of the organization, virtually bringing all the employees under the purview of H.R.D. It represents a variety of historical and contemporary influence on human values and it's approach and applicability has resulted a tremendous transformation over the years and this process would go on with the changes of times.

Nature and Scope of H.R.D.

The nature and scope of H.R.D. is indeed very wide. The scope of H.R.D. covers the manpower planning for ensuring optimum utilization of human resources and improving the work practices. Organizations could use H.R.D. to carryout the activities like recruitment, selections, placement, training and appraisal of the work force. Unless the employees receive attention through systematic H.R.D. activities, organizational effectiveness would not improve. Effectiveness may be in the form of better productivity, reduction of costs, generation of internal resources, better profits and better customer service. The basic philosophy of H.R.D. is directed towards collective responsibility for growth in organizations.

Organizations normally invest huge funds for buying innovative technology and sophisticated equipment but they do give little care for any investment on their human resource. The reason is obvious that they have abundant human resource in this country available at a cheaper cost. Incidentally, organizations do not realize that investment on H.R.D. would yield immense results for them in the long run. This assumes significance in the situation where human resource is becoming a major deciding factor of competitive advantage in a world of constant change. Organizations, of late, find circumstances where top and middle level professional cadre people are not adequately available. Once, they are able to pick up experienced professionals, organizations would try to retain them and show interest to invest on H.R.D. The present day system of liberalization, privatization and globalization particularly in India have undoubtedly posed great threats and challenges on the availability of professional managers for the corporate enterprises. Growing competition obviously demands more efficient and knowledgeable managers.

Broad Areas of H.R.D.: Following are the broad areas of the management of human resource require which careful understanding and consideration

(i) *Man power planning and staffing* :

(a) Methods of recruitment and selection of required number of people for existing and emerging jobs in which knowledge of technology is going to play an important role.

(b) Induction and placement of the new employees in a manner that will enable them to identify themselves with the organization.

(ii) *Training and Employee Development* :

(a) Providing training facilities for developing the specific and specialized skills of the workforce for a strategic operational and managerial functions by appreciating their interdependence with other activities in the environment.

(b) Deciding on an effective performance appraisal system for evaluating employees with a view to improve their present performance and to develop their potential.

(iii) *Compensation and Benefits for employees* :

(a) Formulation of effective compensation plans based on job evaluation and linked to roles, responsibilities, risks and performance.

(b) Management of fringe benefits and other monetary incentives.

(iv) *Integration and Utilization of workforce:*

(a) Reconciliation of individual employees with the organization through job rotation, job enlargement and job enrichment.

(b) Efficiency oriented supervision and leadership for building up a motivated and committed workforce.

(c) Productivity in operation through elimination of all forms of wasteful and redundant activities, improvement in systems and procedures at work and introduction of new technology.

(d) Objectivity in administration by developing a fair, firm and transparent policies and practices in the areas of utilization, transfer, promotion and deputation of the employees.

(v) *Maintenance Functions and Organization Development* :

(a) Employee services covering health, safety, welfare recreation, education and community life.

(b) Employee relations including communication, employee discipline and grievance redressal.

(c) Research covering collection and analysis of relevant data with a view to diagnosing problem areas and providing feedback to the organization.

(d) Management of change and organization development.

Developing H.R.D.: The organization's H.R.D. objective should be to foster an appropriate climate and culture which nurtures employee competence and creates adequate motivational levels for the application of their abilities to assigned jobs/roles with required commitment. They have to realize that investment in H.R.D. would certainly become a source of competitive advantage. A suitable match has to be provided between employee competence levels and company's work requirements. H.R.D. climate and better management styles need to be strengthened. The H.R.D. philosophy of the organization should necessarily enable the employees to seek greater identification with the company with requisite care, concern and developmental approach.

Conclusion

The human factor is an integral part of the corporate plan and the managements should develop and properly utilize the human resource talents in the best possible manner. The failure to do so would certainly cause a great concern to the organizations and also to the nation. Over the years, it has been found that money is not the only factor in getting the best out of the workers in terms of their talents. Gradually, the monetary incentives get replaced by safety, self esteeme and self actualization needs. On realizing this factor, there has been a perceptible change in relooking at the concept of H.R.D. by many organizations. In the light of present day changes taking place in the business world, the organizations and the government should initiate steps to accelerate the pace of H.R.D. Institutes of Management and other enterprises engaged in H.R.D. activities should develop relevant literature, modern techniques and practices of H.R.D. for easy adoption by any business organization. Top management of the enterprises should place the H.R.D. Department at a level equal to other departments like finance in the organizational hierarchy so as to infuse confidence in the workforce. H.R.D. function should be made more creative and professional to achieve the desired results of the organization. Steps should be taken to create training, work culture and learning culture among the employees for making the H.R.D. concept more effective and ultimately enable the employees and the organization to achieve its mission and goals.

18

HUMAN RESOURCE MANAGERS' CHALLENGES

Poornima Y*

Of the various resources that could be harnessed in our Universe by Man, the one that appears to be quite challenging and some times even mind boggling is the concept of harnessing Human Potentialities. Despite the fact that this appears to be quite simple to look at, once we get in to it, then starts the whole drama.

There are several parameters and at the same time, certain limitations which would influence the tapping of human potentialities. Unfortunately, for various obvious reasons, India's potentialities were never considered to such an extent they deserve to be considered as against the world. The first and foremost point that has to be taken into consideration is identifying the right person, for the right job, at the right time. This would demand exhaustive experience, analytical approach and above all, unbiased nature on the part of authorities. Then only one could expect Quality at work place.

It has been perceived that the migration of privileged few from our country to various parts of the world in search of better position as well as financial sustenance, was entirely an outcome of the desperate psychological status of the losers in terms of prospects in our country. May it be the existence of extent of humiliation and suppression they experience in terms of profession or it could even be the lure of Dollars of Pounds.

* Senior Lecturer, Department of Commerce & Business Administration, P.B. Siddartha Post-Graduate Centre, Vijayawada - 520 010

Actually, the present topic namely Human Resource Development as Strategic Strength requires incessant planning, perfect execution of the designed programme and above all, positioning of privileged persons in the perfect places.

Introduction

The conventional way of managing effectively, to organize, co-ordinate, command and control becomes an up hill task, as the business target keeps shifting with greater expectations from the customers, owing to the introduction of latest technologies. The various ways and means of management involve continual experimentation employing new approaches to old problems.

"Successful managers are not born, but they are made"

They are privileged by virtue of their business skills and the interpersonal relationships they maintain at the work place. They develop their own stature and managerial skills based on the situations to encounter people and problems.

In the light of this, the most important functional area of management that demands greater skills is Human Resource Development (HRD) which ensures organizational growth, development effectiveness and aims at long-term broad based activities. It is the elixir of the business enterprise.

Any Human Resource Manager will Aim :

- Primarily at ensuring the participation of sufficient number of executives and managers with the requisite skills to meet the present and future needs of business.
- Encouraging them to grow as efficient persons in their respective capacities to shoulder the responsibility.
- Improving the performance of managers at the various levels in the jobs they perform at that situation and
- Helping managers through out their career, to sustain excellence in performance.

In the present context, it is very apt to mention that Retention of employees appears to be the greatest challenge ever experienced by Human Resource Managers. Employees always tend to look for better opportunities irrespective of their longevity of service in the set organization. Here it is not out of place to quote Public Sector Units (PSUs). Biggest casuality appears to be the exorbitant brain-drain and it is something to be monitored continuously. It is the Human Resources manager who stands accountable for recruitment cost of the organization, causes of employee turn-over and accordingly devise a system to with hold the promising employees.

Normally, why do the employees leave the organization?. The following are some of the causative factors that would give a Human Resource manager better insight into the problem.

- Better monetary compensation else where
- Better promotional avenues
- Inadequate job satisfaction
- Higher perks and facilities in some other place
- Existing work culture may be repelling
- Stress in the job and an unpleasant relationship either with the boss, peers or subordinates in the existing job.
- Domestic compulsions.
- Health considerations
- Education facilities for children
- Inadequate amenities in the existing location for better quality of life
- Cultural barriers
- Foreign assignments
- Decision to set up one's own business etc.

Retention of employees in the organizations is never possible with a uniform system of compensation. For the right kind of people, sky is the limit for growth. Therefore, unless there is a flexible system of compensation that matches with the worth of employees, it is never possible to meet the challenges and retain loyal and efficient employees in the organization. At the same time, these right type of employees tend to become lethargic, discontented and lose their competence in due course of time and ultimately leave the organization. Hence, it is needed to devise a system by which good performers are assured faster growth.

So, most of the Indian managers should agree that people i.e. employees are one of the most delicate factors for success in business in the present Indian scinario. Every organization aims at expansion and diversification at its best possible manner. So, the intake of new personnel is a never-ending process for any dynamic business organization. It is not only very important to attract the best professionals into the Indian organization but also the top talented category is to be retained, the same time.

The basic solution in this context happens to be the exit interviews. Each organization must invariably have a system of exit interview. Analyse of feedback will be the most appropriate remedial measure and the most accepted suggestive solution to this critical issue. Another step that has to be adapted is hiring the right persons, reviewing employee benefits from time to time, and providing a positive work environment. Next to this, the successful employers coordinate creative recruiting strategies by employing effective measures to retain qualified employees. This process begins with an honest evaluation of employee policies, adopting practices and benefits that will ultimately attract candidates and motivating them to stay back in the organization. This is possible through focusing on reviewing the Indian corporate culture so that it would promote employee empowerment in a flexible environment i.e., providing good working conditions, welfare measures, making the job a pleasurable experience, encouraging their ideas and rewarding creativity by providing incentives etc.

One should consider the employees as the internal customers and be committed to build relationship with them. In this context, the major factor is personalization. Managers have to be observant and sensitive to the needs and requirements of each individual. Managers should spare time to listen to each and every employee and determine what actually motivates them. Above all, an increased employee satisfaction will increase productivity, to a greater extent and ultimately this will improve the turn over. Especially in the arenas such as IT, the turn over appears to be quite high. It also necessary to improve the morale of the individuals, to make the organization more effective and competitive. This can be made possible through a comprehensive evaluation of the organization and the successful implementation of equitable human resource policies, programmes and systems that will ultimately improve the relation within the organization.

In this context, it is not out of place to refer to the word "Human Engineering". Human Engineer is one who skillfully manages human beings with good motivation, an expert in the management of human resources. For instance, in Civil Engineering the worn out roads, bridges etc., are discarded and new ones are introduced, in Mechanical Engineering the worn out or rusted parts are thrown away and replaced with new ones, in Electronics old outmoded machinery and parts are thrown out and replaced by new ones. All this is for maintaining quality in this competing world of change. If there is a lifelong worship of the deity called quality, which can only make us survive, let us switch over welfare to warfare in our ethics and ethos. This can happen only if the human engineers follow their counterparts in their disciplines.

BHEL is one of the most progressive Indian organizations in harnessing and utilizing human potential. It is implementing the concept of workers' participation in management in its manufacturing plants throughout the country. It also bought the concept of Quality circles to Indian corporate sector. Quality circles is a small group of employees in the same work area or doing a similar type of job who voluntarily meet regularly for about an hour every week to identify, analyse and resolve work related problems leading to improvement in their total performance and enrichment of their work life. Various other motivational mechanisms were at work. For instance, at BHEL, Tirichirapalli, workers were given cash awards for suggestions that solved problems, upto 1% of resultant savings. It is a ISO 9000 company, constituted 60 odd inter functional task forces to solve problems, each with time bound plans in the early nineties itself.

The effective human resource strategy can be depicted in the following manner.

Fig : Effective Human Resource Strategy

Internal Development of New companies

Dynamic, turbulent environment – changing Competitive requirements

EFFECTIVE HUMAN RESOURCE STRATEGY

Stability in competitive Requirements

Reliance on external sources for new competencies

Many a time employees look for a change over if existing location does not provide adequate facilities for education of children and health care. A care and concern for these things will facilities retention. Hindusthan Organic Chemicals Limited is one of the organizations which has been able to retain people for any reasons but predominantly for a good school and a model hospital for its employees.To retain the most efficient employees, innovative managers find a solution to help them indirectly by combining tours with personal engagements, temporary transfer to near by places, granting of leave etc. It is rightly said that where there is a will there is a way. Thus, Human Resource Development and skill enhancement has emerged of matching the performance of its best, function by function and even excel in the operation.

Conclusion

According to McGregor "If employees are lazy, indifferent unwilling to take responsibility, intransigent, uncreative, uncooperative, the causes lie in managements' methods or organization and control". This statement very well emphasizes the quality of workforce at all levels. The success stories of BHEL, ITC, HINDUSTAN LEVER, LARSEN & TUBRO and several other Indian enterprises are largely due to their emphasis on human resource development. Therefore, this is an important task that lies on the shoulders of every management in managing people effectively and this is a real challenge of retaining people in the Indian organizations forever.

REFERENCES

1. William,P.Antony, et al., (1991), *Strategic Human Resource Management,* Dryden Press.
2. Mukherjee, D.N, (1998), Managing Intagible Assets, *Business World,* November 22 – December 6.
3. United Nationals Development Programme (1998), *Human Development Report,* Oxford University Press, New York.
4. *Management Research* (2002), Ed. G.S. Batra, Anmol Publications Private Limited, New Delhi.
5. The Human Side of Management Consulting, *Journal of Foundation for Organizational Research and Education–Abhigyan* – April-June 2003.

Srivasthava, M.P., (1999), Human Resource Planning, Institute of Applied Manpower Research, New Dlehi.

19

MANAGING TALENT
A MARKET DRIVEN APPROACH

K.S. Venu Gopal Rao*

Employing and retaining talented individuals has become one of the most important challenges for organizations in the present era of globalization. As companies go beyond the confines of their own geographical boundaries getting talent and motivating them to stick to them has taken a whole new meaning. The lack of availability of skilled workforce reflects strengthening demand and a tightening labor market in many countries, consistent with the upward phase of the economic cycle. In India and other developing countries a boom in all round economic activity makes this problem more acute.

How should companies plan for such exigencies? Is there a way out? This paper tries to look at these aspects from a radical view point and tries to identify the ways and means of beating the system rather than living with it. Can employers find out innovative ways and means of arresting the downslide? How can companies ensure that their most valued employees don't leave? Answers are difficult to find but with some smart thinking companies can come with feasible solutions.

In short this paper makes a modest attempt at understanding the management of talent from the Indian perspective in a globalised scenario and tries to suggest some easy means of approaching the challenges.

---

* Associate Professor, Dhruva College of Management, Hyderabad-27.

Introduction

Let's face the tough reality. Major changes are taking place in the business domain around the world and in India. Organizations are unable to figure out reasons as to why their star performers keep leaving them. Companies are struggling to find innovative means of retaining their most valuable stakeholders. Employee retention has become a major challenge. Changes in markets, stiff competition, flatter organizations, smaller product lifecycles and a tighter job market has made the situation worse.

The world scenario is not different. Reasons for attrition are not hard to find. The market for people skills has exploded with the services revolution.. People and skills in certain industries like IT and Consulting have acquired a premium which one could only dream of a couple of years ago. HR managers are groping to find solutions to arrest the slide.

In trying to stop people from jumping ship many companies have fallen back on traditional retention programs. Incentives, ESOPs, time bound promotions etc are passé. Tinkering with compensation programmes, training programs, career paths and the like cannot insulate companies from facing realities. How should companies go about arresting the slide? It will take executives a hard headed strategy to this 'soft side' of business.

Rethinking Retention

Companies should start rethinking about the whole concept of attrition itself. No longer is the company going to determine who stays for how long. It is the market which will determine the fate of your employees. Start living with this fact of life. You can do a lot of things that can make the place a comfortable one to work; you can push people to the limits, send them abroad and provide them with everything under the sun but you cannot counter the pull of the market comprising of aggressive recruiters and attractive opportunities. The old goal of HR management – to minimize overall employee turnover – needs to be replaced by a new goal; to influence who leaves and when. The objective is not to prevent water from flowing out but to control its direction and its speed.

Leading organizations around the world are coming out with innovative solutions which integrate recruiting, retention and training efforts and are geared towards an increasingly mobile workforce. The prescription is not to use the same yardstick for all the problems which the employer might face. Tailor your programs to your retention requirements for various employees and to the level of demand for them in the market place. Some of these mechanisms can be…

Compensation: The most easy and preferred mode of retaining employees is through 'golden handcuffs' – packages weighed heavily in favor of the employee and through deferred compensation. The problem with such a strategy is that it is easy for the competitors to match. Recruiters are smarter and they will buy away your prized employee. Retention amounts therefore end up becoming an additional burden and inflating your wage bill. Companies can now pay for 'special hot skills' where expertise is in short supply. Pay for the critical periods and ignore them once the skills become readily available in the market. Andersen Consulting eliminated its hot skills premium for SAP programmers as soon as it sensed that these skills were easily available and at a much lesser cost.

Paying signing bonuses in stages rather than lump sum can also help keep new employees on their toes, at least in the short run. What is currently happening in the Indian scenario is clearly an act of one-upmanship where a bitter battle is being fought for the skilled worker. This is allowing skilled personnel to float freely in the market and become a target for poaching.

Job Design: In the tearing hurry to retain people through whatever means companies are neglecting this beautiful concept of job design where the employer can look at specific tasks that can infuse confidence in employees. This sort of a commitment on the part of the employer can exert a lot of influence over the retention rates. The UPS example is a very good case of job redesign. Here the organization found out that its drivers who were the main interface between customers and the organization were getting tired by the time they reached the delivery points. When the whole issue was investigated it was found that a whole lot of time and energy was utilized in stacking packets for delivery in their vans. This part of the job was delinked and outsourced to temporary workers who were more than happy with the routine job. The drivers on their part were able to concentrate on delivery with a smile. The results were dramatic. Turnover which was as high as 40 % slid to just 15 % within a six month time span. It also enabled greater coverage of areas in the same time span.

Jobs can also be defined in such a way as to influence when people will leave. By doing so the company is preparing itself for an inevitable situation.

Job Customization: In today's management parlance it is known as job sculpting also. Employees can assess their own interests, values and skills and encourage employees to tailor rewards, benefits and assignments which might satisfy an employee's desire. A case in point can be a flexi time work arrangement.

Social Ties : Man is a social animal. Loyalty to colleagues continues to be high in many organizations. By encouraging development of social ties among key employees companies can significantly reduce turnover amongst employees whose skills are in high demand. Companies which have tried this have seen their turnover rates plunge from 14% to 7%. Arrangements should create a community feeling within an organization. But in times of a crisis or a restructuring programme this can be problematic. This can be offset by another time tested method of creating self designed teams. By involving teams in projects companies can ensure that during the course of the project they remain closely bonded together.

Location : For certain industries location proves to be an advantage. For instance in the engineering and manufacturing industry being close to the location of manpower availability will enable supply. But this may not be the case with the ITES industry where communication skills are at a premium leading to high turnover. It will be wise to set up your office at a location where the swings of employees will be limited due to fewer opportunities.

A good example of taking advantage of location is the industrial belt of Indore in Central Indian state of Madhya Pradesh. Many multinational auto companies like General Motors have set up component manufacturing plants around this area. When the challenge of manpower confronted them they did not rush to the cities. They hired local talent, trained and groomed them and ensured that they were provided with good working conditions and above average salaries. The results of this programme were fantastic. There is no attrition at all and employees in these units are highly cohesive and motivated and are today considered one of the best component manufacturing units in the entire world with several auto companies seeking their services.

Hiring: When companies go out looking for potential recruits they more often end up recruiting those who are the most difficult to retain. Many organizations rush to premier institutions of higher education and flood them with offers in a ratio which is as high as 1:4 and at earth shattering salary packages. By looking at tier 2 and 3 institutions these companies can benefit from not only greater loyalty but at a cost which becomes a win-win for both the employer and the employee. However, an objective assessment of what skills are needed and the problem of switching from a sure shot strategy to a second best options need to be weighed in before such decisions are taken. Companies like HLL, P&G and Infosys are now actively recruiting from campuses outside the no go zone.

How Should Companies Adapt to Attrition?

No sure fire strategies exist and there is no one single panacea that works for an industry. Market forces are too strong. Look at the problems which IT companies in general and the ITES and BPO (India's call center industry, often locally referred to as information technology-enabled services and business process outsourcing, accounts for a quarter of all software and service exports from the country, according to NASSCOM. The market grew 59 percent to $2.3 billion between 2002 and 2003. Total employment in the industry is expected to reach 600,000 by 2007, according to IDC India) What will happen when the stakes are so high.

In the above case the industry has few choices. But in certain industries is will be practical to think of an alternative source. Outsourcing. The world's leading organizations are doing it with great success. Certain companies like GE, AIRTEL, ICICI for example have focused their strategies more on recruitment than on retention.

Lack of leadership is another reason why companies are unable to control attrition. Much of today's business leadership is concerned with occupying the chair for a longer time and personal aggrandizement. There are innumerable examples which tell us how employees and their bosses are no different when it comes to thinking on personal issues and agendas.

Curt Coffman & Marcus Buckingham argue in their best seller First Break All the Rules that "employees don't leave organisations but their managers." There has been a phenomenal change in employee perception of "loyalty" over the last decade and is especially true of knowledge workers. What the organisation can expect from an employee has dramatically changed from "loyalty" to "commitment-to-cause" and so have the factors causing them.

There are ways to adapt to high turnover by simply standardizing jobs and cross training workers in multiple jobs. This reduces the dependence on any one individual. Organizing work around short term projects can make turnover easier to manage and with no explicit need of managing long time loyalty.

Information technology can come to the rescue of the company by storing and preserving what an employee has done all the years with the organization. This also enables the company to immediately find a replacement and train him to take up the job immediately.

Cooperating with Competitors

Many companies view the talent war as an internecine war and view recruitment and retention as competitive exercises – a perspective that has kept them away from their competitors. Cooperative competitiveness can be an effective way of dealing with shortages. It can be taken as a prescription. Companies within the same industry can infact form a consortium which will help them when they need the manpower and help their competitor when projects are hard to find. At the height of the IT boom now sweeping across the Indian sub continent it is timely to form a body which will integrate all the available skills in the market and become a one source contact point.

For this cooperative competitiveness to take root companies will have to stop thinking of their traditional HR roles as guardians of employees and employees as proprietary assets which others cannot share. Those days are numbered and the hard reality is facing every organization.

A positive sign on the horizon is the reported downward trend in all major organizations across India in the last two months. Reasons are yet to be identified. But what is interesting to note is the worldwide trend.

Attrition rates	%
US	42%
Australia	29%
Europe	24%
India	18%
Global Average	24%

Rethinking Loyalty: a smarter look at what employers perceive as loyalty will tell us that loyalty has a different connotation in today's business environment. Loyalty should not mean sticking on to an organization for lifetime. Such behavior and tendancies are detrimental in the long run. Fresh blood has to be infused whenever required. Loyalty must be for the job as long as the employee stays, however short the time is. Loyalty should never be measured in terms of longevity in the organization and fortunately many organizations are looking at talent in a radical manner.

In fact, many new age companies today do not put a premium on the years of experience in a single company or industry. If you are struck in a company for more than three years there is some trouble with the employee and not the company where he/she is working.

Conclusion

Organizations will have to devise innovative ways and means of attracting and managing talent and do so smartly. Easier said than done.

Emerging sectors like IT, Pharma, Communications, Insurance and certain areas in manufacturing have all realized the importance of maintaining a continuous flow of talent and in certain cases given this job to HR consultants who are seeing a major transformation of their business models as a result of this shift. A no strings attached relationship is being encouraged by employers and employees are realizing this reality with a pinch of salt.

The Indian attrition average, although the lowest is no matter for celebration. With majority of the world economic activity being centred around the Asian region, Indian organizations can ill afford to lose the people game.

The framework discussed above is only a broad indication of how companies can shape up their strategies in retaining their star performers. In doing so, we are not only becoming competitive but will be inviting industries from around the world to take advantage of location and people economies. With the largest population of technical and English speaking manpower India only stands to gain at the expense of the rest of the world. The 'soft side' of business stands in the way of success and failure.

20

HALLMARKS OF HIGH PERFORMING ORGANIZATIONS

Dr. Ravi Dasari*

In this highly turbulent tumultuous business environment characterized by globalization, leaders of modern organisations have realized that HR provides a critical source for sustainable competitive advantage. In this paper, the author made an attempt to provide insights in understanding the nature of successful organisations which are following effective workforce practices. The paper highlights the importance of certain workforce practices which ensure peak performance by citing illustrations across the globe. The author argues that organisations which follow these practices can ignite their performance levels to the peak. Finally, a model is presented to guide the organisations to reach high performance levels.

Introduction

Modern organisations are increasingly realizing that, of varied factors that contribute to performance, human element is clearly the most critical. Managers at all levels in organizations are increasingly aware that a critical source of competitive advantage often comes not from having the most ingenious product design or service, the best marketing strategy, state-of-art technology, or most savvy financial management but from having the appropriate systems for attracting, motivating and managing the human resources.

* Associate Professor, Dhruva College of Management, Kachiguda, Hyderabad - 500 027.

To meet the challenges that organisations are facing as a result of the global competitiveness, companies need to demonstrate world-class performance, re-examine the drivers of organisational performance, and create value for society. The drivers of the traditional organizations, namely, physical assets or financial capitals, are no more the prime movers. It is the intellectual or human capital which plays the most significant role in providing competitive edge to the modern organisations. What has already been demonstrated in the past is that some smaller nations with limited natural resources have done better in economic and business development than many nations endowed with rich resources. This indicates that even in the recent past, human capital has played the most significant role in this realm, and it continues to do so.

Building high performance organization is going to be critical for continued success. The practices that can build such work places are employment security, selective hiring, employee ownership, employee involvement, and innovation. Those who make greater use of these practices have much superior business performance.

Employment Security

Security of employment signals a long-standing commitment by the organization to its workforce. Employment security enhances employee involvement because employees are more willing to contribute to the work process when they need not fear about losing their own or co-workers' jobs. For instance, one of the important reasons for the phenomenal growth and low attrition of TCS is the employment security it ensures to its employees.

Selective Hiring

Selective hiring is one of the hallmarks of highly effective organisations. For instance Infosys, although it receives about the twice the number of applications as its competitors, is selective in recruiting employees. In the financial year 2003-04, it received close to one million resumes which went through rigorous selection process, and offers were made to about 1.5 per cent of the applicants. The company focuses on candidates who display a high degree of "learnability". Some other qualities, the company looks for, include analytical ability, teamwork and leadership potential, communication and innovation skills, and a structured approach for problem solving.

Southwest Airlines worries a lot about hiring the right people. In fact, it flies some of its best customers to Dallas, and involves them to the flight attendant hiring process, believing that makes good employee. At Lincoln Electric, hiring is done very carefully based on the desire to succeed and the capacity for growth. One of the practices of many of the Japanese automobile-manufacturing plants opened in the United States that proved especially newsworthy was their extensive screening of employees.

Some companies go to even extraordinary lengths before hiring somebody. According to a study conducted by Hewitt, a leading Indian company was selecting a senior marketing manager, and had gone through several rounds of interviews. The company had identified the person they thought was the right one for the job, and was on the verge of making an offer. The HR head took him out for the dinner and, during the meal, the prospective marketing manager was particularly rude to a waiter in front of his potential employer and peer. The company reversed its decision to recruit him. If he could be rude to the waiter in such a setting, how would his behavior reflect the company image and culture if he were in charge of marketing?

Besides getting the right people in the door, recruiting has an important symbolic aspect. If someone goes through a rigorous selection process, the person feels that he or she is joining an elite organization. High expectations for performance are created, and the message sent is that people matter.

High Employee Involvement

Sharing information is a necessary precondition for high performing organisations. Exploring how to learn together invites participation, which is a key concept in building an ownership culture. In an organization that desires a high-performance culture based on shared ownership, employee participation is a critical element. Successful organisations like GE, Sony, and 3M have leveraged their potential of people resources to improve their efficiency, profitability, and deliver the best to its customers. Be it Sony's miniaturization or 3M's innovation, employee involvement and participation has given these organisations a competitive edge. It is astonishing to know that these organisations receive over 100 suggestions from each employee and the employees themselves get involved in these ideas. Many of the organisations also have culture of employee participation in decision making.

Employee Ownership

Employee ownership offers two advantages. Employees who have ownership interests in the organisations for which they work have less conflict between capital and labor. Employee ownership, effectively implemented, can align interest of employees with those of shareholders too. Second, employee ownership puts stock in the hands of people, employees, who are more inclined to take long term view of the organization.

The research on employee ownership unfolds that organisations which are providing ESOPs (Employee Stock Options) have grown at a phenomenal pace than their competitors in the Industry. In 2004, close to 11,500 US companies had ESOPs involving a total of nearly 10 million workers. An additional 4000 companies sponsored different types of broad based stock option programs covering an estimated 10 million employees. Thanks to these and other programs, roughly 23 million individuals, or about 39% of people working for stock corporations, owned stock, or options to buy stock, in their employers.

Rutgers University's Douglas Kruse and Joseph Blasi, the preeminent scholars in the field of employee ownership, examined 105 publicly traded companies that provided stock options to at least 75% of employees. In the three years following the implementation of their option plans, the companies improved productivity by 17% and return on assets by 2.3% per year. Moreover, the grants made by these companies didn't exact a price from the employees.

In 2003, study by Sibson Consulting found that, dollar per dollar, sharing ownership is the most effective way to lure employees to a new company or keep them at their current jobs. Other studies have shown that companies with substantial employee ownership are more likely than others to offer diversified retirement plans; employee owners usually don't need to fret that their holdings are unduly concentrated in the stock of a single company, namely, their employer.

In India, Infosys Technologies could attract and retain software professionals due to ESOP option extended to them. Many Indian companies are now emulating Infosys. It is observed that in industries like software and biotech, a broad based options program or an employee stock ownership plan (ESOP) is a competitive necessity. Few Indian companies have gone to the extent of offering venture capital to the ideas of its employees.

- At Satyam Computers STEP (Software Technology and Entrepreneurial Programme), invite the ideas from their employees, and help them become entrepreneurs. To fund these ventures, a corpus fund called Satwen has been created. For instance, not more than five people in the company can get together to promote a new company. Satyam will be the majority shareholder; and entrepreneurs are encouraged to pursue some areas like e-commerce, software tools, products in enterprise solutions, etc.
- TEOCO (Totally Employee Owned Company), a US based company funded and headed by Atul Jain, helps its employees to set up their own companies.

Visionary Leadership

Effective leaders have agendas; they are result-oriented. They adopt challenging new visions of what is both possible and desirable, communicate their visions, and persuade others to become committed to these new directions that they are eager to lend their resources and energies to make them happen.

For example, when C.E.O John Carlzon articulated his vision to make Scandinavian Airline Systems (SAS) the best airline in the world for frequent business traveler; he was not saying anything that everyone in air industry didn't already know. Business travellers fly more consistently than other market segments, and are generally willing to pay higher fares. Thus, focusing on business customers offers an airline the possibility of high margins, steady business, and considerable growth. But in an industry known for bureaucracy than vision, no company had ever put these simple ideas together, and dedicated itself to implementing them. John Carlzon did, and it worked.

The importance of vision and purpose lies in the fact that they generate meaning, provide direction, and create a road map to move.

Sony's vision to be as well known as any other company within fifty years; to become a company for changing the worldwide image of poor quality Japanese goods; to be the first Japanese company to go to U.S. market and distribute directly; to create products that become pervasive around the world; and beat U.S. companies in innovations, created a new purpose among its people. It provided a new direction to people and triggered their thought and action for the new march. Purpose not only gives energy to the leader; it provides rallying points around which others willingly connect to move with the leader towards the goal.

During Licence Raj in India Aditya Birla gave a vision of transforming A.V.Birla group into a multinational company, 30 years ago. In contrast, other Indian organizations were busy criticizing the scenario, rather than expanding the horizons. Today A.V.B group is an Indian multinational company having presence in countries like Thailand, Malaysia, Indonesia and Egypt.

Great leaders, thus, demonstrate the capability to communicate the grand vision into smaller goals with clear road map without losing a sense of larger purpose and bigger picture. People move with the vision and purpose because it is exciting to be a part of something big. It creates meaning and charge people to channelize their energies. Modern organisations need visionary leadership who steer the organization to the path of progress and prosperity.

Nurturing a Facilitating Culture

The character of an organization's work environment, particularly as perceived by a member, has long been recognized as a potent influence on employee cognitions, attitudes and behavior. Such environment influences job satisfaction, organizational commitment, employee turnover, vocational adjustment and occupational stability. While much work has been done in the field of understanding organizational performance and the underlying objective determinants (e.g. contextual features such as structure, technology and size); little empirical work is found in the literature identifying discriminating influences that climate may have on performance. Where studies have taken place, they have tended to concentrate on "growth" (sunrise) industries. Baker and Hart and Guest have highlighted some of the limitations of studies hitherto (e.g. Peters and Waterman, 1982), especially the evidence and the methodology tending to examine only successful companies. Baker and Hart further suggested that such an approach could often mean that it is difficult to say whether companies are successful because of their climate or in spite of it. The evidence for the impact of climate upon performance is limited. Other scholars like Campbell *et al*.; Payne and Pugh; Schneider and Reichers; Joyce and Slocum; Rousseau; Rentsch and Schneider have made some useful contribution through their review of climate and organizations but have not reshaped the discourse for the purposes.

Most IT companies consider an informal and conducive work environment necessary for retaining employees. The physical work environment and facilities at the work place as well as the organizational culture were emphasized by most companies as important elements

Since software engineers like informal environment, many Indian IT companies have designed their work place that resembles very much like a college environment. Sports activities such as table tennis, tennis and badminton courts, swimming pool, gym, and open cafetaria are very much part of many software organizations. A number of fun activities such as debate, fancy dress and quiz competitions are organized for organizational members and their families.

The physical work environment reflected open offices, with as little symbols of hierarchy. Open workspaces for relaxing, gym and work out facilities, and where possible facilities for outdoor games were provided. Companies in Bangalore especially have done a lot in terms of the physical work environment, and providing a campus type atmosphere of fun and youth. Several of the large companies had a large campus such as Infosys, Satyam, TCS at some locations, Texas, Kanbay, etc

The locations of some of these campuses have made many companies provide transport to work and other facilities such as lunch, childcare facilities, etc. Several companies did provide benefits such as lunch though employees were charged a nominal amount for these. In fact, provision of snacks round the clock was considered important.

Several companies also attempted to provide convenience to employees by providing facilities for attending to personal issues such as paying telephone and electricity bills, purchasing tickets for concerts, booking travel tickets, etc. These were provided through outsourced agencies who provided help lines and implants in the company. Employees had to pay for these services but the company managed to negotiate favorable rates. This practice was more prevalent in Bangalore.

Culture is a DNA to the organisations. An organization which provides an enabling culture is built to last.

Open Communication

A high performing organization has a high degree of openness and responsiveness. Openness to listen and continuously seek feedback about the performance, and taking appropriate corrective action is a characteristic of a high performing organisation. In Indian IT companies with a young work force, the importance of open and frequent two-way communication was recognized. Employee opinion surveys, "town hall" meetings with the CEO, intranet chat boxes were various means used. Many companies shared the findings of these surveys with employees to create an atmosphere of trust and transparency. Such surveys were also used as benchmarks to evaluate the success of interventions.

Team building exercises to build stronger bonds were especially encouraged in project groups. Picnics, employee recreation activities sponsored by the company were also common. Team celebrations were considered important and companies did have their own "events". Many groups were also actively involved in social work on a voluntary basis, and were encouraged by companies. In fact, some of the companies seek to provide active encouragement to employees to work in the community.

Employee involvements in recognition programs by having awards based on employee voting were also practised in some companies. Recognition programs for a variety of technical, managerial and off work activities were common in all companies.

Successful companies take a regular and continuous feedback from their employee resources, and work on them to make improvements in work design and processes. It is extremely necessary to have a transparent and open culture for employees to give feedback for the improvement of organisation's performance.

Promoting from Within

Promoting from within encourages training and skill development because the availability of promotion opportunities within the firm binds workers to employers, and vice versa. It facilitates decentralization, participation and delegation because it helps promote trust across hierarchical levels. Promotion from within means that supervisors are responsible for coordinating the efforts of people whom they probably know quite well.

At Nordstrom, even those with advanced degrees start on the sales floor. Promotion is strictly from within, and when Nordstrom opens a new store, its key people are recruited from other stores around the country. This helps perpetuate the Nordstrom culture and values but also provides assurance that those running the store know what they are doing and have experience doing it the Nordstrom way.

In a research conducted by Jim Collins and Porras of Stanford University, it was found that organisations which developed home grown CEOs have out played their competitors in terms of profitability and market share. In fact, world's renowned leader, Jack Welch was a home grown CEO who transformed GE as a learning organization which is built to last.

Conclusion

In this highly competitive and ever changing global business environment, organisations are expected to perform exceptionally in order to remain competitive. Research unfolds that organisations which are providing employee security not only ensure employee stability but also guarantee high performance. Successful organisations are treating their employees as partners by providing employee ownership.

Organisations of twenty-first century need visionary leaders who provide direction to the organisations by instilling passion and commitment among the employees. Since employees of modern organisations are knowledge workers, involving them in decision making is a vital factor which ensures high performance.

Progressive organisations are following the philosophy of selective hiring to acquire candidates who are likely to remain with the organizations. Creating enabling culture, and promoting within motivate the employees to learn more, and contribute to the success of modern organisations.

REFERENCES

1. Burt Nanus (1992) "Visionary Leadership", Jossy-Bass Inc. Publishers, 1992.
2. Dutta Rajan (2003), "Let Learning Spur Us On", *Human Capital*, August.
3. James C. Collins & Jerry I.Porras (1994), "*Built to Last*", Random House.
4. Pfeffer Jeffrey (1995), "Producing Sustainable Competitive Advantage Through Effective Management of People", *Academy of Management Executive*.
5. Ravi Dasari (2005), "The Dynamic Synchronization of Leadership - A Model For Twenty-first Century", *HRD Newsletter*, January.

INDIA SHINING WITH HUMAN STRATEGIC STRENGTH

G. Anitha*

The paper highlights the need for a multi-pronged approach to train and harness the resources of the youth in the country to productive avenues of employment and wealth creation. One of the approaches referred to is young professional entrepreneurial development (YPED) activity. It is reflected as business creation by motivating people who have commitment and potential. Various programmes of training and improving the skills of the vast majority of youth for wage employment and self employment are presented. Emphasis is on self employment for income generation and wealth creation. There is need for human resources to be fruitfully deployed; and there is also need to satisfy their urge for identity; and their own emotional, intellectual and physical concerns.

Introduction

India is the largest democracy in the world. It has a federal structure with a written constitution had a parliamentary system of government. It achieved the independence on 15th August, 1947 and since then the development of human potentialities has been given a prime importance. Demographically India's population is 846,302,688. The density of population is 273 per sq.km. and sex ratio is 927 females per 1000 males. Literacy rate is 52.19% (males 64.2; female 39.19). Emergence of human resource as a powerful

* Department of Business Administration, NNS Vidya College of P.G.Studies, Chirala

social group is one of the most notable features in India in recent times. It has been, therefore the endeavor of government of India to mobilize the potential, human resource in different fields and to build up a strong India. The devolution of decision-making over operational and financial matters is central to public management reform which also provides greater flexibility in public service delivery – includes human resource management. At some point, these structural and organizational changes have repercussions on employment security for many public service workers and have an impact on the contractual terms and conditions of an even greater number of employees.

However, these repercussions may not be uniform and affect various groups of workers differently. Cutting jobs and streamlining an organization can improve its viability and provide better employment security for the remaining staff – although this might be small discomfort for those who have lost their jobs in the process. If increased functional flexibility is accompanied by appropriate training, workers may acquire a wider range of related skills, thus improving their chances of being employed; in other words, their employment security in the long term is increased even if they are in a vulnerable situation within the organization currently employing them. Gender may also be a significant factor in the way jobs are affected – but not necessarily. While some elements of reform have undoubtedly had far more serious repercussions on women workers than on men, there are striking examples to the contrary.

Human Employment

The nature of employment and unemployment in India, as in many developing countries, are largely determined by the rate of growth of economy as well as by the growth of labour force, which is itself influenced by demographic changes and a host of other factors. Self-employed and family labour account for a major portion of the total agricultural labour force in India. As the labour force increases, extra labour available is absorbed in the traditional and informal sectors.

The major unemployment sectors in India are:

- Rural agricultural labour accounts for 47 per cent of the total daily unemployment.

- Unemployment rate was also highest in other rural sectors.
- Self-employed sector had lowest share of unemployment.

Manpower development in terms of employment creation and unemployment alleviation coupled with developing the available human resource if properly directed till build up the work force which will be self-sufficient, professional, productive and high dedicated. The manpower thus developed constitute an overall initiative directed toward the improvement, creation and development of quality manpower which will be productive, efficient, effective, having the spirit of entrepreneurship. Hence the developed manpower will be able to fill up, create and expand the employment as well as business opportunities.

This statement was extended the main 7 policies of the Ministry of Manpower, namely 'Saptakaryatama'. One of these policies is called Tenaga Kerja Mandiri Professional meaning Young Professional Entrepreneur Development (YPED). This policy becomes a program. It reflected in creating business by motivating the people who have commitment and potential.

During the REPELITA VI, the new additional work force in India is estimated at 12.7 million persons. If the economic growth is estimated at the average 6.2 percent per annum, the employment opportunity can only accommodate 11.9 million persons, meaning 0.8 million people are not employed. Thus, the YPED is one alternative employment creating opportunity. To implement this YPED, the Ministry of Manpower, Govt. of India has various programmes for that work force at different education background levels:

Meaning, Objective and Target

1. *Meaning*

- Self-reliant, has an attitude, optimistic, willing with great expectations to become success by developing the productive economic activities.
- Young Self-employed (entrepreneur) is Indonesian youth of 15-25 years old who have spirit, own idea and high self-motivated, independent, and able to produce a realistic work in terms of productive business activities which are useful to communities.

- Professional is a person who has capability based on own talent, willingness to exist it into the realistic work in creating either goods or services and able to provide the income source for own-self and satisfaction for others.

2. *Objective*

- To improve the technical and entrepreneurship managerial skill for youth work force.
- To improve the work force's capability to be self-reliant and self-sustained on creating and developing a productive economic activity.
- To create the small productive business for young educated which offers employment opportunity for others.

3. *Target*

- Young Educated People who have talent, spirit of entrepreneurship and commitment to be entrepreneur.
- Young Educated working People with family business background or with a business facilities and own potential to create a business.
- Drop out of school and village community who are willing to improve their life and income in rural areas.

Assessment of Situation in India

The need for opening up opportunities for developing the personality of young persons; upgrading their functional capabilities; making them economically productive and useful, and preparing them for life and work is fully recognized in India. The basic goals towards which the Indian youth programme is directed are as follows :

- Enabling young people to be better individuals through self improvement and self service
- Promoting awareness among young people about the variety and richness of India's culture and traditions and need to preserve and promote the same which is unique in its basic unity and apparent diversity
- Restructuring the educational system to relate it meaningfully to employment opportunities specially among youth

- Training the youth to use new technology in all areas, especially agriculture, where it matters most for economic and social emancipation of young women in India
- Paying special attention to young women's welfare particularly in providing equal access to education, equal wages, maternity and child benefits, special health care, eliminating existing social discriminatory practices to eliminate the social status of young women in India
- Educating the youth about the family control in an effort to tackle the problem of physical, mental and social well-being of young people; and
- Preparing young people for their future role as good citizens by helping them to realize their duties and responsibilities towards themselves, their families, society and the country.

The potential of human resource, if is to be properly tapped requires a good understanding and support. Youth is a very special time with special challenges and is period during which the body, personality, intellect and social attitude will be developing erratically usually independent of one another and frequently explosively. It is a time of life that is full of potential and problems. Breakdown of the traditional socializing structure, urbanization, migration, unemployment and the effect of the mass media have affected the life and growth of youth significantly.

Social values are undergoing significant changes everywhere. Hence, there is a need for them to be fruitfully employed and there is an equally important need to satisfy their search for identity and their own emotional, intellectual and physical concerns.

New Direction to Employment Situation

One of the primary tasks ahead of the planners in India must be the harnessing of the country's abundant youth resources and improving their capabilities for development with equity. The traditional skills of rural artisans require upgrading in tune with changing village culture and to improve their competitiveness. Training facilities will have to be organized for categories of manpower where shortages have been identified and for the formation of new skills that are emerging. Training in intermediate skills needs to be undertaken on a large scale for provision of various services, including primary health services. Policies to attract and develop the required manpower for the hill and tribal areas will have to be pursued with vigor. India's youth have to be trained to use new technology in all areas. Modern advances in genetics and related technology have to be brought to the doors of India's enterprising and hard workers. New horizons are opening in the field of unconventional sources of energy, in the spread of new knowledge to top areas of subsistence agriculture and in agro-industry. Indian youth has to be involved in the process of spreading this new knowledge and this enables expansion of the country. Recognizing the changing context of scientific enterprise in the era of globalization, India seeks to develop paradigms in exploration and application of science and technology for the benefit of all human kind through its new science and technology policy. In a bold departure from the linear paradigms of the west, India offers a holistic policy framework, which directly integrates human resources.

Policies to attract and develop the required manpower for better performance of the Indian industries in various sectors to have world-class success with first class operations. To develop the Indian industries the role of individuals is often important. The traditional skills of rural artisans require upgrading in tune with changing village culture and to improve their competitiveness. There is need for human resources to be fruitfully employed and there is an equally important need to satisfy their search for identity and their own emotional, intellectual and physical concerns.

22

HUMAN RESOURCE MANAGEMENT WITH SPECIFIC CASE STUDIES IN INDIA

N. Kiran Kumar*

Human Resource is only resource that can show their emotions back. So, human resource should be carefully and effectively tackled. To develop Human Resource so that it becomes strategically strengthful, there is a necessity of effective Human Resource policy.

A Human Resource policy is a directive, usually written, to help Human Resource Department in accomplishing its objectives or functions. A Human Resource policy is dynamic to meet fundamental changes or the current situation. It is in this context the paper covers Principles of Good Human Resource Policy and tries to highlight the lively situations existing in various companies like Bombay Oil Industries, Birla Group etc.

Introduction

Personnel management is planning, organizing, Directing and controlling of the procurement, development, compensation, integration and maintenance of people (i.e., employees) for the purpose of contributing to the organizational goals.

Planning means determination in advance of a personnel programme. It involves ability to think, analyze and to reach decisions. Organizing means (after determining a course of action) establishing an organization by designing the structure of relationships among

* Lecturer, Department of Management Studies, J.B. Institute of P.G. Courses, Tirupati

jobs, personnel and physical factors to attain the company objectives. Directing, motivation or actuation means getting employees to go to work willingly and effectively. Controlling concerns with regulating activities in accordance with the personnel plan (formulated on the basis of organizational goals). Procurement means obtaining proper kind and size of personnel necessary to achieve company goals. To maintain the quality factors that are to be taken care are Recruitment, Interviewing, Testing, Induction, Placement, Follow up of new employees for adjustment. Development involves increasing of employee's skill, through training, that is necessary for proper job performance. Compensation means (adequate and equitable) remuneration of personnel for their contribution to achieve organizational goals. Factors considered are Merit rating, Promotion, transfer and discharge, Employment records. Integration is concerned with the attempt to effect a reasonable reconciliation of individual and organizational interest. Maintenance means sustaining and improving the conditions (e.g., health and safety measures, employee services programme, etc.), that have been established.

A Human Resource policy is a directive, usually written, to help Human Resource department in accomplishing its objectives or functions. A Human Resource policy is dynamic to meet fundamental changes or the current situation.

A Human Resource Policy Contains the Information Regarding

Recruiting Employees

Recruitment may be described as the process of getting potential employees willing to apply for a job with the concern or firm. Sources of new employees may be from within the company (Promotion, Transfer etc) or from outside the company (Through press and other advertisements, through employment agencies etc).

Selection Process Includes

- *Job Description:* Combination of short statements that describe both the work to be performed and the essential requirements of the particular job.
- *Application Form:* Application form tests an applicant's ability to write, to organize his thoughts and to present facts clearly.

- *Employment tests:* Measures selected psychological factors such as ability to reason, capacity for learning, temperament, specific aptitudes, physical or motor abilities etc. (Achievement tests, aptitude tests, Intelligence tests, interest tests, Dexterity tests and Personality tests.
- *Interviewing:* It is a conversation between a applicant and the interviewer and much of the interaction between these two is carried on by gestures, postures, facial expressions and other communicative behavior (patterned interview, unpatterned interview)
- *Physical Examination:* Physical Examination as a step is finding whether applicant has unusual stamina, strength or tolerance in unpleasant condition.
- *Induction:* Introducing or orienting a new employee to the organization.

Employment Conditions

How +ve Are You?

A positive approach to work can mean the difference between success and failure for employees and organizations!

Companies are taking major initiatives to create "stress free" environment for their employees. But to fight office blues, one needs to have a positive attitude and willingness to make 'joy at workplace' more of a practice than just an idea, says Aditi Joshi.

How's your work? If you have this sluggish look on your face and a tiring answer - "it's going on" then perhaps its time for you to make a change in your attitude and experiment with the way you have been working.

Work Place Negativity

A major reason for workplace negativity is the structure of work in the 21st century. New economic realities have driven us to embrace a 24x7 and 365-days-a-year schedule. Advances in technology, growth of Internet, e-commerce and globalization are major factors that have added to the stress and competition levels. Companies have been devising ways to help employees fight office fatigue. Ranging from swanky interiors, fitness programs, recreation programs, training modules to meditation classes, organizations are focusing on de-stress initiatives to raise productivity and satisfaction levels among employees.

Essential Factors to Promoting Positive Atmosphere At Work Place

Creating A Positive Workplace: A positive work environment can mean the difference between success and failure for an organization. There are many ways in which managers and supervisors can create positive workplaces for their associates. To begin, they must define what a positive workplace is by establishing good relationships, improving teamwork, and fostering innovations.

The next thing is to develop a "diagnostic eye" - an eye for finding those values, practices, and organizational habits which support joy at work. Identify principles that facilitate positive work environments.

Need for Mutual Understanding: Creating positive workplace is not about facilities alone, it is about creating a positive work culture. It involves self-evaluation and understanding what practices are rewarded in the organization and how well does one fit in to them. Companies need to understand that a positive workplace is about building relationship with employees and making them feel part of the entire process.

There are specific principles that facilitate joy at work – and conversely, promote misery at work.

The Balance : Timing : Clarity Equation : The manager-subordinate relationship is the variable that often has the greatest impact on associate performance. It is important for managers to listen and communicate sincerely with their associates and provide positive reinforcement. Three ways to develop a sincere manager-associate relationship are balance, timing and clarity. Balance means having set standards for reinforcing actions. Timing means recognizing actions or achievements when they occur. Clarity means keeping praise simple and specific.

Interpersonal Relationship : In addition, managers must also promote interpersonal relationships between associates. Teamwork increases productivity, quality, and customer service. It encourages associates to get involved and share information, which improves the overall quality of the organization. By working together, associates disseminate new information to each other, which can produce fresh insights and innovations.

Happy Employees Promote Better Business : Positive workplace relationships also can have external effects. Customer satisfaction can be increased by associates' ambience-happy associates lead to happy customers. It is common for management to overlook the associates and focus only on customers. It is easy for customers to spot dissatisfied associates. Therefore, it is important to create and maintain associates' morale to improve customer satisfaction and increase productivity.

Mission Statements: Another good way of creating a positive interactive workplace is creating a value-centered group mission statement that is endorsed by management. Workshops should be conducted on a regular basis to empower the mission statement and rewards and punishments should be used to enforce the mission statement. It is important for managers to define a purpose, set clear goals, and use appropriate positive reinforcement to motivate associates. One way to do this is by creating and enforcing a mission statement that is beneficial to both associates and customers. By defining what is acceptable behavior and vigorously facilitating a harmonious environment, management can create positive workplaces that benefit everyone.

The Individual Effort: As an employee it becomes one's responsibility to participate in all such initiatives introduced by the company. The management wants to serve their employees with the best and employee feedback is invaluable to them. If you think you need to improve communication with your colleagues and there is lack of free flow of information, then be prompt in discussing it with the management. Let them know what you would consider as a positive workplace. It is not surprising to see how smaller organization with little or no modern day means of appeasing their employees have been successful in creating joy at workplace. In a system where both the employee and the employers are able to set up a symbiotic relationship, people become more adaptable and much better team members, more effective communicators, more creative and innovative in their thinking and more committed to lifelong learning.

Key Rule: Understand what motivates negative co-workers, and take steps to ensure these negative attitudes end. Identify areas in your organization that foster negativity, and then try shifting organizational norms to create a more positive and productive workplace.

The simple rule that you should keep in mind while formulating strategies for a positive workplace or creating joy at work is - If you don't feel well, you don't work well. If you don't work well, your full potential is never realized. You become a liability to yourself and to your business! If you can't manage you then how can you expect to manage others?

Promotions: Promotion may be defined as a significant enlargement in job responsibility but also any increase in pay, prestige, rank or status. There should be a well-developed system of making promotions. Lines of promotion should be clearly defined and a real promotion policy should be formulated. A sound personnel policy demands that promotions should be made from within the industry if suitable persons are available, which will motivate employees, develops employee loyalty, employee morale, increases job satisfaction and enable the formation of an efficient and stable workforce.

Factors forming the bases for promotion from within the organization are

- The results of merit rating
- Productivity and quality record of employees
- Attendance and punctuality record of employees
- Seniority of the employees
- Qualifications and experience, if any possessed by the employee as per demands of the higher job etc.

Discharge: Discharge is most severe penalty that an organization can give to its employees. Discharge is also called as Industrial Capital Punishment. Discharge means ending the services of an employee. In other words, separating or removing the employee from the pay roll for following reasons :

- Serious or habitual infractions of company rules and policies.
- Dishonesty.

- Poor job performance.
- Miscellaneous damage.
- Intoxication.
- Fighting.
- Insubordination.

To support a case for discharge, it is often essential to have a permanent merit rating of the employee.

- Memoranda indicating attempts to correct the employee faults.
- A copy of the final warning.
- A letter of discharge stating the reasons for the action.

Safety Practices: The modern safety movement started around 1912 with the First cooperative Safety Congress and the organization of the National Safety Council in U.S.A. The importance of industrial safety was realized because every year millions of industrial accidents occur which result in either death or in temporary and permanent disablement of the employees and involve a good amount of cost such as resulting from wasted man hours, machine hours etc. Loss of lives and accidents costs gradually led to the formation of Factories act, Office, Shops and Railway Premises Act etc. safety training/ education gives knowledge about safe (and unsafe) mechanical conditions, personal practices and of the remedial measures. Causes of accidents are unsafe mechanical design, improper machine guarding and material handling, broken safety guards and protruding nails.

Safety measures to be adopted are:

- Power should be switched off before repairing the equipment.
- Provide wire mesh safety guards to all rotating parts, e.g., pulleys etc.
- High voltage equipment and other machines that cannot be properly guarded should be fenced.
- Electrical connections and insulation should be checked at regular intervals.

Training

On the Job Training

- Learning by experience
- On the job coaching
- Understudies: The trainee is kept understudy and he learns the ways of his superior under whom he is at study.
- Position Rotation: Rotation an executive from one position to another broadens his background in the business.
- Special Projects : a special assignment, e.g., " to develop a system of dust collection in the foundry" is highly useful and flexible training device.
- Committee assignments, unlike special projects, committee assignments are regularly constituted.
- Selective reading e.g., going through business magazines etc.

Off the Job Training

- Special courses conducted at colleges and universities.
- Role playing : It involves constructing artificially a conflict situation in which the trainee is given a strategic position to play. Role playing increases the trainees skill in dealing with other people.
- Sensitivity training : It develops executive awareness and sensitivity to behavioral pattern of oneself and other people.
- Simulation: Trainees are asked to make decisions about production, cost, inventories, sales etc for a simulated firm.

Financial aid: Financial aid is given as Insurance benefit (including group insurance), Retirement and Pension plans, Health and accident services, Paid holidays and Credit unions (It is a organized group of people who pool their money and agree to make loans to one another at the time of need).

Health Standards to be followed: For adequate lighting, ventilation etc., the heights of the working rooms should be of 3 meters. A high noise level at the workplace impairs men at work and may even endanger them. Noise develops from riveting, grinding, forging, engines, compressors etc. To reduce noise level and to minimize detrimental effects (e.g., deafness) arising out of it:

- Select, purchase and make use of machines and processes, which produce little noise.
- Isolate and keep noise producing machines in separate closed cabins.
- Use silencers to minimize the hissing sound of compressed air escaping from blow-off valves in pneumatic tools and machines.
- Use suitable machine mounts to damp down the vibrations.

Separation

Separation may be due to

- Non-availability/shortage of material fuels or power.
- Accumulation of excess stocks.
- Breakdown of machinery etc.

Various Characteristics/Principles of a good Human Resource policy which foster a strategically superior Human Resource department are

1. It should have due regard for the human equation, the employees, the employers and the consumers (or public).
2. An employee should be able to approach Human Resource manager to express his grievances.
3. It should guarantee permanent employment to competent employees.
4. It should be flexible enough to meet varying needs of employees and the changing conditions.
5. It should have provision to train competent employees for promotion.
6. It should be easily understood by all concerned persons.
7. It should guard employees against unfair dismissal.
8. It should have a fair wage agreement system.

9. It should provide good working conditions, safety and medical benefits.
10. It should recognize individual differences in capacities, interests, emotional reactions.
11. It should motivate all the employees and it should reduce labor turnover and absenteeism.
12. It should avoid opportunism and be stable.
13. It should not contain ambiguities and uncertainties.
14. It should provide good working conditions, safety and medical benefits.
15. It should organize and encourage social facilities.
16. It should be above religious, social or political discrimination.
17. A worker or workers should have formal recognition in phases of management of their vital interest. It should maintain effective consultation between employers and employees.

A look at Six emotions you need to handle if your decisions have to be sound

(According to Vikas Dhoot & Supriya Kurane)

- *Over confidence:* If you have made several investments decisions recently that have been really good, you tend to get over confident about your ability to pick winners.
- *Shame:* Your investment decisions, whether taken in the capacity of an individual or fund manager, are tracked by your peers and you don't want to be seen making the wrong calls. That may keep you from taking the path less travelled.
- *Anxiety:* Coupled with a lack of real information, anxiety makes you apply your fantasies to external events and then you are convinced about it.
- *Experience of Time:* Individuals who feel time is passing quickly are better equipped to handle volatility than those who experience time moving too slowly.

- *Loss:* Risk is intimately connected with loss. People with unresolved real or emotional losses get terrified every time a stock starts dipping. It brings back their past feelings of loss. Reflecting on these past losses and incorporating the knowledge in your investing area will get rid of your panic.
- *Herd mentality:* Often you may take in higher rewards for actions based on imitation rather than independent thinking. Trust your own judgement even if it goes against the tide.

India has developed maturity especially as we have moved up the value chain developing web-ized products. HRMS (Ma Foi human resource management systems) encompasses a wider spectrum of employer HR needs. It helps capture, track, store, modify all information concerning on employee in that organization.

Lively situations exisisting in various companies which results in developing strategically strengthful Human Resource Department

Case-I : Bombay Oil Industries Limited

Views of Bombay Oil Industries Limited regarding their people are

- We offer our existing and new entrants not just a job, but a career and even beyond that, the membership of an organization community.
- We believe that people have a variety of untapped potentials and we shall provide them the opportunities to harness the potential.
- We regard the competence and achievements of a person as more important than age, qualification and experience. Competent and talented people will be natured through varied roles, responsibilities and attractive compensation based on the intrisinic worth of the person and the job.
- We seek to provide our people not just autonomy and job satisfaction but continuos enrichment of their task roles and beyond by empowering and inviting people to take on and perform organizational roles.

- We believe that flatter and leaner organization is more conductive to speed, effectiveness, personal growth and contribution.
- Alongside the above values for quality of work life, we believe in firm action to curb lapses in integrity, system disciplines and non-performance despite feedback and opportunities to measure up.

Views of Bombay Oil Industries Limited regarding their way of working are:

- We believe that people perform better with clarity of goals and result orientation. We will invest in continuously upgrading the goal setting and accomplishment process.
- We will support experimentation, calculated risk taking and innovative approaches. If per chance there are some failures, we shall focus on learning from these.
- We are convinced of the power of participation. We shall involve people in most of things we do. We believe that truly involved people have a sense of ownership and can achieve almost anything.
- We value openness and criticism in our everyday interactions. We prefer 'Constructive no-men' to 'Spontaneous yes-man'.
- We realize the motivational power of praise and the public acknowledgement of genuine and ever-raising standards of high performance.
- We prefer to foster unilateral trust and its reciprocation, to an excess of rules, regulations, checks and balances.
- We believe that organizational and interpersonal care and concern make people want to give their best.

Views of Bombay Oil Industries Limited regarding their Business associates are:

- We regard our business associates as our "Partners in progress". We believe an enduring long-term relationship which meets each other needs, will be mutually most beneficial.

- All such partnerships should be based on merit. We will select and retain associates on merit.

Case-II : A.V. Birla Group

The various steps undertaken to align human resource department by A.V. Birla Group are:

- Involving top management- Vice presidents and above in the H.R initiatives consisting of training and development activities, aimed at developing professional skills, promoting esprit de corps, and enhancing the self-confidence of employees.
- Setting up of an Rs. 16 crore training and self-development centre.
- Secondment abroad of high-potential employees to provide international exposure.
- Designing of performance appraisal systems for managerial employees of the level of general managers and above in order to track high-potential talent. The focus in appraisal was on results consistent with the larger business goals.
- Implementing a group management trainee scheme at the entry-level to attract the best talent.
- Developing managers for leadership roles in order to create a distinct group identity.

A.V. Birla group engaged in inculcating performance orientation, ideas generation and customer focus of employees in a planned manner.

Case-III : Modi Xerox

Human Resource Department in Modi Xerox

Customers are being divided into segments and respective accounts are handled by specialized account managers, global accountant, local accountant, named account and general and mass market managers. Sales promotion agents (dealers, partners) handle the rest of the customers. Through this method there is a fleet of 1000 feet of street people for the products.

The company also has telemarketing and telesales programme. Tele marketing plays a support role, marketing mostly to small organizations with around 20 employees. The telesales team is able to access relevant geographical customers spread on computers each district is split up into defined areas that each person must top.

Apart from this the company has made available various facilities like housing buses, canteen, club, fair price shop, school, bank, and hospitals for the employees. The company also provides training for its employees at regular intervals.

(MXTC) Modi Xerox Training Centre is fully equipped to carry out training programmes for all Modi Xerox employees. The company also has a Research and Development Centre. Every employee goes through a training programme on quality within 90 days of his/ her joining.

Case-IV : Reebok

Practices of Reebok

The well known athletic shoe multinational, Reebok will seek business partners that don't discriminate in hiring and employment practices on ground of race, colour, national origin, gender, religion, or political or other opinion. Reebok will seek business partners who share our commitment to the betterment of wage and benefit levels that address the basic needs of workers and their families so far as possible and appropriate in light of national practices and conditions. Reebok will seek business partners that strive to assure employees a safe and healthy workplace and that do not expose workers to hazardous conditions.

Case-V : Co-eff Friction Bands Pvt. Ltd.

Human Resource Department in Co-eff Friction Bands Pvt. Ltd.

Co-Eff thinks that its team members are its greatest assets. Co-Eff shall provide encouragement for innovation and entrepreneurship and full opportunities for its employees to grow to the limit of their desire and ability.

Co-Eff believes in career development of its employees through need-based training and development, object oriented appraisal system, atmosphere of open, honest communication and thrust.

Co-Eff's endeavor is to create a culture of motivation for excellence and sense of pride, belongingness, pleasure and social fulfillment in being a member of Co-Eff.

It calls upon every employee to instill a collective commitment to a common mission and goals to foster distinctive competence for achieving superior performance and above all to treat customer delight as the core mega value of Co-Eff family.

Case-VI : Scooters India Ltd. (SIL)

Leadership Characteristics responsible for the Success of Scooters India limited (SIL)

- Transparency in dealing
- Genuineness and concern in dealings
- Values were maintained
- Keeping the promises
- Courage and conviction: sticking to the guns where necessary
- Understanding of the business
- High stress threshold
- Environmental sensitivity
- Empowering skills
- Integrative skills
- Ability to develop plans and confidence to achieve them
- Innovation skills

Case-VII : MRF Ltd.

Personnel Policies at MRF Ltd

The Personnel policy is development-oriented. Managers down the line are provided systematic exposure to technology. There are product managers for each category of tyres. Empowerment to departmental heads is encouraged. The effort of the company has been to change its perception of being a low-profile organization to one, which has a new image and corporate identity. The style of management is professional and policy matters are decided by the top management, while day-to-day affairs are left to professional managers. MRF is a multiplant company and disruption of production is avoided if work stoppage occurs at some of its plants.

Case-VIII : Metlife India Insurance Company

Metlife India Insurance Company - Managing Director's opinion on Leadership

As per MD, Leadership is fundamentally about people management. It is about having the right people in the right jobs. A good leader is one who has the ability to feel the pulse of people and never tries to put a square peg in a round hole (that done, half the battle is won). A good leader is one who understands that It does not cost much to show your people some appreciation and exploits it to the hilt.

MD also thinks that no Company is perfect and the same applies to the individuals who work in them. There are many ways of dealing with the problem of underperformers. Just sacking them is one option, but that in turn could create negative vibes in the rest of the organization and cause general demoralization.

Case-IX : Amway India

Amway India - Managing Director & Chief Executive Officer's Opinion on Leadership

Leaders show the way in organizations, while clear vision, Sound Judgement, Knowledge and Passion are qualities essential for successful leaders, there are some other essential traits that define good leadership.

- *Ethics:* They must consistently espouse and act upon their values, Standards and principles in their public as well as Private lives.
- *Knowledge:* Knowledge helps develop perspective. It also opens up the mind and removes biases.
- *The ability to Listen:* Good leaders need to be patient listeners. They must listen to their colleagues and collaborators, to market and constituencies and ultimately to themselves.

- *Decisiveness:* Good leaders listen to all but do what they think is best for the companies.
- *Communication:* Through communications leaders inform, convince, unite, motivate and direct their flock.
- *Exemplification:* Stepping back while others take risks simply doesn't work for leaders. They must be where they are expected to be- ahead, infront, leading the charge.

Case-X : Tri-State Solutions

Tri-State Solutions for Human Resource

Tri-State offers a comprehensive set of solutions to help you manage your human capital. Our programs are designed to enhance, not replace an existing HR department. Or, if your company isn't large enough to afford a HR department, our program can help you with the basics.

- Developing and updating employee handbooks, workplace policies and procedures
- Developing and managing HR forms
- Maintaining personnel files
- Assisting with employee performance reviews
- Assisting with job descriptions, screenings, hiring, orientations, disciplinary actions, terminations and exit interviews
- Provide legally required labor postings
- COBRA administration, unemployment claims, hearings & appeals management

Case-XI : People-Track Solutions

People-Trak is a PC/Web based Human Resource Information System (HRIS) for organizations with 10 to 10,000 employees. The unique combination of performance, passion, and price make it the most comprehensive, affordable HRIS on the market today. From our products to our people to our performance, we are passionate about what we do. Please select the solution below that best suits your needs and discover how People-Trak is the best solution for you!

Small business solution : People-Trak is the leading HRIS solution in the market today. Developed with your business in mind, we offer an easy-to-use, robust system that allows you to manage the needs of your company today and long into the future. People-Trak's HRIS solution offers comprehensive employee data management and reporting; training and benefits administration; recruiting; and much more. No matter what your needs are, People-Trak has the solution for you!

Enterprise solution : For companies that have a distributed workforce or that have outgrown their current HRIS solution, People-Trak now provides a truly powerful solution for all of your unique needs. Our web-native technology combines all of the easy-to-use, powerful features that you would expect in an HRIS solution with the power of the Internet. Add to that our fully integrated Employee and Manager Self Service, you have a solution that will last a lifetime. Experience how Technology can make all the Difference.

Education Solutions : Now Educators and Students can take advantage of people track solutions. Whether you need to evaluate their software for your continuing education, or would like to use their software and training material in you classrooms, People Trak is ready to help. Through their online Demo World and partnerships with Educators around the country, they can provide you with access to all of their solutions. Personnel Management takes employee information out of the filing cabinets or your obsolete HRIS and puts it at your fingertips. Now you can respond immediately to management, employee, and government requests making you a real information provider.

Safety Management : It provides for detailed accident/incident reporting. This allows you to produce all the government compliance reports and documents you need including the OSHA 300, OSHA 300A, and OSHA 301 reports. Safety Management also tracks workman's compensation details including costs for rehabilitation, liability, medical, and more. In addition, there are many reports included that help you schedule training, pinpoint problem areas, control costs, and take corrective actions.

Training Administration : It works in conjunction with Personnel Management to track detailed information about internal and external training programs. At the trainee level, course history, skills acquired, and costs accumulated are added to Personnel Management as classes are tracked and completed within Training Administration. At the course level, you can maintain an extensive catalog of courses and track instructors, facilities, equipment, and costs. You can establish schedules for facilities, instructors, and equipment and Training Administration will prevent you from double-booking resources. In addition, you can define pre-requisite courses for trainees and these pre-requisites will be validated when trainees are enrolled.

REFERENCES

1. *Business Policy and Strategic Management*-Azhar Kazmi-Second Edition-Tata McGraw-Hill Publishing Company Limited.
2. *Business Policy and Strategic Management*-Sukul Lomash & P.K.Mishra-2003 Edition-Vikas Publishing House Limited.
3. *Industrial Engineering and Management* - O.P.Khanna- 1992 edition-Dhanpat Rai Publication (P) Ltd.
4. *Business Environment* - Francis Cherunilam-2003 edition-Himalaya Publishing House
5. *Business Today* dated 1 February 2004
6. *Business Today* dated 4 January 2004
7. *Business World* dated 11 March 2002.
8. *Business India* dated 29 September to 12 October 2003
9. INTERNET
   http://www.seeq.com/popupwrapper.jsp?domain=humanforce.com

23

HUMAN RESOURCE MANAGEMENT
CHALLENGES IN NEW MILLENIUM

Sk. Khamurddin*

The present study focuses on the functions, changing environment to of Human Resource Management, the role and significance and the challenges to Human Resource Management in the new millennium. Most changes in this world do not take place in a vaccum – artists and poets create their works in response to the times in which they live, wars change out of economical and political pressures and companies change their structure in response to the need to follow their customers overseas, for instance.

Therefore, to better understand HR's role in organization's today, it is useful to understand how companies themselves are changing and the trends that are causing these changes to occur perhaps most importantly, organizations today are under intense pressure to be better, faster, and more competitive – HMO's are squeezing more productivity out of hospitals, companies are merging and downsizing, and the universities are working hard to boost enrollments and faculty productivity. Why is this case? Globalization, technical advances, and deregulation are three of the trends accounting for these competitive pressures. Other trends include diversity and other workforce changes under this changing business environment the likely challenges HRM will face in the days to come.

Such being the challenges and the role of the HR function is not realized and respected. In most organizations, the HR function receives the attention of the top management when there is a breakdown in

* Lecturer in Management, Vignan School of P.G.Studies, Guntur

industrial relation. To meet the above challenges, the need of the HRM is a proactive approach, a strategy which helps HR managers foresee events and take appropriate actions before the events occur proactive strategies call for awareness about the likely challenges the HR managers will fall in the days to come.

Introduction

The world is in a state of flux. Rapid studies are being made in most areas of human behaviour. We are poised to witness a far greater mobility of capital and labour. Distances are shrinking. In this era of lib and globe a manager can hardly function effectively unless he continuously updates his knowledge and hones his skills; he is also required to keep his eyes and ears open to the happenings within the firm he works and the experiences of the related system.

The 1990s have brought a revolutionary change in Indian business. Post-liberalization is marked by a shift from command economy to market driven economy; from sheltered market to competitive market; from monopoly to competition; and from domestic made to global made. Such a shift calls for a different approach to Human Resource (HR) problems. The need of the hour is proactive approach, a strategy which helps HR managers to foreseen events and take appropriate actions before the event occur. Proactive strategies call for awareness about the likely challenges the HR managers will realise in the days to come.

What is Human Resource Management?

Human Resource Management (HRM) is a management function that helps managers recruit, select, train and develop members for an organization. Human Resource Management is concerned with people's dimension in organization. HRM refers to practices and policies need to carry out the people or personnel aspects of management job. HRM refers to a set of programmes, functions and activities designed and carried out in order to maximize both employee as well as organization effectiveness.

The Changing Environment of Human Resource Management

Most changes in this world do not take place in a vaccum– artists and poets create their works in response to the times in which they live, wars emerge out of economic and political pressures, and companies change their structure in response to the need to follow their customers overseas, for instance. Therefore, to better understand HR's role in organizations today, it is useful to understand how companies themselves are changing and the trends that are causing these changes to occur. Perhaps most importantly, organizations today are under intense pressures to be better, faster, and more competitive - HMO's are squeezing more productivity out of hospitals, companies like Citigroup are merging and downsizing, and the universities are working hard to boost enrollments and faculty productivity. Why is this case? Globalization, technical advances, and degeneration are three of the trends accounting for these competitive pressures. Other trends include diversity and other workforce changes.

Globalization: Every Country's economy is gradually getting integrated with the global economy. Globalization has vastly increased global competition. Throughout the world, firms that formerly competed with local firms – from airlines to automakers to banks – now face an onslaught of foreign competitors. Globalization has considerable influence on HR functions, employee hiring, training, motivation, compensation and retaining are to be guided by the global perspective etc.

As every advanced nation is increasingly becoming globalized, skills and cumulative learning of its workforce become its competitive assets. All developed countries can design, produce, and distribute goods and services with ease and speed. It is all fungible – capital, technology, raw materials, information – all except for one thing, the most critical one, the element that is unique about a nation – its workforce. A workforce that is knowledgeable and skilled at doing complex things keeps a company's competitive advantage on prime rating and attracts investment.

Technological advances: J.K. Galbraith defines Technology as a systematic application of organized knowledge to practical tasks. During the last 150 years, technology has developed beyond anybody's comprehension. Science and technology enabled man to overcome distances; common birth rate; save lives; generate, preserve and distribute energy; discover new materials and substitute existing ones; introduce machines to do the work for humans; substitute mental work with computers; unravel the mysteries of the seas and space; and provide himself with a lot of leisure and comfort in the present.

The technology affects the HRM in the following ways :

- With the advent of technology, jobs tend to become more intellectual or upgraded. A job which can be either handled by an illiterate or unskilled worker previously, now requires the services of an educated and skilled worker.
- The introduction of new technology dislocates workers unless they become well equipped to work on new machines. This makes obligatory on the part of HRM to train workers and to rehabilitate those, whose are displaced or cannot be trained.
- For those employees who pick up and acquaint themselves with new technology, the job will be challenging and rewarding. In general working class will always gain through increased productivity, reduced prices and increased real wages, – which are all by-products of technological advancement.
- Technology has its impact on human relations. Technology lays down the requirements for much of the human interaction in organizations.
- Job holders will become highly professionalized and knowledgeable.

Deregulation: Even though this situation is a problem to some industries over subscribed by Govt. but for many others it is an opportunity to elevate themselves to better faster and more competitive International positions with less shackles.

Trends in the nature of work: Globalization, deregulation and technology are also changing the nature of jobs and work. There has been a pronounced shift from manufacturing jobs to service jobs. These service jobs will in turn require new types of "knowledge" workers, new HR Management methods to manage them and a new focus on human capital.

The challenge for managers is that skill workers can't be managed as were their earlier counter-parts. As one expert put this, the centre of gravity in employment is moving fast from manual and clerical workers to knowledge workers, who resist the command and common model that business took from the military 100 years ago. In other words, workers like these can't just be ordered around all closely monitored. New HR system and skills will be required to select, train and motivate such employees and to win their commitment.

Workforce Diversity: Workforce diversity is another major work related trend. Specifically, the workforce becoming more diverse as women and other workers flood the workforce. Diversity has been defined as "any attribute that humans are likely to use to tell themselves, that person is different from me" and thus includes such factors as religion, caste, sex, age, values and cultural norms.

Major Challenges to Human Resource Management

Globalization: The demise of communism, the breaking up of trade barriers, and the rise of networked information in business. Market capitalism guides every country on the earth; goods and services flow across borders more freely than even before. The information networks instantly link nations, companies and the people.

Globalization is increasingly viewed as a growth strategy by several companies. As table 1 shows, major shares of revenue and profit of multinational corporations originate from their overseas operations.

Table 23.1: US firms with the largest foreign revenues

Rank	*Company*	*Foreign Sales as % of Total*	*Foreign Net Profits as % of Total*
1	*2*	*3*	*4*
1.	Exxon	76.9	60.0
2.	General Motors	28.6	43.4
3.	Ford Motor	32.3	24.4
4.	IBM	58.4	61.0
5.	MOBIL	59.4	59.6
6.	TEXACO	55.6	50.4
7.	GE	29.7	20.7
8.	HP	55.5	64.3
9.	CHEVRON	47.2	61.7
10.	CITICORP	62.2	69.6
11.	Phillip Morris	35.3	18.8

(Contd...)

1	*2*	*3*	*4*
12.	P&G	48.8	36.3
13.	American Intel Group	53.8	68.8
14.	E.I.du Pont de Nermours	41.0	51.6
15.	Intel	55.9	32.5
16.	Motorola	45.2	93.9
17.	Xerox	57.4	55.8
18.	Coca-Cola	65.5	75.1
19.	Dow Chemical	56.3	40.5
20.	Compaq Computer	45.4	38.9

Source: Forbes, July 27, 1998.

Growing internalization has its impact on HRM functions. The HR Department is required to cope with the problems of unfamiliar laws, languages, practices, competitions, attributes, management styles, work ethics and more. HR Managers are required to know that international operations has

1. More functions, such as taxation and coordination of departments.
2. More heterogeneous functions, such as coordination of multiple salary currencies.
3. More involvement in the employees personal life, such as housing, health, education, and recreation.

HR functions such as planning, staffing, remunerations and the like, therefore, will be affected by globalization.

Corporate Re-organization: The early 1990s brought us news about corporate mergers, takeovers, and massive reorganizations to bend off reorganizations resulting from acquisitions, mergers, divestitures or a take over threats. The organizations will have impact on organizational levels and employees. Employees experience anxiety and uncertainty about their places in a new organization.

The employees of both the 'taking over' as well as the 'taken over' will have anxious moments because of:

- Fear of loss of jobs,
- Job changes, including new roles and assignments,

- Transfers to new geographic location,
- Changes in remuneration and benefits,
- Changes in career possibilities,
- Changes in organizational power, status and prestige,
- Staff changes, including new peers, supervisors and subordinates,
- Changes in corporate culture and loss of identity of the company.

There is little indication that the place of mergers and acquisition will slacken in the near future. To a greater extent than ever before, companies consider acquisition managers, or dive statures as routing business transactions. But an important key to the success of almost any merger or acquisition is the management of HR.

Close to the corporate mergers and takeovers is the internal restructuring of organizations themselves. Competition from Multi National Corporations and domestic industries has compelled many companies to resort downsizing and centering their organizational structures. A Business Today Survey (Dec 7-21, 1993) revealed that more than two dozens of the biggest companies were busy reducing the number of management grades, eliminating layers, and redrawing reporting lines with their organizations. ITC, HLL, Godrej, Boyce, RPG Enterprises, Raymond woolen mills, Shawallace, Ballarpur Industries and Crompton and Graves are only some companies which have embarked certain flattering exercise.

New Organizational forms: The practice of HRM is shaped by the organizational forms in which people are employed. Elsewhere, economies have been undergoing fundamental changes and the structures of organizations and the relationships between them have been transformed. Big organizations have grown bigger in the sense that the world economy is dominated by trans-national organizations. Between a quarter and one-fifth of the total GNP of the world is, thus accounted for by just 600 companies. But the employment potential of these giant corporations is declining. Large production units have become increasingly a thing of the part, and large companies now tend to consist of business units managed relatively independently.

The consequences have been a higher profile of medium sized and small sized firms and employees.

This trend affects HRM functions in various forms :

1. Smaller firms and establishments mean a more personalized style not more face to face.
2. Smaller units may require complex and sophisticated systems of personnel management but may also be less able to sustain them in areas like management development.
3. Smaller units are less able to sustain to specialist personnel management functions.
4. On the other hand the business and human challenges of operating in this kind of environment are becoming greater. The contricenfied of HRM will then be in facilitating the processes which support the development the enterprise, rather than, as a traditional personnel management has done, in administering system for controlling people.

The basic challenge of HRM an enterprise management comes from the challenging of competition. The issue is not large firms, medium firms and small firms. Competition in many sectors is no longer between individual firms, large or small, but between constellations of firms. In the international for instance, major companies operate through a complex web of strategic of varying degrees of per.

Changing Demographic of Workforce: The major challenge that has resulted from changing workforce demography concerns dual career couples, couples where both partners are actively pursuing professional careers. Organizations have accustomed of using job moves and physical relocation as an important means of developing talent. Men or women moving through organization ranks to upper level position need experience in variety of roles in different organizational units. Frequently physical relocation is required. The increasing number of dual career professionals limits individual flexibility in accepting some assignments and may render organizations flexibility in acquiring and develop talent.

Another change in the workforce demographics is related to the following number of employees who are young. Companies which were set up in the 1940's and the 1950's have employees who are now superannuating. Enterprises which are newly established obviously prefer young men and women. The Bangalore based Infosys, for example has employees whose average age is just 25 years. Employees of Infosys are taken to the office by a company bus and the day starts with breakfast. It is positive consideration for the employees who are single.

The other demographic changes in the workforce are:

(i) Increasing number of working mothers.

(ii) A steady decline of blue-collar employees who are giving way to white-collar employees, and

(iii) Increasing awareness and education among workers. All these have their own implications for HR managements.

Changed Employee Expectations: With changes in workforce demographics, employee expectations and attitude also have shifted. Traditional allurements such as job security, attractive remuneration, housing and the like do not attract and motivate today's workforce. Employees demand empowerment and expect equality with the management. Previous notions about the managerial authority are giving way to employee influence and involvement along with mechanisms for upward communication and due process. Empowerment results in redefining jobs, both on the shop floors and in board rooms. As workmen are given more control over their jobs, a whole of inspectors may become redundant, not because they will do bad jobs, but because there shall be no need for them. Expectation of equality breaks up the traditional relationship between employer and employee, top and bottom. Another expectation by the employee is that the electronic and telecommunication revolution will improve the quality of work life. Innovation in communication and computer technology will accelerate the pace of change, and as a result lead to many innovations in HRM.

One possibility that is increasingly becoming a reality is the opportunity to work at home. Alvin Toffler estimates that the information revolution will shift millions of jobs out of factories and offices back to the home front. Also today's average worker demands better treatment, challenging jobs and career advancement. For example, the worker's unions of Otis, Hindustan Lever, ICI, TOMCO, Blue Star, Webel Electro and Central Bank are rewriting their agenda to include quality and better customer service and are even accusing the managements of malpractice. The HR management must, therefore redraw the profile of the worker and dissever new methods of hiring, training, remunerating and motivating employees.

Proactive Industrial Relations Strategy: There is almost a metamorphosis at the industrial relations front. Strikes, lockouts and loss of man-days are declining considerably as is evident from Table 2. This transformation is the result of socio-economic and political reasons.

Table 23.2: Declining strikes, lockouts and man-days lost

Years	*Strikes*	*Lockouts*	*Total*
1986	1458	434	1892
1987	1348	451	1799
1988	1304	441	1745
1989	1397	389	1786
1990(P)	1459	366	1825
1991(P)	983	445	1428
Worker Involvement(in thousands)			
1986	1444	200	1644
1987	1495	275	1770
1988	937	254	1191
1989	1158	206	1364
1990(P)	1162	146	1308
1991(P)	551	440	991
Man-Days Lost(in millions)			
1986	18.02	13.92	32.75
1987	14.03	21.33	35.36
1988	12.53	21.42	33.94
1989	10.70	21.97	32.66
1990(P)	10.64	13.45	24.09
1991(P)	5.26	10.47	15.73

P- Provisional.

Source: Labour Bureau, Shimla.

Trade unions are affected because of the realization on the part of the workers that strikes and militancy will be a loss to the company which finally leads to the loss for themselves which consequently brought down the negative role of trade unions. Hence trade union membership has fallen drastically all over the world, and the future of labour movement itself is in danger. The need, now is to adopt a proactive strategy towards industrial relations, an approach which should enable HR specialists to look into the challenges unfolding in the future and to be prepared to convert them into opportunities.

Contribution to the Success of Organizations: The biggest challenge to a HR manager is to make all the employees to contribute to the success of the organization in an ethical and socially responsible way. The well-being of a society to a large extent, depend on its organizations and particularly business organizations. It is the business organization which makes goods and services available, provide jobs, generate wealth, and lend stability and security to the people. Failure of organizations will affect the society, particularly the lowly placed people in the social hierarchy , when NGEF, a Bangalore based Engineering company, was about to be declared sick and handed over to BIFR, the workers gave a statement against the move, as the close would effect them more than any other interest group. Similarly when Railway Ministry stopped placing orders with the Bangalore based BEML for supply of railway coaches, it was workers, conscience which was priced most, as back of orders meant back of adequate work lent not wages.

It must be the endeavour of everybody to ensure success and stability of organizations. Responsibility is more on the HR manager as it is he/she who coordinates people's activities and it is the people who make or mar organizations. The ethical and socially conscious dimensions of business are too obvious.

Renewed focus on the people: There is renewed focus on the people in organizations. For too long managers believed in structures, strategies and systems. For decades this philosophy served companies well. It supported many successive ways for growth when companies started integrating horizontally in the 1950's and diversifing in the 1960's and finally when they expanded into global markets in 1970's and early 1980's. But over the last decade the technological advancement with competitive and market changes have eroded its effectiveness. The problems of companies as diverse as GM and IBM in Europe, and Matsushita and Hitachi in Japan can be solved at least in part, if the top management can understand the changing philosophy. The structure, strategy, system approach, which worked during post-war era, is no more relevant in today's economic environment which is characterized by overcapacities and intense competition. What is needed now-a-days is, people's approach. Adopting this approach does not mean stripping the organization of all it's formal systems, policies and procedures. It requires redefining them so that they support and not subvert the top management's ability to focus on the organization's people.

The top management must therefore:

1. Reduce it's reliance on strategic planning systems by influencing the organization's direction through the development of key people.
2. Lighten the burden of control system by developing personal values and interpersonal relationships that encourage self monitoring, and
3. Replace much of its dependence on information systems by developing personal communication with those who have access to vital intelligence and expertise.

The role of HR manager in the present scenario is to make the role of people either justifiable or sustainable.

Managing the Managers : Managing the managers is another challenge before the HR managers. A dangerous trend is emerging in the post-liberalization era. Freedom given to the managers is grossly misused to get rid off talented and hard working juniors. Managers feel slighted when their juniors turn out to be better performers. Managers, instead of only managing their allotted functions assume the role of employers and for those employees whom they feel are too smart even without the knowledge of the real employer. Consequently, many talented and able young men are forced to leave the organisation. This situation is a real challenge for the H.R. Managers and study their commitment to morals and ethics of their profession.

Protect the Interests of Weaker sections: Another important challenge for HRM is to protect the interests of weaker sections of the society. The dramatic increase in women, minorities and Other Backward Communities (OBC) among the workforce has resulted in the need for organisations to re-examine their policies, practices and values. The general belief is that a lot has already been done to minorities, SCs and STs and OBCs but facts reveal a different story. Table 3 depicts the figures about recruitment of Scheduled Castes in Govt, PSUs, banks and insurance corporations.

Table 23.3: Recruitment of Scheduled Castes in various organizations

	1989-90		*1990-91*		*1991-92*		*1992-93*	
	Vacancies	Filled-up	Vacancies	Filled-up	Vacancies	Filled-up	Vacancies	Filled-up
Govt.	35647	31243	31928	19878	20041	9271	19692	8271
PSUs	11000	8125	10461	6316	12149	7196	8542	2369
Banks	8822	8084	3142	2197	2242	1384	1319	1139
Insurance	8822	8084	3142	2197	2242	1384	1319	1139
	58554	50475	46559	29415	39236	18231	30259	12346

In the name of global competition, productivity, and quality, the interests of the weaker sections of the society should not be sacrificed. With the gradual decline in the role of government in economic activities, weaker sections feel helpless and insecure. It is the responsibility of every manager, more so of the HR manager, to ensure that people belonging to weaker and poorer sections will be encouraged to get right jobs, and are not discriminated while in service, either in remuneration or promotion.

The Job Ahead : The job ahead in this vital area of management of human assets is clearly a difficult and challenging one and the men in this field must arise to the occasion and ealing themselves with all the weapons to combact the ongoing changes. They will need more technical competence and better professional training. They will need to identify and develop potential leaders and this process of identification and development may require constant sharpening of their tools of selection. They must develop the ability to through clearly the kind of problems, needs, aspirations and motivations of people and have sagacity to aid management to deal with successfully. They must be aware of latest literature, experiments, tools and techniques, theories and principles in their chosen avocation and they must also endeavour to use the constantly growing body of knowledge by learning to improve on personnel functions.

Conclusion

It can be concluded that HRM is more crucial today for the success of any organization than ever before. The question that arises at this point is what measures should be organization take into influence the human resource outputs. The issues that are need to be considered to move towards this goal are:

(a) Workers must no longer be seen as a liability, but as a key resource which needs to be carefully gestured and constantly developed.

(b) While organizations are becoming conscious of potential of new technologies, they must also realize the crucial role that human being plays in managing that techniques.

(c) Those organizations which are able to give relevant training to their personnel and maintain their willingness to learn new ways to do things can hope to survive in today's economic environment.

(d) There is serious need for all of us to try and transform at least that part of organization, where we have the power into learning segments could then be synthesized into learning whole.

REFERENCES

1. Gary Dessler, *Human Resource Management*, Pearson Education (Singapore) Pvt. Ltd., New Delhi, 2002.

2. David A Decenzo and Stephen P Robbins, *Personnel/Human Resource Management*, Prentice-Hall Incorporation, New Delhi, 1989.

3. Kandula, *Human Resource Management*, PHI, New Delhi, 2003.

4. William B Wrether, and Keith Davis, *Human Resource Management and Personnel Management*, Tata McGraw-Hill Publications, New Delhi, 1994.

5. Edwin Phillip, *Personnel Management*, Tata McGraw-Hill Publications, New Delhi, 2002.

6. Biswajeet Pattnayak, *Human Resource Management*, PHI, New Delhi, 2002.

7. *Forbes*, July 27, 1998.

8. *Indian Management* Vol 42, December 2003

9. John Sullivan, "HR in 21st Century", *HRM Review*, March, 2003, ICFAI Publications.

10. Aswathappa K, *Human Resource and Personnel Management*, Tata McGraw-Hill Company Ltd., New Delhi, 2002

M.N.Rudrabasavaraj, *Dynamic Personnel Administration*, Himalaya Publishing House, Mumbai, 2000.

TRADITIONAL PROFESSIONAL COMMUNITIES

THEIR REORIENTATION

Dr. K. Sudhakar Reddy* and **Dr. V. Narasimha Rao****

Traditional professions and professionals associated with these occupations were given considerable support prior to liberalization of the Indian economy. The support included programmes of the decentralized sector industrial organizations such as Khadi and Village Industries Commission, Handlooms, Handicrafts, Sericulture, Coir and Wool all India bodies, apart from small scale sector organizations associated with modern small industries. Council of Scientific and Industrial Research (CSIR) is implementing the Leather Technology Mission since 1995 to introduce technological improvements in the leather sector. In the era of liberalization, artisans, particularly in rural areas, are not getting sufficient support from the state for their long term survival and growth strategies. They are forced to take care of themselves, without enough support from the Government. Providing substantive support in the modern economic environment is one part; and the other equally important aspect is to introduce a comprehensive Human Resource (HR) reorientation programme to address the following issues : (1) attitudes, (2) thinking, (3) emotions, (4) self-concept, (5) health and habits, (6) work culture, (7) inter-personal skills, (8) communication skills, (9) money management,

* Associate Professor, P.G. Dept. of Business Administration, Akkineni Nageswara Rao College, Gudivada.

** Associate Professor & Head, P.G. Dept. of Business Administration, Akkineni Nageswara Rao College, Gudivadass.

(10) leadership, (11) customer reorientation, (12) self motivation, (13) team culture, (14) risk management, (15) ethos and values. These should be sensitively and appropriately presented to artisans to motivate them to become dynamic, and competent to meet the challenges of globalization.

"India's way is not Europe's; India is not Calcutta and Bombay. India lives in her seven hundred thousand villages" –Mahatma Gandhi.

Introduction

Indian village reflects Indian society, civilization and its basic values. Indian viilage shaped the thought, culture and economic life of the Indian. All the artisans are originated from Indian village only. Artisans, the traditional professional communities have been the custodians of the heritage of India. The country artisans now and then enjoy the appreciations from all the corners across the globe for their creative, innovative and unique contributions. Indian handicrafts were once the focal point of global market for their masterpieces. The golden age of India in the history was nothing but the glorious days of our artisans. The ancient weavers surprised the world with the saris that were packed in matchbox size. The idols of ancient India still cost in lakhs in foreign markets. Despite its rich image the socio economic conditions of the artisans are not satisfactory. They have been struggling for existence.

In the 1950s second largest employers of labour force after agriculture were cottage and village industries. Even today two crore craftsmen are employed in traditional professions across India. Bulk of the labour were involved in the production of cotton, silk and woolen fabrics. The asset of cottage and small-scale industry is traditional accumulation of capital and skill. It was mentioned in the Industrial Policy Resolution of 1956 that cottage and small sector enable more equitable distribution of the national income and effectively mobilize resources of capital and skill, which may otherwise remain unutilized. Taking care of traditional professions will solve the problems arising due to unplanned urbanization. Most of the traditional industries carried on household or cottage are using traditional skills such as pottery, basket making, hand spinning, hand weaving, hand made paper, toys and dolls, embroided articles, coir, sericulture etc.

The review of literature reveals that traditional professions have been well taken care by state with the inspiration of Gandhi's Swadeshi movement. Khadi Village Industries Commission was initiated to promote the Swadeshi movement and it has been employing around eighty lakh people through protecting the traditional profesions. The Rural Employment Generation Program has been contributing significantly for the safeguard of traditional professions. During the past nine years 1.9 units have been established and they are employing 22.73 lakh people. KVIC is taking care of this program with the help of government of India. The artisan welfare trusts have been formed in all major states. KVIC launched the "Viswakarma Abhigyan" in 2002 with an eleven-point charter and a detailed action plan. KVIC grew to a vast sector of around five thousand institutes and 1.8 lakh entrepreneurs. It has so far signed MOUs with thirteen reputed institutes.

The CSIR has been implementing a mission mode program namely Leather Technology Mission (LTM) since 1995 in leather industry. It has commissioned around two hundred activities in seven states, which had tangible and traceable impact on the artisans. Sixteen training centers including Chennai and Guntur were established for leather products and they are producing hundreds of shoemakers including women. Regarding the manufacturing of Kolhapuri cheppals, improved process of bag tanning to produce leather was successfully demonstrated. However, to meet the challenges of global environment a brown revolution for leather in India need to be initiated. In cane and bamboo sector local artisans are competing with large scale users like paper and rayon mills. In India over 130 species of bamboo are found and some of these are widely exploited by traditional communities on a selective basis. The Indian artisan can benefit from this emerging opportunity if an integrated development plan can provide a sustained supply of raw material along with product and market knowledge that can generate a great deal of employment. Cane is also another area where skills are available very widely and this too can be made use for the benefit of the crafts persons. The Small Industries development and Employment Program have covered various sub programs like jute, nonmulberry silk, wool, hand knotted carpets along with bamboo and cane under 'Fibers and Handicrafts Program'. The Development Commissioner (Handicrafts) is responsible for implementing various development schemes of the Government of India. The efforts of state governments are supplemented by the Central Government. During the Ninth Plan emphasis was laid on marketing, skill upgradation, modernization, welfare and preservation of craft heritage. The Ninth Plan addressed the need of train the trainers programs, computerized design development, design development through reputed institutes, development of improved tools and kits. This plan document acknowledged the need of helping the artisans by providing quality raw materials, new designs, improved manufacturing techniques, marketing support and other welfare measures. The success story of 'Aparajitha' project reported be Elisa Patnaik, a Bhuvaneswar based journalist is an inspiration for artisan community of India. The devastated artisans of 1999 super cyclone in Orissa ar taking international orders today. They travel the country seeking out new ideas and incorporating quality controls. The contributions of renowned designers from reputed institutes like NIFT and NID supplemented the efforts of Aparajitha.

Despite all these significant efforts traditional professions are gradually disappearing in the global trends. In the era of liberalization and globalization artisans particularly rural India are not getting sufficient support from the state for their long term existence. The WTO negotiations under structural process made the governments to withdraw from welfare measures and civil society is not so strong that it can't take care the responsibility. The empowerment of traditional professions is the need of the hour. Capacity building and entrepreneurship development are to be initiated on war foot basis in order to protect existence of traditional rural artisan, where India lives. They are simply left to their own fate and asked to survive on their own in the global market of sharks. Under WTO regime India simply can't afford to protect these traditional professions unless radical changes take place in their functioning. Meanwhile the HR issues of artisans haven't been addressed adequately.

HR Issues Relevant to Traditional Professionl Communities

Any development or growth can't be imagined without human concern. Profession .... Organization ... Society ... Country ... all these are collective human systems. The glory of any of these systems is attributed to human capital. As a women entrepreneur once mentioned, if people are taken care of they will take care of any thing either in the organization or in any profession. That's why HR issues play vital role in any development. Mostly to many organizations HR means training and development. The soft aspects of human resources are hardly considered. Training is important, but capacity to assimilate and work with improved technology is very important. The effect of training or capacity building basically depends upon the attitudes of the individual. Attitude determines altitude. Attitudes ar determined by core values and ethos of the individual. Self-image is a key factor that contributes for the success of any individual in traitional professions. Along with positive self-concept, the higher level of needs like self esteem, self-actualization and need for achievement should be addressed. Ultimately the objective of HR initiation should be making the individual to feel pride for being the part of the traditional profession. Today no traditional professional enjoys the comfortable future or career and has to stretch every minute for existence imparting employable an entrepreneur skills is also very essential in the case of traditional professions.

As most of the traditional professions are largely located in clusters spread throughout the country, their level of literacy is also very low. In the existing generation more than sixty percent are even illiterates and semi literates. So facilitating informal education is the first prerequisite apart of HR initiations. Health needs of the artisans should also be taken care of. In order to address higher level of needs of traditional professionals, basic needs fulfillment is very necessary. They need to be ensured the security needs also. Like wise HR initiatives should be in the direction of Maslow's hierarchy of needs.

The comprehensive HR reorientation programs in the current global trends should address the following issues comprehensively in practical and realistic orientation. The program should be included (1) Attitudes (2) Thinking (3) Emotions (4) Self-concept (5) Health and Habits (6) Work culture (7) Inter personal skills (8) Communication Skills (9) Money management (10) Leadership (11) Customer orientation (12) Self motivation (13) Team culture (14) Risk Management (15) Ethos and values.

Artisans are very flexible to change and very responsive to technical changes and innovation, if they are sensitively and appropriately presented. Their strength lies in conversion costs associated with their work, the existence of strong community structure and the tradition of household based activity including participation of women at different stages of production. If such kind of HR orientation is facilitated, the traditional professionals will be very dynamic, competent and will certainly meet the challenges of globalization and liberalization. Our products will enjoy good appreciation across the world and one fine day our artisans will be leaders to the world of traditional professions. Lets await that day .....

25

HUMAN RESOURCE DEVELOPMENT AS STRATEGIC STRENGTH

N. Lakshmi Soujanya* and **B. Raghava Satya Murthy****

The paper highlights a few tasks of economic governance on which special attention needs to be paid, such as physical infrastructure, agriculture, accessibility of information technology to the youth in vast rural areas, and rural housing. The focus of the paper is on emphasis to be given to human resource development (HRD) for managing corporate excellence in the 21st century. HRD could be the means, and cannot be an end in itself. The new systems call for reengineering not only processes but also internal mindset of the people working in the system. An empirical study on rigidity of software professionals from various angles to shift to the changing requirement has been presented. Out of the seven rigidities analysed, emotional and creative rigidities have changed. In the other five rigidities - intellectual, dispositional, social, behavioural, and perceptual – the software engineers have shown consistency in their rigidity, before training and after training. The study reveals that this model could be a tool for reorienting the employee mindset to respond better to the changing environment.

Introduction

Excellent first half results. Sensex crossing 6000. Foreign exchange reserves at over $100 billion. Quarterly GDP growth

* Lecturers, P.G. Dept. of Commerce & Business Administration, KBN College, Vijayawada.

** Lecturers, P.G. Dept. of Commerce & Business Administration, KBN College, Vijayawada.

exceeding 8%. We haven't seen India usher in a new year with such confidence. The big question is: How can we translate this 'feel good' factor and the achievements of 2003-04 into higher decadal growth? But, as we begin 2004, the theme bears repetition. Irrespective of party or alliance comes to power after the elections, it would do well to single-mindedly pursue four goals which will faster greater economic governance.

Goal No. 1: Physical Infrastructure

Much has happened for the National Highways Authority of India's Golden Quadrilateral project. Equally much needs to be done. Even if we focus only on national and state highways – and most state highways are so poor that they don't deserve to be called roads, leave aside highways there is work that needs to done on another 187, 500 Km. Also, not enough has happened for developing the village roads, for which an extra Rs 0.50 / litre was levied in the last Union budget. A third of these roads were supposed to be rebuilt with concrete. Up to October 2003 less than Rs. 5 Crore has been spent on doing so.

Similarly, Indian rail needs major reforms Cargo traffic has been steadily moving away from rail to roads because of high tariffs arising out of cross – subsidization. There is excessive congestion on main lines, a rapid deterioration of rolling stock, and a decline in safety standards. The Indian Railways needs major Investments. Just as the roads in the country are gradually improving through fuel gas and prime importance given to the national highway development programme, so too can the Indian Railways be transformed if such importance is given by the highest authority in the country.

Goal No. 2: Agriculture

The decadal growth of agriculture has been under 3% per year with 2/3rd of the population dependent on the rural economy, this must be raised to around 4.5% in this decade. How ever, agriculture has to grow at 4.5% for India to consistently achieve about 7% GDP growth. That won't be easy because agriculture is a state subject, and most states aren't in fiscal position to devote resources for irrigation, seeds and extension services. But it has to be done through fiscal incentives, changes in laws, encouraging new technologies and marketing methods and far greater public- private partnership.

Goal No. 3 : Using IT for Educational Empowerment

By 2020, India will have 231 million people in the 15-24 age group who will need gainful employment, plus another 232 million children between 5 and 14 years. For then, IT has to be the lever. Even if half of them get access to community computers, India will be an unbeatable force in the knowledge age. This requires a dramatic expansion in laying fiber optic cables and ensuring that the basic computer costs no more than Rs.15,000 so that each village can have at least three.

Goal No. 4 : Rural Housing

According to the 2001 census, only 41% of the rural households have pence houses, and just 21% have concrete roofs. Why should this be so? Why can't the boom in loan – financed urban housing be replicated for rural India? Why can't public sector banks offer housing and home improvement loans to formers at 7.5% floating for 15 years? The benefits are enormous. There will be more rural housing. There will be a surge in rural employment; there will be greater broad basing of the demand for brick, cement and steel.

These are some of the tasks of economic governance.

In the context of the borderless world, heightened competition and opening up of the domestic economy. People have become pivots around which successful firms function. Businesses today strive for all round excellence in their entire rage of activities. The managerial focus has, over the last few decades, shifted from 'efficiency to efficiency and 'effectiveness', then to efficiency, effectiveness and 'excellence'. Efficiency orientation creates 'I' versus 'You' divide between employees and management whereas in the effectiveness orientation, 'We' and 'Us' concerns emerge. When the organization strives for 'excellence' at a global level, it starts inculcating among is community a dislike of 'mediocrity' and encourages them to strive for 'superiority'. In a market-driven competitive economy, only the fittest firms survive and with in the forms, the fitter of its employees fare better where performance appraisal plays a significant part as a tool and technique of management development and growth. Usually, performance will be assessed periodically and potential appraisal on a long- term basis with a developmental objective will be focal. The potential appraisal system offers more possibilities for personal growth and development for the best performers in the company.

Change is said to be the only constant and how one responds to change decides one's growth and evolution as an individual. A high performance knowledge based organizational system is a community of such dynamic individuals designed to survive and grow against the rigors of emerging global technological and market conditions. Its long life depends on its continuing ability to re-adapt, renew or reinvest itself in an organized way in response to disruptive discontinuities in its environment. It needs to be fast, focused, and flexible, as ell as positive and proactive. It is possible only through its human recourse and hence, its people must therefore continually engage I the learning and use of knowledge, in accelerating their decisions, activities, work processes, continuously integrating and co-ordinating these functions as a single organism through information and communication technology and as a parallel process dynamically re-examining their assumptions concerning changes in and with the external environment. However, the efforts put in by domestic firms to develop human resources do not appear to be commensurate with the challenge before them if one accepts the measure of the number of training days as a reflection of such a strategy. They did not even reach, on an average, one man-day of training per year per employee.

The challenge of attaining international competitiveness is inspiring and exciting for any organization. The road map calls for an appreciation of the potential value of the organization 's human capital and the readiness of organizational leadership to commit itself to continuous improvement in the area of human competitiveness as the essential imperative for survival and growth. The need for emphasis on Human Research Development(HRD) for managing corporate excellence in the 21st century arises for the reasons such as, (a) the single most critical constraint to survival and competitiveness will be the dearth of managerial skills in the emerging competitive environment, (b) the imperatives of business growth with increased complexities such as problems of size, technology and competition (c) unsettled political, economic and social conditions. These complexities call for an altogether different orientation and competencies than hitherto followed from the managerial community. While business has moved into the dynamic mode, people and models still remain at a static/linear mode. This mismatch needs to be resolved to meet the demand for intelligent managers for the 21st century. The potential performance programming model has been an attempt at resolving these issues, considering the present and future needs of both organizations and individuals. The model is a map of the dynamics involved in the process of personal/organizational growth. The model facilitates the process of orienting oneself to the rigours of the professional world from a systems perspective, envision the potential from a much broader perspective, position oneself with a cleared focus on the opportunities/roadblocks in responsibility for continuous learning and improvement. Such a realization of the higher potential in a person is in fact the first major step towards reduction in wastage of human potential. Being a framework, is has the necessary flexibility to accommodate both the universal and the situational experiences, making it extremely effective in diverse contexts.

The Approach

The emergence of the knowledge industry exemplified by firms like Infosys and Wipro also points to the emergence of the knowledge worker. The Indian professional today is better educated than their predecessors. They expect more intelligent leadership and more considerate treatment. The concept of self-management is more appropriate to the Indian business environment and to the current global context. The approach reinforces one's own responsibility for personal growth without sacrificing overall objectives of the firm, offers a well defined path for self- development consistent with the cultural traditions and practices. The model is designed around a very basic premise that 'Nature' is the source of all learning, the master trainer and frame of reference against which the person validates the map of his internal world. The core processes involved in personal growth/ business are mapped out using very familiar symbols from nature or the cultural context to facilitate accelerated learning. The big picture of the micro and macro/global environment creates the necessary orientations and further in depth understanding is brought about in the organizational context of work. The focus is on enhancing the shared areas in terms of organizational goals and values. The organizational relevance of one-ness, harmony, quality and such other basics along with approaches to problem solving are a very much amenable to be clarified, using very ordinary symbols from daily routine. Thus, one-ness is the quality of one and duality is the quantity of two. Duality is division, separation and the origin of problems.

Trinity is the quality of three. It is more of completeness like the three dimensions of the physical world. The concept of trinity is common to predominant religious systems and thus a part of every one's daily life. Employees are oriented to the concept of self-expression is the purpose of such a *reorientation*. The model facilitates the process of aligning personal goals with that of the organization. The result is the capability of the organizational system to behave as an organism to respond to its environment. This model was tested in very diverse situations and also in some domestic companies as a tool to enhances their human competencies.

The remnants of the past achievements still linger with most of the firms. The business process continue to be inefficient and ineffective. Re- engineering strategy, business process, technology and human resources become inevitable for meeting challenges in the new millennium. Approximately, 70% of private businesses in the U.S. or Europe have run or are running some form of re-engineering projects. The failure rate of reengineering attempts has also been equally high-over 70%. The reasons for such a debacle can most often be traced to the management of the human interface with the new systems. New systems call for reengineering not only processes but also the internal mindsets of the constituents. In such contexts, the approach to HRD assumes an altogether different dimension. HRD could be the means and cannot be the end in it self. This end, or to use a better word, direction, is journey of evolving and sustaining an organizational work culture and environment where maximum satisfaction of not only one's basic needs but higher order needs of recognition, achievement, self-esteem and self actualization are met. These organizations will be working under a philosophy of *'Caring and sharing'*.

The Empirical Study

Software exports registered a high growth rate of 50% consistently over the last five years through information technology business trends at present indicate negative growth rates. Hardware exports slipped by 19% in 1998-99 when compared with the previous year. However, the demand for software professionals continue with different skill sets. The industry operates under tremendous pressure since global competitiveness is extremely critical growth, which depends on the creativity of its human resources. Creativity provides the cutting edge of organizational excellence. It is reflected in the organization's ability to achieve improvement after improvement and innovate both incrementally and radically in its continuing quest for growth. Against this background, the following objectives were set for the study:

- To identify and locate the existing level of intellectual, creative, emotional, behavioral dispositional and social rigidities among the trainees and
- To undertake comparative analysis among the trainees *vis –a – vis* various dimensions after the training programme, assuming that variables are predominantly a function of the potential performance programming learning process.

Methodology

The model was put to test in a number of software firms. It is important to note the fact that employees of the firm are working in a highly competitive environment. A well structured 'rigidity scale designed by Dr.N.K.Chadhe had been used for the purpose of collecting primary data for the study. The various dimensions of rigidity scale are as follows.

Intellectual Rigidity

- Not accepting anything or idea without logical reasoning
- Believing in setting high standards for oneself and striving for the best.
- To have an inclination towards thinking about and discussing intellectual and philosophical matters and
- To have definite ideas about things.

Emotional Rigidity

- Lack of emotional reaction even when the situation demands it.
- To have definite ideas about what type of emotional reactions should be aroused in particular emotional situations.
- Arousal of similar, unchanged, emotional response to stimuli and
- To exert strict control over one's emotions.

Dispositional Rigidity

- To have very definite and rigid habits and/or ideas about habits of eating, sleeping, reading, dealing with things etc.,
- To be inclined to finish work once started.
- To hold extreme attitudes (positive or negative) regargin persons, things, problems etc.,

Social Rigidity

- To find it very difficult to feel comfortable in a social gathering or a new situation
- Not developing too many new acquaintances
- To have very defined ideas about society and the social responsibilities of the people and
- Giving too much importance to friendship

Behavioural Rigidity

- To stick to traditional ways of dressing and
- To have strict and definite attitude towards Indian traditions and customs.

Perceptul Rigidity

- Not to accept or believe in anything without a proof supporting it
- Generally misperceive something for some other things
- Not able to perceive abstract relationships among things and a tendency to stick to obvious relationships and
- To perceive one's knowledge about things to be always correct.

Creative Rigidity

- To be able to think of diverse ideas at a time
- Not able to think about a thing or problem from many different angles and
- To show stereotype in ideas

Major Findings and Interpretation

Rigidity is a tendency to persevere and resist conceptual change, to resist the acquisition of new patterns behavior and to refuse to relinquish old and established patterns. Accordingly, higher the score, higher the rigidity along that dimension. For the purpose of analysis, mean scores, standard deviation and coefficient of variation have been calculated.

Out of seven dimensions that have been studied, in as many as five dimensions, software engineers have shown consistency in their rigidity, except that of emotional and creative rigidities during pre-training session. This shows that the overall engineering personality is rigid before attending the programme. How ever, after attending the training, they have scored minimum co-efficient of variations for both emotional rigidity and creative rigidity.

The study implies that the education and training that the employees undergo exercise a significant influence in the personality to meet the requirements of their profession. The model could be a tool for reorienting employee mindsets to respond better to the changing environment. However a lot more has to be done in terms of improvement and amendments in communication and value setting proves, delivery mechanisms, and perhaps restructuring authority relationships so as to successfully achieve the objective of positioning dynamic, enterprising and responsible professionals, who are capable of handling and responding to socio-economic pressures in diverse contexts. In the context of software development, creativity of its employees moved the company for being market driven to market driving. The result of the study validates the fact that PPP could enable the software firm to deliver unique and superior value products to its global customers and continues to improve itself during the period of the study.

26

HRD AS A STRATEGIC POWER

P. Purnachandra Rao*

The article stresses that HRD is the ultimate goal of development of the country. Network of educational institutions and cooperatives can transform the lives of the poor in rural areas to become conscious of the need for education, health, self respect and other social basic human needs. The development of human resources focuses on education and health, for improving productivity, and for accelerating economic growth. The experience of East Asian economies can serve as a model for India on the stages of development by focusing on development of human resources, including technical skills at the post secondary stage. The article also underlines the importance of business process outsourcing, and development of a knowledge society in the country, for transforming the country into a developed nation.

Introduction

In the emerging knowledge & innovations coupled with human development and effective utilization of them will hold the key to sustainable food and livelihood security as well as to national well being. It is the time to inspire our youth power, which represents the best part of the production to fire them with enthusiasm to build a modern India. The emergence of a caring, sharing and innovative India in the coming century, is a prospect well within our reach. It is our duty and privilege to work towards such a dreaming nation. With only 2.4% of the world's geographical area, India's share of the world

* Faculty Member, Dept. of Commerce & Business Administration, ANU P.G. Centre, Ongole

population is 16.7% i.e. 102 crores. India is adding 17 million people every year, roughly equivalent to the total population of Australia. We are second in the world next to China in terms of population.

What is needed now is a renewed focus on the Labour & Human Resource Policies that views development as a sustainable process of expanding the capabilities of people and seeks to mobilize the human resources. This new approach necessarily emphasizes the centrality of human initiative in the development process. This approach provides holistic concept which should guide every policy. It acknowledge the human being as the engine of development.

Needless to say, HRD is the ultimate goal of development of India. The changing economic environment in the world in the wake of globalization and the resultant pace of technological development also necessitates the formulation of an appropriate of HRD policy for the workforce. The policy has to inter-alia meet the challenge of rapidly changing technology, the changing nature of job – slots and the consequent rapid change in the social organization. The policy has to design, redesign and continuously upgrade the potential of human resources so that the labour can contribute to the process of development in a productive manner.

The experience of Pravara Nagar, Maharastra shows that it is possible to make significant progress towards empowering rural people, particularly the poor through a network of committed educational institutions and cooperatives. It is worth noting that today even the poor in the Indian rural areas are becoming conscious of the need for education, health, self-respect and other social basic human needs. They are a more enlightened and vocal with increased capacity of articulating their voices as a recent study reveals by the "Institute for Human Development" has shown.

In this direction, the state has to become an efficient, active partner in promoting HRD. It is responsible for providing an enabling environment in which all individuals can develop their capabilities to the full and can thereby become more productive members of the society. The state must ensure that the weak and vulnerable sections of the society are not being neglected but are enabled to develop their capabilities and play their part in economic and social life.

The development of human resources can be achieved by focusing on education and health and thereby increasing the productivity of the economy which is an important factor in economic development. The experience of East Asian economies shows that they could face a lead over other developing countries by making investment in human capital formation. In the 60's these providing universal primary education and later by increasing the availability secondary education. The experiences of East Asian economies also show that they were successful in reducing in the birth rate and thus brought about a sharp decline in their population growth. Consequently, declining fertility becoming available for child education. Coupled with this, these countries made more investments in generating technical skills at the post secondary stage. The result of these policies has been to create a broad, technically trained human capital base well studied for improving productivity and thus ensuring rapid economic development. The experiences have significant lessons for India.

Some Selective Demographic Indicators

% millions

	1981	*1991*	*2001*
Rural Population	76.70	74.30	72.22
Urban Population	23.30	25.70	27.78
Literacy	43.56	52.21	65.38
Male Literacy	56.37	63.86	75.96
Female Literacy	29.75	39.42	54.28

The table reveals that about half of the women are illiterates and also 1/4th of the males are illiterate. Hence, the state has to focus the areas where its interference is very much required. The first area which needs to be improved is literacy. In certain situations new ways of giving education have to be thought of, such as tele-education and open schools and universities. Another important area is health care. Modern methods like tele-medicine can be applied for treating patients in remote areas.

Role of India in the Business Process Outsourcing (BPO)

Business process outsourcing means "Contracting with an external organization to take the primary responsibility for providing a business process or function". The changing Economic Environment in the World of globalization and the resultant phase of technological development. Business process outsourcing (BPO) paves the way to global competition and ensures strategic focus on core capabilities for improving stakeholders' value, by increasing efficiency and there by reducing operating costs. The identified benefits of BPO are quality improvement, enhanced access to technology, lower operating costs, greater efficiency and strategic focus on core competencies. BPO covers the activities like finance & accounts, human resources, real estate related matters, internal audit, tax compliance, applications process, procurement, knowledge management etc.

India can provide educated, technically qualified and efficient manpower at a much lower cost than the west as it has a potential human resources base. A study reveals by Nasscomm KPMG on "Attractiveness of key locations in India for IT enabled services (ITES). The national capital region (NCR) housed 103 BPO companies, out of which Bangalore has 65 firms followed by Mumbai with 59 entities. Other regions like the Hyderabad-Secunderabad cluster accommodates 43 firms while Chennai has 34 and Chandigarh-Mohali cluster consisting of 12 companies, upcoming BPO destinations include Pune, Kolkata, Kochi, Ahmedabad, Gandhi Nagar and Ghaziabad and others. Despite the outcry in the united states (anti BPO bill passed by the US Congress), BPO is here to stay and India will continue to retain its competitive edge for obvious reasons such as a large and highly skilled workforce with good knowledge and extremely low wages in comparison with European and American standards. As long as these positive factors continue in its favour, it seems India will retain its competitive edge and bans could end up having little effect on the burgeoning BPO industry.

Knowledge Society–Role of India

The veda means knowledge. They are not religious books but a perfect guide to living. Hence, they are relevant even in the modern age. They speak of everything on staying healthy, social evils, improving concentration/knowledge, and tenets of behaviour. All vedic rituals are techniques for leading a harmonous life. All scientific developments of the modern age, including dotcoms, have their roots in the Vedas. In the 21st century, knowledge is the prime production resource instead of capital and labour. There will be a shift from the molecule-centric agricultural area to the electron-centric knowledge era. The efficient utilization of knowledge alone can create comprehensive health for the nation in the form of better health education, infrastructure and other social indicators. The ability to create and maintain the knowledge infrastructure, develop knowledge workers and enhance their productivity through creation and nurturing and exploitation of new knowledge will be the key factors in a nation becoming a knowledge superpower.

As the world transforms into a knowledge society, India has the tremendous advantage due to its core competence in certain technologies including IT, Vast natural resources and above all 300 million ignited youth. This strength must be harnessed fully for the transformation of society towards developed nation. As we know, both sectors viz. Economic & Social are complementary to each other and investment in one at the cost of another is likely to produce disastrous consequences. Hence, the state has to balance these two sectors by proper treatment investment for the overall development of the nation.

REFERENCES

1. The Week.
2. The Hindu.
3. Times of India.
4. The Indian Journal of Labour Economics.
5. Business Line,
6. Eenadu.
7. Yojana.

27

DEVELOPING HUMAN RESOURCE AS A STRATEGIC STRENGTH

Suja S. Nair* and **Dr. C.S.G. Krishnamacharyulu****

Progress of any nation depends on its human resources development, participation and contribution. People fortify organizations with their creativity and productive capabilities and help fructify their goals. The globalization and liberalization scenario has changed the value systems and new challenges are in the offing for H.R. professionals and senior managers.

The work force diversity, multi-skilled needs of jobs, cross-cultural operations and switft changing technology would place pressure on the hiring, training, appraising and developing activities. The practices like buying talent would take back seat giving over riding preference to developing and retaining capable, creative and competitive resources.

India, a country of unity in diversity, can leverage its resources to full extent if its human potential can be extracted. India is known for the availability of world class scientific, technical, managerial and professional manpower. Indian human resources can do far better if provided necessary environment.

Strategically the efforts should address the areas like quality education, health care services, infrastructure, training and counseling,

* Lecturer, Department of Management Studies, J.B.Institute of P.G.Courses, Renigunta Road, Tirupati.

** Professor and Chairman BOS, School of Business Management, S.V.University, Tirupathi.

social security and protection of constitutional rights like right to work. This paper discusses these measures in detail.

Introduction

Progress of any nation depends on its human resources development, participation and contribution. People fortify organizations with their creativity and productive capabilities and help fructify their goals. The workforce diversity, changing technology and multi-skilled needs of jobs and cross-cultural operations would place pressure on the hiring, training and developing activities of organizations.

In the new environment, technology, information and capital are found to cross borders easily and thus effective human resource management has become the competitive edge for corporations. Indian industry is realizing that technology, IT, infrastructure, large-scale operations and capital are "entry criteria" and not competitive tools any more. In other words, people and their effective management is where Indian businesses will have to invest in. It is the social responsibility of employers towards employees and society at large, which includes primarily contribution to quality education, healthcare, infrastructure and protection of human rights.

Modern HR

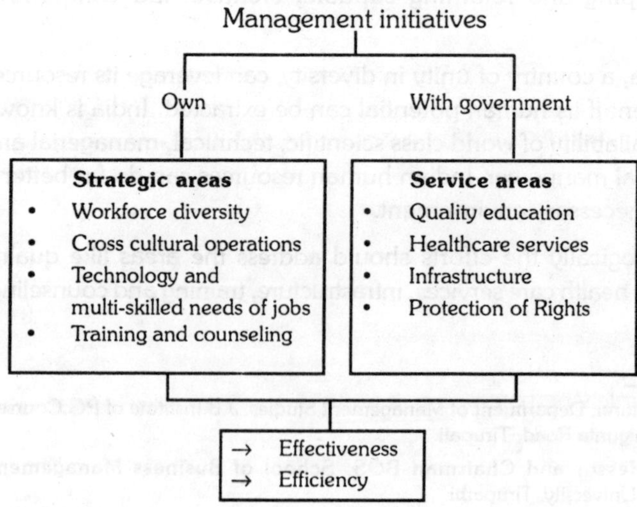

HR Strategies

What kinds of challenges are inherent with the emerging environment? What kind of strategies HR personnel have to evolve?

Workforce Diversity: Workforce diversity refers to varied background of workers of an organization. Because of globalization many changes have taken place and people of different cultures, races, genders, ethnics, attitudes, customs, religions, social classes etc., come together to work. Understanding the differences will make them more constructive but misunderstanding would lead to disruptive problems. These trends have implications for HR managers. The decision alternatives are to manage them or to fight against them.

The organizations that thrive will be the ones that embrace the new demographic trends instead of fighting them. Diversity is a business imperative. There is no way to achieve business strategy unless we develop and utilize diversity in the work place to achieve competitive advantage. A growing number of companies now realize that their workforces should mirror their customers. Similarities in culture, dress and language between workers and customers creates more efficient interactions between them and better business for the firm. When companies discover they can communicate better with their customers through employees who are similar to their customers, those companies then realize they have increased this internal diversity. And that means they have to manage and retain their new, diverse workforce. There is no going back: diversity breeds diversity. Managing it well is an essential part of HR strategy.

Managing diversity means organizing a heterogeneous workforce to perform to its potential in an equitable work environment where no member or group of members has an advantage or a disadvantage. The challenge is to create a work setting in which each person can perform to his or her full potential and therefore compete for promotions and other rewards on merit alone.

Cross-cultural Operations : Many organizations have cross-cultural operations through mergers, acquisitions and strategic alliances etc. unleashed by LPG reforms. They know how important it is to knit together the new partner's financial, technological, production and marketing resources. However, the reso urces of the new enterprise also include people and this means creating a partnership that spans different corporate cultures. Corporate cultures may differ in many ways, such as the customs of conducting business, how people are expected to behave and the kinds of behaviors that get rewards.

Corporate culture has been called,

"the DNA of organizations invisible to the naked eye,

but critical in shaping the character of the workforce."

A key source of problems in these organizations is differences in corporate cultures.

As the Chairman of Unilever cited,

"achieving diversity is about bringing together a rich mix of people, with different perspectives, creating an environment in which their differences are valued. A vibrant and open culture, a culture where ideas flourish, people thrive, grow and have fun. A winning culture of the 21st century."

Both workers and managers need to understand and capitalize these cross-cultural problems as companies combine their efforts to offer products ands services to customers in far flung markets.

The management of culture needs assessment and definition of different cultures, identifying the common factors and modifiable differences and activating integrating forces.

Technology and Multiskilled needs of jobs: In the creative economy, the most important intellectual property isn't software or music, it is the intellectual capital that resides in people. When assets are physical things organizations own them. But when the most vital assets are people, the best that organizations can do is to create an environment that makes the best people to stay. However, this is easier said than done due to the new challenges in the offing. One such force is technological change.

New technological changes, facilities like computers and availability of internet all create fast channels of communication and vast changes in nature of work. Continuous learning is the main requirement for the modern workers who at the same time should be multi-skilled and team oriented and adjusting to changes. Globalization has made worker as mobile as capital. Indeed they can be thought as globalized people who are employable almost any where in the world. These changes in communication, mobility and nature of work all need worker to have different skills to manage the changes and adapt to these changes. Thus world of work has become complex and diverse. With technology and competition the very existence of their jobs has become a major area of concern for the workers.

Clearly it is a great challenge for human resource professionals to synergise the roles of labour and capital and build a relationship based on mutual trust between them. It is necessary to lay emphasis on concepts such as teamwork, retraining, multiskilling and rewards. Hiring, training and development, performance appraisal should all be monitored on a fair basis. Sustained development and competitive advantage is based on creation of wealth, improving environment and ensuring social equity. These values have to be put into action through integrity, commitment, transparency and accountability.

Training and Counselling: Training and counseling help remove performance deficiencies in employees. Training contributes to employee stability in at least two ways. Employees become efficient after undergoing training. Efficient employees contribute to the growth of the organization. Growth renders stability to the workforce. Training makes the employees versatile in operations. All rounders can be transferred to any job. Flexibility is therefore ensured. Even dissatisfaction, complaints, absenteeism, and turnover can be reduced if employees are trained well. Further needs of employees will be met through training and development programmes. Training is an investment in HR with a promise of better returns in future.

As a result of emerging workforce of diversity, the concept of diversity training in the work place is an area of increasing interest and challenge.

Diversity training helps in many ways.

- It provides organizations with a competitive advantage. With such training, employees are more likely to appreciate and utilize, increased heterogeneity of their markets, customers and colleagues.
- Diversity training can be a catalyst to unlocking innovation by providing the opportunity to utilize multiple perspective rather than adopting a unitary view.

Diversity training comes in many ways. ASKE model suggests the guidelines for factors on which diversity training has to be developed.

Exhibit 1 : ASKE Model

ASKE MODEL Learning elements	*Examples of the components of diversity training*
Attitudes	• Understanding your own attitudes • Understanding different attitudes • Openness to cultural difference
Skills	• Inter personal communications • Cross-cultural communications • Problem solving • Team work • Leadership • Conflict resolution
Knowledge	• Legislation • Company policy and procedures • Professional standards
Emotions	• Re-organising emotions • Managing emotions productively

Source: Workplace diversity training, Dr. Philip Frame and Jennifer O'Connor, *Human Capital*, vol.7, No.8, January,2004, p. 35.

HR Services

In response to the forces, what kind of services HR should envisage?

Quality Education: Education is imperative for development of any society or nation, whose objective and purpose necessarily would be to add value to individual, organization and society. If it serves, the education is effective and that is the quality education. Quality education is one, which serves as a tool for development of values of individual and in the process facilitates growth and development of society.

For quality education the process should start at the primary level and span the entire education spectrum. It can be seen that the number of educational institutions have been increasing but the quality delivered is in the opposite swing. What is frustrating is that there is no linkage between the growth of the institutions and the industry's requirement. In this background organizations can take education as a social responsibility and serve in the following two ways.

- Provide basic education to the people by providing primary and secondary education to its workers. They can also think broadly to provide education to the poor by providing night schools, evening classes and awareness programmes. Organisations can plan these measures to provide basic education to people with hand in hand with other voluntary organizations.
- Management of technical education by sponsoring scholarships, contributing to faculty development, encouraging research and donating to equipment and building, industry can help teaching faculty with modern techniques of teaching and developmental programmes.

Indian Government has been trying to make education reachable to the poor-providing free education through Government schools, free lunch for poor students. Many measures go ineffective because of flaws in implementation and maintenance. Corporate HR managers can play a role collaborating with the government agencies.

Health Care Services : Development of healthcare sector is the toughest challenge for the Government. Since this is a vital sector and it faces several problems. The challenges include vast population, paucity of resources and non availability of affordable healthcare to the poor. We have to leverage the traditional strengths of Unani, Ayurveda and Yoga systems, harmonise them with modern systems and evolve an integrated model of affordable healthcare for the poor. Therefore we have to scientifically establish elements of traditional systems and at the same time take advantage of new technologies, which will surely provide a new dawn in the horizon of health care.

What can be the role of organizations in this regard?

- Organisations can also take means to improve infrastructure and other facilities for public health and this investment must be exempted from tax liability.

- Organisations may take necessary steps to build sanitary facilities and monitor the standards of public hygiene throughout.
- Organisations may monitor health education programmes for workers and make them health conscious and make them aware of different schemes and utilize them provided by government.

Infrastructure: Development of infrastructure like Telecom, Highways, Railways, Posts, Power, Constructions etc., are important for development of any nation. There is direct correlation between the availability of infrastructure and a country's economic growth. In a vast country like India penetration of all the infrastructural facilities should be made to facilitate economic development. Infrastructural facilities give Indian human resources to have higher freedom of mobility and development of living standards.

What then is the role of corporate bodies? While the organizations engaged in provision of infrastructural facilities like Roads and Buildings(R&B department and construction companies), Post, Telegraph and Telecom (P&T, BSNL, ITI and others), Electricity (GENCO, TRANSCO and Power sector companies) have to develop human resources to enhance quality of services. The user organizations have to train the users to utilize the services optimally and productively.

Protection of Rights: Some Fundamental Rights observed in all the developing nations include Right to work, Right to equality, Right to express and Right to seek justice. Perhaps this is one area that is more sensitive and challenging. corporate democracy for protecting right to bargaining and for participation in decision making of, employees is highly desirable.

India has put in place laws meant to protect worker interests in the matter of minimum wages, collective bargaining, safety and gender equality. These laws cover less than ten percent of total workforce. Also many pieces of legislation such as factories act and law on minimum wages are hardly enforced. The dynamic changes in work environment and its consequent erosion of rights at work is the main cause of tension, conflict and low productivity in labour. The conventional view about rights at work is limited. More often than not, it is confined to existing labour legislation. If human well being is the purpose of development, meeting basic needs for all and ensuring decent work for people must be fundamental objectives. The mismatch between legal perspective and broader perspective of rights can be bridged only through corrections and interventions in national development strategies that would make for a more egalitarian development, which can only be introduced by the state because, unlike markets, governments are accountable to their people. The realization of rights as a part of the development agenda would also reshape the world of work and livelihood.

Conclusion

Ignoring human face will prove to be a spoke in the wheel of the much hyped second generation (2G) reforms of government. Differences in political parties, unions, etc., make the introducing of reforms in labour laws in India a pause. Competitive labour policy is being pursued by the other developing countries like China, Thailand, Malaysia and South Korea to attract investment and create employment avenues. India with huge human resources in unorganized and organized can no longer wait and see. Rather we have to join the race sooner than later. Thus Indian HR can give better results with proper background that may be provided by respective government and employers.

REFERENCES

1. Personnel Today, *The Indian Journal on Personnel Management*, Vol. XXIV. No.1, April-June 2003(p-52).
2. *The Indian Journal of Labour Economics*, Vol. 46 No. Jan-Mar, 2003 (p-3).
3. *Human Capital*, Vol. 7. No.6 November-2003 (p-46).
4. Analyst, *Chartered Financial*, December-2003 (p-66) & November-2003 (p-76)
5. *Industrial Economist*, 15-29 October-2003 (p-9).
6. *Industrial Economist*, 30th October-14November-2003 (p-33).
7. *Industrial Economist*, November-2003 (p-33).
8. *The Hindu Business*, Friday, 19th December-2003 (p-9)
9. *The Hindu*, Wednesday, 10th September-2003 (p-10).
10. *The Hindu*, Monday, 22nd September-2003 (p-22)

11. *The Hindu*, Sunday, 16th November-2003 (p-8)
12. *The Hindu Business line*, Saturday, 15th Novemebr-2003 (p-4).
13. *The Economic Times*, Saturday,1st Novemeber-2003(p-6)
14. *The Economic Times*, Satuday,13th December-2003(p-1).
15. *Human Capital* Vol. 7 No. 8 Jan 2004 Page 35.

28

TRANSCULTURAL HUMAN VALUES

Ch. H.K.S. Kumar* and **Dr. Talluru Sreenivas****

A business that is committed to ethical norms and code of conduct develops a high sense of responsibility for quality standards. Some core values, which determine the 'absolute moral threshold' have to be accepted by countries in matters of management. Respect for humanity, which is a core value, implies respect for human dignity and basic rights, and in business matters, various stakeholders have to be treated with respect. Differences in cultural values and local conditions have to be respected, as it is an accepted ethical principle.

Values have both content and intensity attributes. The content attribute says that mode of conduct is 'important'. The intensity attribute specifies 'how important' it is. When we rank an individual's values in terms of their intensity, we obtain that 'person's value system'. Values are the motivating force for human action. Culture is a set of beliefs, values, attitudes, habits and forms of behaviour that are shared by the society, and are transmitted from generation to generation within that society. While trans-cultural values promote cultural congruence, the culture-specific values have to be nurtured. The article suggests a few norms and values which need to be ingrained in the culture of a society in general, and in industrial culture in the context of globalization.

* Lecturer in Management Sciences, Alhabeeb College of Engineering, Hyderabad.

** Reader, Dept. of Management Sciences, R.V.R.& J.C. College of Engineering, Guntur.

Introduction

India is known for its rich contribution in the areas of cultural, social spiritual values since immemorial times. Even today Indian contribution is acknowledged on a higher side in many developed countries. But now we are living in the period of moral crisis. There is degeneration in the values which have been basis of ethics and culture. We also formally celebrated with great pride the completion of 50 years of independence recently. However in the heart of the heart we were in doubt whether we did even our minimum obligations to our country after independence during these fifty years. Did we do any thing honestly to protect the noble Indian traditions and values? Did we expect to build nation of rampant poverty, illiteracy, unbridled corruption, poor governance, utter callousness and lack of concern? Some people are even undermining the past glory and the contributions of the greatest scholars. So far nobody is sure whether industrialisation has resulted in the increase of quality of life or destroyed human values. But ethics and values in the human life went to back seat resulting in immoral, unethical and illegal ways of leading life. There is degradation of our heritage, ethics and human values.

The situation in the developed countries doesn't differ from that of developing countries. Unhealthy competition and rivalry dominate business environment. The news about the recent massive bankruptcies in the US Corporate Sector is the best example. For the record it may be stated that World Com Inc. filed the largest US Bankruptcy : its total assets before its bankruptcy were reported to be around $107 billion. About five years ago, the Asian economic system had collapsed for whatever reasons. South Korea, in particular, was in bad shape. The blame is laid at the door of the auditing firms who were able to compromise their auditing skills for a fee. But the most important element in this tragedy is not the failure of the system but the dishonesty and deceit of the men and women who run this system.

Globalisation has added a new dimension to the problem with the growth and dominance of multinational organisations in the corporate sector. Cultural differences between countries result in conflicts and tensions. The cultural values of a company of one country may not be accepted by another country. Technological developments may have impact on the value system and may result in undesirable outcome. In order to come out of this situation, a moral and value based system has to be explored.

A human being is a mixture of complex set of values, attitudes, personalities, perceptions, culture, behaviour etc. it is the divergent situation, which determines the usage of requisite quality to suit that specific condition, shows the "flexibility" of human being. This flexibility has laid foundations to the variation of suitability to volatile conditions of business. In order to face the challenging business conditions, the human beings are also modifying (or trying to modify) their so called inner set of basics, to match the outer set of conditions. Now, the problem comes at the transition phase, which many times causes lot of friction.

In this context, there is a need to understand the conditions which force the business professionals to continuously change their way of approach, which allows to go thorough a structural evaluation of certain facts. They are

The Inner Set of Basics: Though there are abundant concepts available in the language, we ourselves confine to few important concepts, which will play vital role, in determining a specific behaviour of a person or human being. The front seat (or driving seat) goes to "Values". Value represent basic conviction that " a specific mode of conduct or end-state of existence is personally or socially preferable to an opposite or converse mode of conduct or end-state of existence". Values have both content and intensity attributes. The content attribute says that a mode of conduct or end-state of existence is "important". The intensity attribute specifies " how important" it is. When we rank an individual's values in terms of their intensity, we obtain that person's "Value System". Every one will have a hierarchy of values that forms his value system. This system is identified by the relative importance we assign to such values as freedom, pleasure, self-respect, honesty, obedience and equality. Values lay foundation for the understanding of attitudes and motivation, because they influence our perceptions, hence the behaviour. Values are relatively stable and enduring. If they are stable and enduring, how comes the question of "deterioration"? Here the point to be observed is "Relativity". So, one has to compare with what, whom, where? Answers could be,

What – Another value system

Whom – Other person i.e., business professional

Where – At a business transaction

One can explain this through the process of Globalisation. When touching the nooks and corners of the globe, there is every possibility of encountering the local or other MNCs. The Transaction would not be smooth if they don't understand each other's value system. For example: a Japanese professional style of wishing can be considered here against an Indian professional style of wishing.

Values are the motivating force for human action. Some societal values are related to survival of species, security of life and material prosperity, while some are related to mental and spiritual progress. Intellectual values and morality are the two basic qualities of spirituality. Mental progress results in realization of full potential of an individual. These core values are the corner stones of a society.

Another brick of foundation is "Culture". Culture is " a set of learned beliefs, values, attitudes, habits and forms of behavior that are shared by society and are transmitted from generation to generation within that society." Culture is not an outcome of genes. It is learned either formally or informally through family and friends and the environment. Cultural norms are effective when they become internalised by an individual. When we learn a new culture that is not our native culture, we call it "acculturation".

When Globalisation activates, the citizens of various countries will commonly share the designations of the companies and involve in communication. In doing so, they need to honour the cultural aspects of members who involve in communication process, failing which, problems arise. Conflicts arise. Dishonour generates disbelief, which leads to disturbance in the harmony of company. Other part of culture is dynamic, it keeps on evolving to meet the newly emerging social needs. The second part of cultural values most of the time is congruent with corporate culture and considered to be the lesser influence. The influence is heavy if there is incongruing in core values, like dharma, artha and kama. India is a deeply religious and spiritual society. It has a long tradition of trade and commerce too, which cannot be seen alone without core values.

A study of human society is a study of its culture. Culture is a complex whole which includes knowledge, belief, art, morals, law, custom, etc., of the people of a society acquired from time to time. It refers to a whole pattern of human behaviour as reflected in the language and activities of the members of a society and the various aspects of living which are passed on to 'succeeding generations'. The material and non-material aspects of people's realization of values in the modern society constitute an important part of culture. 'Culture is the integral sum of values which individuals, groups of individuals and the society at large conceive and practise'. It "is the acquired knowledge people use to interpret experience and generate social behaviour".

Values and Culture at a State of Flux

"Cultural Values", a term generally used by us shows the inseparability of culture and value system. When the citizens of various countries as representatives of their native companies, i.e., business professionals, meet other business professionals, there comes the sharing of each other's values and cultural values. These cultural values will be passed on from one generation of employees to the next generation as policies. These policies see deviation when situation demands them; nobody can judge the degree of deviation. The negative deviation and positive deviation, depends on perceiver to think of.

The "economy is a product of cultural values:. It is a product of "human choices and values". While economic activities of a society are managed under a "system" of its choice, traditions, practices and age old institutions do influence the structure of organizations, methods of production etc., Management, which is concerned with the work of planning, organizing and controlling, has to follow a code of conduct. While it has to perforce function within the legal framework, it has to clearly articulate its mission and values. The organizational values should be in harmony with societal values. The organization is expected to follow ethical norms in discharging its responsibilities and fulfilling the expectations of various stake-holders. Business practices reflect organizational culture and values; firms have to conform to commonly accepted ethical principles. Integrity, that is, "unimpaired moral state", should be the corner stone of management practices.

The Influencing Parameters: There are various factors where there is scope of breach.

- Distortion, selling out corporate information, diluting secrecy.
- Discrimination towards employees from hiring to firing
- Avoidance of tax payments, against movement to law
- Sexual harassment
- Using advertising as a deceiving agent, as unwanted usage of lady models
- Making use of criminals, underworld dons, terrorist groups to reduce competition
- Bribing employees seeking top secretive information

The Outer Set of Conditions: At first sight, professionals who are in need of Power or Achievement, try to sort out issues, opting the back door strategies, to get their things done. They want to creep up in the organisation, very fast, turn themselves into practice, resulting in the violation of cultural values. Secondly, professionals with deep desire for money may choose unethical behavior and they don't mind how they are earning. Thirdly, job security or struggle for existence. The companies, falling down in sales, compel their employees to somehow show higher sales. This forces employees to adopt unwanted activities, to survive themselves.

Transcultural Human Values

Some human values are universal. These values have to be respected irrespective of cross cultures. The members of any society should have a right to secure and healthy life and improved standard of living. These rights arise from the core values of human being, that is, a person's values as an individual with basic rights.

Some 'operative' human values of society may result from universal or core human values. For example, the importance Americans give to liberty of individual is an expression of their faith in the core value of humanity. Similarly in India respect to elders is an expression of this value in action. Paying homage to nature is a core human value and this is translated into culture-specific value of offering worship to Sun, Trees, animals etc. While the trans-cultural values promote cultural congruence, the culture-specific values have to be nurtured since they constitute the basis for separate identity of culture and Ethos. Several moral principles acquire importance in the context of particular culture of a community and religious spirit.

A careful consideration of various categories of human values suggests that the universal values of Truth, Trust, Equality and Integrity are of great importance in interpersonal relationship. Some of them are observed in Indian family living to a greater extent even today. The importance given to women in family is an expression of faith in feminine qualities of compassion, affection, tolerance and forgiveness. These qualities will be equally helpful in business organizations. The value-system of a management may consist of end-state values like productivity, profitability, growth, innovation etc., which is not wrong. But what is more important is the question of values as means where the focus is on the qualitative aspect; it is not so much as 'what is value' but how the value is achieved. The values accepted by a company should distinguish between 'good and bad' and the 'desired and desirable'.

Suggestions

Integrity is the foundation of ethical management and good governance and code of conduct is one of the tools. It may not be possible to have a common code of governance for all companies because of differences in local conditions, but the code of conduct should be integrity-based. There should be clear guidelines about illegal payments and business practices. Codes of conduct must be explicit. Secondly the rules and code of conduct of an organization should be voluntarily followed, rather than imposed by law, which implies self-governance. One has to define the mission and purpose of the organization and present a statement of its values. It should focus on spiritual qualities of divinity in work, customer satisfaction, detachment from ego, fairness, courtesy and humility, top quality service etc. They should reflect our culture and ethos, the organizational policies and strategies should be based on integrity as reflected in the values and work culture. The ethical policy should be institutionalized by focusing on important measures. Another important measure is that the values of the organization should be integrated into normal channels of decision making of management for sound ethical decisions.

Conclusion

A business that is committed to ethical norms and code of conduct develops a high sense of responsibility for quality standards. Some core values, which determine "the absolute moral threshold" have to be accepted by countries in matters of management. Respect for humanity, which is a core value, implies respect for human dignity and basic rights; and in business matters the various stakeholders have to be treated with respect. Secondly, respect for differences in cultural values and local traditions is an accepted ethical principle.

29

RATIONALISATION

A COMEPETITIVE ADVANTAGE

T. Sree Krishna*, Dr. T. Nagaraju** and **Dr. C. Ramachandra Prabhu*****

The Indian Government after realising the importance of the need for rationalization in major industries like the cotton textiles, jute, sugar etc., in which the machinery became obsolete, has been trying to implement rationalization in a phased manner without loss of jobs for labour. However, in the Indian industries like cotton textile, jute, sugar, steel and coal etc., there is an urgent need for rationalization because the methods of production processes are traditional and a large number of units in each industry are below optimum capacity. Several committees and commissions have recommended from time to time, the implementation of rationalization schemes in various industries. This paper presents the positive impact of rationalization on the Indian labour, particularly in creating the need for welfare measures to be undertaken by the Government to help the working community in India and paving the way to make comprehensive labour laws. This paper emphasizes the need for proper implementation of the concept of rationalization in Indian industries for having a competitive advantage in India's economic growth particularly in the time frame of Vision-2020. This paper also highlights

* Faculty Members of Management Sciences, RVR&JC College of Engg, Guntur.

** Faculty Members of Management Sciences, RVR&JC College of Engg, Guntur.

*** Faculty Member of Physics', Department of Applied Sciences, Higher College of Technology, P.O. Box 74, Al-khuwair-133, Muscut - Oman.

the rationalization in Indian service sector with reference to the needed reforms on rational and scientific basis in all its factors, viz., men, material, management and money, with a view for achieving the maximum output with the minimum cost and effort.

Introduction

The term rationalization means the organization of a business according to scientific principles of management in order to increase efficiency. It can be defined as systematic organization which means the act of organizing something according to a system or a rationale. Rationalization can also be thought as the cognitive process of making something seem consistent with or based on a reason. Based on the work of 19th century utopian thinkers such as St Simon and Fourier, the scientific management of industrial production was developed by Frederick W. Taylor in his essay «The Principles of Scientific Management» (1911). The objective of this production worker turned engineer was to save time, eliminate wasted motion, and separate planning from organization, based on a scientific analysis of industrial processes. Theoreticians such as Carl G. Bath and C.B. Thomson adopted these concepts and made them part of a system.

Henry Ford, founder of the Ford Motor Company in Detroit in 1903, quickly realized that these theories could bring huge benefits for industry. He put them into practice for the Ford T, a vehicle that heralded a new industrial concept: mass production. As a result, Henry Ford became the pioneer of mass consumption. Taylorism increased productivity and promoted the employment of unskilled workers. The rise of Fordism paved the way for the spectacular development of Taylor's theories. However, production workers were discouraged to see the intellectual content of their work decline into a series of monotonous and repetitive tasks. New research, such as that conducted by Elton Mayo in the 1930s, highlighted the advantages of developing human relations within the company. At the same time, Hyacinthe Dubreuil – production worker and trade unionist – published "Standards". This book emphasized the importance of making tasks varied and interesting and also introduced such innovative themes as decentralization and self-management

The rationalization of industrial plants has led to the development of a stringent quality policy, in which seven zeros symbolize the challenges to be met: zero breakdowns – zero lead times –zero paper – zero contempt – zero defects – zero stock –zero accidents. In the automotive sector and elsewhere, the limits of the Ford model were reached more than thirty years ago. Today, industrial organization is guided by quality, service, ergonomics and task variety. As part of this process, employees have a real role to play rather than just carrying out orders.

In the earlier days the term 'rationalization' was used to indicate the application of principles of scientific management. But later the distinction between the two terms have been recognized and appreciated in many quarters. Rationalization has a wider scope than scientific management. In fact, rationalization includes not only scientific management, but also many more things. While scientific management is implemented by an individual concern, rationalization is concerned with the problems of industry as a whole. It is also said that the scientific management is concerned primarily with increased efficiency of existing production processes whereas rationalization covers a number of other activities too like simplification, standardization, mechanization, etc. Rationalization covers financing and distribution, which are untouched by scientific management.

The Initial Phase of Rationalisation in India

The rationalization movement, initially started in Germany, has spread to almost all the Western countries, although its nature and scope differ from country to country. Though the need for rationalizing the major industries of India was keenly felt even during the first quarter of the 20th Century, rationalization in its complete sense is not adopted in India except in a piecemeal and tentative fashion. Majority of employers meant by rationalization a combination for replacement of man by machine or for combination to exploit workers. As the industrialists have not made rational use of the movement, all the important trade unions such as Indian National Trade Union Congress (INTUC), All-India Trade Union Congress (AITUC), and Hind Mazdoor Sabha (HMS) have opposed rationalization on the ground that it leads to un-employment. The trade unions have been advocating that rationalization should take place firstly on organizational and managerial sides rather than on the labour side.

The Government, realising the importance of the need for rationalization in major industries like the cotton textiles whose machinery became obsolete and worn-out, has been trying to allay the fears of labour. A Sub-Committee of the Industries Development Committee of the Planning Commission consisting of employers' and employees' representatives under the chairmanship of Gulzari Lal Nanda discussed the issue of rationalization in detail and arrived at the following conclusions in 1951

1. Rationalization should be introduced in the Indian industries with a special care to avoid retrenchment of workers and to keep it to the minimum if it is there. This was to be achieved by
   (a) Not filling the vacancies caused by death, retirement, etc.,
   (b) Absorbing the surplus workers in other departments without breaking the continuity of services and without reducing their total earnings
   (c) Granting gratuities for voluntary retirements; and
   (d) Extending machinery wherever possible to absorb some of the displaced workers.
2. Workload should be standardized and if there is any dispute it should be investigated and the standards be fixed by experts selected by both the parties.
3. The Government should prepare a scheme for the rehabilitation of the retrenched workers.
4. An equitable share in gains of rationalization should be given to laborers.

All the above views were embodied in the Second Five Year Plan which observed that "rationalization should be attempted when it does not lead to unemployment and is introduced in consultation with the workers and is affected after improving the working conditions and guaranteeing a substantial share of gains to workers."

The Seventh All-India Conference of the Indian Institute of Personnel Management (1957) discussed the problem of rationalization. The Conference has reaffirmed its faith in rationalization and suggested the following measures to curb the adverse effects of rationalization

1. Before the rationalization schemes are taken up it is necessary to have preliminary planning and thorough investigation of the conditions in the particular industry.
2. Prior consultation with the employees and their unions so as to secure their co-operation in the successful implementation of the schemes is desirable;
3. There must be proper phasing of the schemes
4. It would be beneficial to have an agreement on the details of the scheme with a clause providing for voluntary arbitration to remove doubts.
5. Wherever necessary proper arrangements should be made for training workers to fit into the changes inherent in rationalization.
6. An agreeable method of sharing of gains of rationalization by capital and labour should be evolved; and
7. Rationalization, as far as possible, be planned in such a way as to eliminate retrenchment, and where retrenchment becomes inevitable, efforts should be made to secure alternative employment for those workers.

Positive Impact of Rationalisation in India in Labour Protection and in Increasing Productivity

The labour scenario in the country has witnessed two major turning points since Independence. The first can be identified with the period from Independence upto 1990 while the second can be related to the post-1991 era when the entire gamut of liberalization policies was initiated. At the time of Independence, the level of industrialization was very low. Also, the over-riding concern of the Labour Acts that existed at that time was limited to enhancing the skills of the labour working in the factories.

After Independence, while rapid industrialization took place on the one hand, the welfare approach of the Government led to a host of initiatives for labour protection such as Minimum Wages Act, 1948, Factories Act, 1948 and Employees State Insurance Act, 1952. The positive impact of rationalization in India can be seen to a great extent at this stage especially in protecting the interest of labour, their welfare and making laws. The impact of rationalization was so great that by the early 60s a need was felt to rationalize the existing labour laws in India to bring about a degree of cohesion and also to examine the ways and means of extending the labour welfare measures beyond the organized sector. Accordingly, the first National Labour Commission was set up in December 1966 under the chairmanship of Justice P.B. Gajendragadkar. The recommendations of the first National Labour Commission covered issues like recruitment agencies and practices, employment service administration, training and worker's education, working conditions, labour welfare, housing, social security, wages and earnings, wage policy, bonus to workers and employers and industrial relations machinery.

The recommendations of the first Labour Commission were sought to be implemented through amendments to existing labour laws as well as by identifying the areas where fresh legislation would be necessary. Examples of the former are amendments to labour laws like the Workmen's Compensation Act, 1923 (for removal of wage ceiling for coverage) and the Industrial Disputes Act, 1947 (mainly in respect of the unfair labour practices). The Employees State Insurance Act, 1948 (for enhancement in the wage limit for exemption from payment of Employees' Contribution), Factories Act, 1948 (for making penalties more stringent for violation of safety requirements and provision of welfare facilities) and the Employees' Provident Funds and Miscellaneous Provisions Act, 1952 (enhancement in the rate of contribution and making default of dues a cognizable offence). New legislations that were brought up in the light of the recommendations made by the first Labour Commission, include the Contract Labour (Regulation & Abolition) Act, 1970, Equal Remuneration Act, 1976 and Child Labour (Prohibition & Regulation) Act, 1986.

In the areas of wage policy and minimum wages, employment services, vocational training, labour statistics and research and workers' education also, the recommendations made by the Commission have been largely taken into account in modifying the policies, procedures and programmes of the Government.

Unfortunately, however the first Labour Commission could not bring about any meaningful initiative for reducing the exploitation of labour in the un-organised sector. As a result, the labour in the un-organised sector is still subject to exploitation. The post-1991 policy reforms in almost all sectors of the economy are guided by the need to make the Indian economy globally competitive. This obviously raises a set of questions with regard to the protection of labour in the country. At the same time, attention must also be accorded to the fact that the existing labour laws may not be fully consistent with the changes. Industrial associations have demanded that the multiplicity of the laws and acts have to be reduced and brought to a minimum if Indian industry has to become globally competitive. The proposal for setting up the Second National Commission on Labour was first mooted on the basis of the recommendation of Indian Labour Conference held in September, 1992. Various Central employers and trade union organisations also wrote to the Ministry of Labour suggesting it set up the Second National Commission on Labour and accordingly the Commission was setup and submitted its report in 2002.

So far as the organised sector is concerned, the main focus of the Second National Commission on Labour was suggesting a rationalisation of the existing laws so as to make them more relevant and appropriate in the changing context of globalization and opening up of the Indian economy. In addition, the Commission also reviewed the implications of the recommendations made by the Jain Commission set up in May, 1998 and councils set up by the Indian Prime Minister to review the various administrative laws. The task for the Labour Commission was really very challenging. While the labour, particularly from the un-organised segments were benefited by atleast having a written set of recommendations that will improve their living conditions. The requirement of increasing the global competitiveness of Indian industry was also translated into another set of recommendations. The Second National Commission on Labour was a success because of the synthesis and balance achieved between the aforesaid two major concerns, which is indirectly a concept of rationalization of existing labour laws, and prevailing situations with foreseeing the future of India.

Some strategies highlighting the need for proper implementation of the concept of rationalization in indian industries for having a competitive advantage in india's economic growth particularly in the present days of globalisation and within the time frame of vision-2020.

The globalisation that we see today has been triggered off by modern technology. History testifies to the fact that a mix of motives has fuelled the growth of technology. It also shows that the use to which technology is being put, has been influenced by a variety of motives and objectives. Knowledge of the technique of splitting the atom has led to bene-ficial uses as well as to holocausts and fear for the survival of humanity. Knowledge of techniques of propulsion has been used not only to launch spaceships that explore outer space, but also to launch satellites that can provide bases for 'Star Wars.' Technology has been used to concentrate power, and bolster regimes of terror. It has also shown the possibilities of universalising, or near universalising access to knowledge, and therefore, power, and the possibilities of a vast increase in accountability, transparency and participation in decision-making. It has led to concentration of production, but it has also demonstrated the possibility of decentralising production without diluting efficiency or expedition.

The main factors that have contributed to the globalisation that we see today are the revolutionary advances that have been made in the use of technologies in the fields of transport, communication and 'Information Systems' like the computer. Advances in transport and communication have replaced distance with proximity. Many barriers that the world considered insuperable have disappeared like mist before the rising sun. They no longer provide one with immunity or permit one to live in isolation. Knowledge and information travel fast, giving one a glimpse of what is happening elsewhere and what can happen in one's own area.

If the effects of the achievements that technology has chalked up have traveled across frontiers, so have the effects of the pollution that modern technology has caused to the environment, poisoning the soil, water and air on which humanity and other species depend, endangering health and life, and the environment on which all life and bio-diversity depend. Thus, it can be said that globalisation is both a consequence and a reminder of the paradigms of inter-dependence within which humanity lives, survives and prospers. If the paradigms of inter-dependence are unalterable, they impose limits on the role of competition. If competition is the paramount paradigm, the weak may be enslaved or allowed to be eliminated through visible or invisible forms of violence. It may be too much to assume that the weak will meekly submit rather than struggle to survive, and if necessary, to use whatever power they have, to turn tables, or at least to protect themselves by seeking changes in systems and policies. Seattle, Vienna, Genoa, Gothenburg and other places are reminders of the indignation and power of the weak who feel deprived, exploited and tricked.

The fields of industry, agriculture and the services show that they acquire their viability through inter-dependence. Industry is not an end in itself. Its raison d'être is itself the ability to serve society and the needs of the consumer. In that sense, therefore, industry depends on the consumer, and the consumer depends on industry. Industry depends on technology, capital, the worker, the entrepreneur, management, and the consumer, and society in general. Both workers and employers therefore, depend on industry and the cooperation each gives to the other. One cannot prosper at the cost of the other, if industry rather than the individual is to prosper.

The needs of society can be met only if industry prospers. In the ambience of globalisation, our industry can survive, and our workers and employers can survive only if we fine-tune our ability to compete in the world market. We cannot achieve this if the human factors that determine the success of industry are in conflict with each other. Our economic security and the success of our efforts to abolish poverty, to generate and maintain employment and to improve the standard of living of our people will, therefore, depend on our ability to identify the conditions that can ensure cooperation between our workers and employers.

Globalisation will not permit us to remain in a state of isolation and stagnation. Horizons have expanded. New paradigms have emerged. Old clichés and mindsets have lost their relevance. We cannot negotiate the rapids before us unless we revise the mindsets of the days of isolation and confrontation. Attitudes of confrontation must give place to an attitude of genuine partnership. Mechanistic views of industrial relations should yield place to a view that recognizes that industry is an organic entity. Internal competition will only weaken our ability to increase the competitiveness that we need if we are to hold our own in the face of the new configurations of forces in the world which may adversely affect our progress. Organisations of workers as well as employers, and the State itself, should identify and create the conditions on which the harmonious relations that we need can be created and maintained. It is in this spirit that we have attempted to do justice to the task that has been entrusted to us.

In almost all the major Indian industries, viz, cotton textile, jute, sugar, and coal, there is an urgent need for rationalisation. In all the industries the methods of production are traditional. The machinery used is antiquated and worn-out. A large number of units in each industry are below optimum capacity. Our industrialists are not able to compete in the foreign markets because of the poor quality and high cost of the products. There is a fear that India may lose international markets for some of the traditional export items like jute and textiles. In view of all these, several committees and commissions have, from time to time, recommended the implementation of rationalisation schemes in various industries. However, it is imperative that problems do arise in securing finances for modernization schemes. To solve these, efforts must be made within the industry for self-financing and also encouragement should come from the Government through loans at concessional rates from the public financial institutions. Trade unions also should recognize that rationalization in industries would aid the betterment of workers and the working environment.There is a good relationship between the development patterns and the dynamics of connectivity between nations, especially in trade and business. The world has few developed countries and many developing countries. What is the dynamics between them and what connects them? The answer is that, a developed country has to market its products in a competitive way to different countries to remain a developed country. The developing country, to get transformed into developed country, they too have to market their products to other countries in a competitive way.

Competitiveness has three dimensions:

- Quality of the product;
- Cost-effectiveness; and
- Supply in time.

Indeed this dynamics of competitiveness in marketing of products by developing and developed countries is called the law of development. India is today a developing country and we have a vision to transform India into a developed nation by 2020, using technology as a tool. With the growing economy and strong internal market, India is destined to make competitive products using technological innovations. Software and pharma products have shown the lead and the emergence of steel technology, space technology and defence systems going to the international markets in addition to conventional products is a good sign of implementation of Vision-2020. The initiatives taken in solar farming to generate energy, desalination plants to generate drinking water will soon be mission mode programmes offering a large business in India and outside.

The small-scale industries sector plays a vital role in the growth of the country. It contributes almost 40 per cent of the gross industrial value added in the Indian economy. It has been estimated that the turn over to capital employed is approximately 4.62. The small-scale sector has grown rapidly over the years. The number of small-scale units has increased from an estimated 0.87 million units in the year 1980-81 to over 3 million in the year 2000. The small-scale industry sector in India creates largest employment opportunities for the Indian populace, next only to agriculture. The SSI sector plays a major role in India's present export performance. About 45 per cent to 50 per cent of the Indian exports are contributed by the SSI sector. Direct exports from the SSI sector account for nearly 35 per cent of the total exports. Besides direct exports, it is estimated that small-scale industrial units contribute around 15 per cent to exports indirectly. This takes place through merchant exporters, trading houses and export houses. It would surprise many to know that non-traditional products account for more than 95 per cent of the SSI exports. The product groups where the SSI sector dominates in exports are sports goods, readymade garments, woolen garments and knitwear, plastic products, processed food and leather products. The strategy for enhancing the exports of goods and services from SSI sector has to be based technology upgradation, value addition techniques, credits support and exports marketing zones. Big industries should ensure timely payments for the products they receive from small-scale industries. Also IITF should find from the international traders where Indian SSIs can fare better in global competition in areas of quality, quantity and schedule. This promotion will enable the SSI industry to grow much faster towards its target of Rs 5 lakh crore (Rs 5,000 billion) of export performance by the year 2020. The small- and medium-scale industries need an exclusive umbrella organisation to promote productivity and market their products, including exports. The Indian industry must develop quality products in time and cost effective manner, for becoming globally competitive and must penetrate into entrenched market by fully tapping the principles of rationalization.

In fact, the balance of opinion is swinging around to the view that bad times might not be such an evil, after all. Korea went through a downturn in the early nineties- an ideal time to restructure, but then the economy took off again, and nobody did anything. Like the above-mentioned situation there is a great opportunity for restructuring and rationalisation in India. Accept and enjoy change and it seems to be a primary condition for survival and success. If the leadership can create an atmosphere where people thrive on challenges and uncertainty that alone is a guarantor of success. The onus for creating this mindset is squarely on the top management. Clarity of values, vision, and a near-term strategy consistently articulated by the leader, and a strong motivated top management team which shares it with the leader are the critical factors for survival in today's environment. That's a tall order for most of India's hitherto sheltered business leaders. There's no ready-made solution. Reactions range from the attacking mode to the defensive mode - for instance, companies like Reliance, Ranbaxy and HLL are considered to be in the process of developing businesses which are globally competitive. They're affected, but not dictated to by what happens in the short run. Defensive action implies building up reserves and hunkering down to wait out the storm, hoping to take advantage when things change. But it can be done. First of all, get your ship in order - both business portfolios as well as organisationally. Corporations have to become very clear about goals, objectives, businesses - and if necessary restructure and consolidate to achieve an effective shape. The days of big conglomerates are over. The Korean crisis has proved that. Companies have to stick to core competences and acquire the right size. During a demand slack, companies are forced to merge. Strategic choices have to be made. Operations have to be streamlined, competitive advantages of the corporation and competitors have to be identified, non-value added activities junked, costs reduced and resources conserved.

This is not only beginning to happen, it's going to become the order of the day. Most experts see the number of JVs, spin-offs, sell-outs and mergers increasing drastically in the near future. Next, get your organisation in fighting trim. The buzzword1998 - the year of gloom? Wrong. Having lived with uncertainty for well over two years, Corporate India today knows that money is made when there's blood on the streets For India's corporates, the world is getting meaner, tougher, more complex. Long accustomed to depending on the government to dictate the course of industrial activity, as well as to blaming policy-makers for most of their woes, Corporate India is suddenly finding that there's no longer any point. Nobody's listening. The government is not only out to lunch, it's likely to stay that way for some time to come. The message is crystal clear- the ball's in your court. Managing uncertainty has been, for a while, a way of life. If there was no uncertainty, management skills would become redundant. In the year ahead, therefore, managing chaos effectively will be the single most critical factor affecting any corporation. In a regulated economy you had to keep watching the government instead of the customer. Today the situation has changed. Stability is desirable, even awfully important, but it's not happening in a hurry. Environmental uncertainty is a new thing here - it's common the world over. Indian managers have to understand that the environment will stay this way for the short to medium term, and only those who can manage the environment effectively will survive. Political shenanigans are no longer by any means the only destabilising factor. Thanks to the moves towards a market economy, world events, international trends, competition, as well as policy direction are all strong forces interacting together to produce a general environment of uncertainty. At the macro- level it might mean less efficiency. But overall uncertainty leads to opportunities and is not at all restraining.

It also means more opportunities for the entrepreneur It is a 'reconfigurable' or 'flexible organisational structures based on project teams built around business processes are required. Team members can be successfully redeployed and reconstituted around new opportunities and new sources of competitive advantage. Communication flows - both internal and external - are an essential. Information needs to move across the hierarchy, and fast. It's also great opportunity for taking hard decisions, cutting flab, costs, improving operational efficiencies, and quality, making assets more productive and harnessing and husbanding every resource available, mainly human and financial. One needs to have strong financial fundamentals, which means that cash flows should be positive. Naturally, this implies strict cost-controls, improved productivity and making the best use of technology. Planning, naturally, is crucial to managing an uncertain environment - corporations are quickly beginning to realise the importance of planning for contingencies. We'll see more companies spending time and resources on tracking the external environment, and on strategic planning. HLL already does it. Mahindra & Mahindra has been using techniques like scenario creation and quantitative methods like Game Theory techniques to create plans for possible alternative scenarios. Booz.Allen goes a step further - and recommends that scenario planning, or war games as they like to call it, should involve a cross- section of managers and be conducted in a workshop environment, instead of just by one group.

Additionally, it's important to have early warning systems in place - to pinpoint changes in the environment that will require an internal re-orientation. Essentially, it's the old adage - be prepared for the worst, and plan for the best.

All this should lead to creating a flexible and fast organisation which can change tack with every need and move fast. The agenda for micro-units is to be able to quickly adjust the sails to changing winds without losing the basic sense of direction. Flexibility - or by any other name, agility, nimbleness, ability to adapt, is critical. Being flexible in approach demands that a corporation should have broad directional plans, rather than deterministic ones. Arvind Mills response to the changing demand patterns for denim has been to move definitely towards value- added products and brands. Sharad Bansal, executive director, Coopers and Lybrand explains C&L's approach -

when its international clients stayed wary of entering India, C&L moved on to woo Indian business houses. It's important to be able to identify and take advantage of the windows of opportunity that arise. In the Indian context, nimbleness is even more important - Indian managements tend to stand still and assume that nothing is going to change, especially if they are relatively better placed. That's suicidal. In many cases, Indian corporates tend to benchmark with industry standards instead of benchmarking with international competition. Speed, efficiency, and ability to adapt will ensure an evolving corporation - everyone knows what happened to the dinosaurs. Bringing about stability is not necessarily a key objective.

Companies should look for ways to derive competitive advantage by thriving on uncertainty.

Indian industry needs to transit from relative protection to tomorrow's global market. That calls for a major change in mindset and skills. A consistent growth rate of 9 to 10 per cent per annum needs to be sustained over many years before millions of our disadvantaged countrymen can hope to gain access to a minimum standard of living and dignified existence. It is impossible to realise such a challenging vision of growth with social equity without fashioning an effective development and growth strategy for rural India. Growth in rural incomes is both a means and an end of India's economic development. The slowdown of industrial growth has highlighted even more starkly the vital need to sustain rural demand. One of the key objectives of second-generation reforms should be to create a climate that enables the corporate sector to pursue its objective of creating shareholder value more readily by contributing to the prosperity of the Indian farmer.

In this context, the criticality of accelerating the reform process cannot be overstated. The fundamental purpose of reform is to create a climate in which investments in India can become productive and internationally competitive. It must create robust market institutions that foster investor confidence, upgrade social and physical infrastructure and mobilise even higher rates of private, public and international savings. Purposeful channelisation of savings would entail a fundamental re-ordering and rationalisation of the terms of tax assignment between the Centre and the states to align the structure of responsibility in a manner that promotes fiscal discipline, expands the tax base, and unlocks the potential of a larger Indian common market. The reform process must extend to financial markets, labour markets, environment, public health and education systems, the legal framework and much more. Acceleration of reforms can sustainably come about only through a growing political consensus on the fundamentals of a long-term growth strategy that cuts across ideologies and short-term sectarian interests.

The Indian corporate sector bears a critical responsibility, particularly in the context of the internal and external challenges confronting the Indian industry. The priority for Indian industry should be the rapid attainment of international competitiveness by successfully transiting from an era of relative protection to the fully globalised markets of tomorrow.

Global competitiveness demands a major change in mindset. It also calls for organisational vitality, backed by substantial investments in modernisation, scaling up and skills upgradation. Such strategic investments would naturally entail gestation drags that would severely test managements for their staying power and commitment to their businesses. Business portfolios would need to be rationalised and restructured for focussed attention, so that the deployment of scarce resources is confined to those areas that best match organisational capability with market opportunity. It is, therefore, imperative for business to shed preoccupation with the mere maximisation of tactical financial results, and instead focus on building strategic capabilities. A wholesome balance will have to be struck between the short, medium and long terms.

Frustrations arising from a slow pace of reforms, together with competitive pressures generated by the fast pace of trade liberalisation arising from the WTO time-table are severely testing the resourcefulness of Indian companies and their commitment to the Indian economy. In this context, I would like to draw a distinction between an «Indian' company and a company operating in India. The difference lies in the depth of commitment to the Indian economy. An 'Indian' enterprise would, given its fundamental orientation, favour value chains within India by supporting their competitiveness wherever feasible. On the other hand, any other enterprise1 would not necessarily demonstrate such a commitment in pursuit of shareholder value. An «Indian' company, while recognising the need to create a fair reward for shareholders, would go the extra mile in partnership with other participants in the economy to create conductive conditions in which Indian value chains can become internationally competitive. Thus an 'Indian' enterprise is borne out by its commitment to the Indian economy rather than by the source of its capital.

Anecdotal evidence appears to suggest that hitherto well established manufacturing companies are now increasingly looking for sources of supply from outside India to service the Indian market. This downgrading of focus from «leadership to dealership» does not augur well for the ambitious growth agenda of the Indian economy. «Dealership» will only serve to exploit the Indian market to create economic surpluses for value chains residing outside India. This phenomenon underscores the need for an even closer and deeper spirit of partnership within the Indian economy in shaping and effectively executing the reform agenda, so as to create and capture the lion's share of value creation within the Indian economy.

Every industry should be inspired by the vision of enlarging its contribution to the Indian economy with a strong belief that creation of shareholder value provides the only basis for sustainable contribution to the super ordinate goal of creating national value. Every industry should practices this philosophy by not only driving each of the businesses towards international competitiveness, but by also consciously contributing to enhancing the competitiveness of the larger value chain of which it is a part. All industries have to make a significant contribution towards enhancing farm productivity and rural incomes with a mission to enhance the wealth-generating capability of their company. Fundamental to creating such capability is organisational vitality, market-standing and profitability. All industries should adopt a corporate strategy which aims at exploiting market opportunities thrown up by the emerging nature of the Indian economy to create multiple centres of growth by harnessing and blending its unique and diverse core competencies residing in its various businesses. Over time, these blended competencies will, in turn, spawn newer capabilities thereby imparting a multiplier effect to its growth strategies. Every industry should have a vision to create and sustain a special position for themselves as one of the most valuable contributors to the Indian economy through world-class competitive performance, creating growing value for the Indian economy and superior value for the company's shareholders.

The Rationalization in Indian Service Sector

The services sector has emerged as the torchbearer of the Indian economy and its importance in the same is increasing with every passing year. In this backdrop, concerns have been raised regarding the sustainability of growth in the services sector and the likely impact it can have on an economy, which is witnessing a growing reliance on this sector. Before we delve deeper in to this aspect of the Indian economy, let us get a historical perspective of the various constituents of the economy and their performance over the years.

Agriculture, Industry and Services: Shares in GDP (%)

Year	*Agriculture*	*Industry*	*Services*
1950-51	57.2	14.8	28.0
1960-61	54.7	16.6	28.7
1970-71	48.1	19.9	32.1
1980-81	41.8	21.6	36.6
1990-91	34.9	24.5	40.6
2000-01	24.2	27.3	48.5
2001-02	24.3	26.7	49.0
2002-03	22.1	21.8	56.1

Source: Central Statistical Organisation.

The table above indicates the contribution of various sectors, namely agriculture, manufacturing and services to the GDP of the country at different periods of time in the last five decades. The table highlights the growing contribution of the services and the industrial sectors to the overall economy. While the growing contribution of the industrial sector is in line with the standard growth characteristics of a developing economy, the high contribution of the services sector is anomalous. What we are trying to indicate here is that, these high levels of services contribution to the economy is only observed in the status of economically developed countries. To that extent the Indian economic status is an aberration.

Sectoral and Overall GDP Growth Since 1990-91 (%)

Year	*Agriculture*	*Industry*	*Services*	*GDP*
1990-91	4.1	7.7	5.3	5.6
1991-92	-0.02	-0.6	4.8	1.3
1992-93	5.8	4.0	5.4	5.1
1993-94	4.1	5.2	7.7	5.9
1994-95	5.0	10.2	7.1	7.3
1995-96	-0.9	11.6	10.5	7.3
1996-97	9.6	7.1	7.2	7.8
1997-98	-2.4	4.3	9.8	4.8
1998-99	6.2	3.4	8.3	6.5
1999-00	1.3	5.3	9.5	6.1
2000-01	-0.2	6.3	4.8	4.0
2001-02	5.7	3.3	6.5	5.4
2002-03	-3.2	5.7	7.1	4.3
2003-04	9.1	6.6	8.2	8.1

Source: Central Statistical Organisation.

The table above indicates the performance of the services sector over the last decade and it indicates that despite the slowdown in the GDP growth over this period, the contribution from the services segment has only risen. This may be attributed to the fact that while the economy may have witnessed volatile growth trends in the last decade, the services sector growth has been rather stable and this has led to the steadily improving contribution by the same. The decade between 1990 and 2000 has been of significance for the services sector.

The services sector entered the decade of 1990s with a growth of 5.3%, which was lower than the GDP growth of 5.6% in 1990-91. In 1991-92 however, due to the balance of payments crisis when both agriculture and industry encountered a negative growth, services posted a positive growth of 4.8%, ensuring an overall GDP growth of 1.3%. During 1994-95 to 1996-97, when the economic growth stood in the 7% region, growth in services also ruled over 7%. In the subsequent years till 2001-02, the services growth remained higher than those of the other sectors barring 2000-01 when it was lower at a mere 4.8% primarily gravitated by the negative growth in non-bank financial companies. Overall, the services sector posted a growth of 7.6% in 1990s up from 6.6% in 1980s.

As per the Economic Survey, 2000-01, liberalisation of the economy in the 1990s and encouragement of private investment in industry and infrastructure have induced sustained high growth in services sector. A rapid increase in expenditure on public administration and defence, social services, and rural extension services also has an impact on the growth of services sector. Besides, IT software and services has emerged as one of the fastest growing segments of the economy with a compound annual growth of over 50 per cent during 1990s.

Another reason that could be attributed to the rapid growth in the services sector could be the rising reliance of the manufacturing sector in the services sector. With the increasing complexities of modern industrial organisations, manufacturing activities have become more and more service intensive, both upstream (e.g., design and R&D) and downstream (e.g., marketing and advertising). Competitive advantage of a firm now depends more on providing specialised services like financing and after-sales facilities than on production, which has increasingly become routinised.

Coming back to the question of the direction and sustainability of the services sector growth, we believe that the Indian services sector has strong potential to maintain growth rates seen in the last decade and probably even outstrip it going forward. This optimism stems from the fact that strong growth has been witnessed in established sectors like travel and tourism, financial services and IT sector, as well as emerging sectors like telecom, insurance and healthcare. Moreover, we expect the same to be continued going forward. Having said that, we still believe, that in order to realise the full potential of the services sector, the industrial sector needs to be promoted to its maximum potential. Since the services sector is not a significant employment generator, the industrial sector can act as a fuel for the services sector by providing a growing populace of consumers that are increasingly demanding different range of services. Thus there is a strong need for rationalization of Indian service sector with reference to the needed reforms on rational and scientific basis in all its factors, viz., men, material, management and money, with a view for achieving the maximum output with the minimum cost and effort.

Conclusion

This paper presented the positive impact of rationalization on the Indian labour, particularly in creating the need for welfare measures to be undertaken by the Government to help the working community in India and paving the way to make comprehensive labour laws. This paper also emphasized the need for proper implementation of the concept of rationalization in Indian industries for having a competitive advantage in India's economic growth particularly in the time frame of Vision-2020. This paper also highlighted the rationalization in Indian service sector with reference to the needed reforms on rational and scientific basis in all its factors, viz., men, material, management and money, with a view for achieving the maximum output with the minimum cost and effort.

INDEX

A

B